TAKING CHARGE

TAKING CHARGE

CHARGE

Collected Stories on Aging Boldly

By Herb Weiss

Taking Charge: Collected Stories on Aging Boldly

Visit our website at **www.StillwaterPress.com** for more information.

First Stillwater River Publications Edition
ISBN-10: 0-692-68870-6
ISBN-13: 978-0692-68870-0

Library of Congress Control Number: 2016938614

  2 3 4 5 6 7 8 9 10
Written by Herb Weiss
Published by Stillwater River Publications, Glocester, RI, US

Dedicated to my wife Patty Zacks, Samantha, Ben, Lilianna, and Abby.

"CARPE DIEM, QUAM MINIMUM CREDULA POSTERO"

Which can be translated as "Seize today, put very little trust in tomorrow."

Taken from the Roman poet Horace's *Odes* (65 BCE - 8 BCE)

FOREWORD

Herb Weiss charges boldly into the great universal experience of aging in this eclectic collection of newspaper columns written over the course of a long and distinguished career.

In these weekly columns, the Pawtucket-based writer breathes life into the endless stream of statistics, reports, plans, policy initiatives, reventatives, successes and failures related to aging that inundate the public consciousness on a daily basis. Through the voices of people who live with and through the challenges and rewards of aging, he tells their personal stories as they deal with issues ranging from the everyday annoyances of daily routines to the greater matters of life and death, joy and sorrow, love and loss.

Robert Frost once said "In three words I can sum up everything I learned about life—it goes on." Indeed it does, and Herb chronicles the journey integrating the research and the real-life happenings with wit and wisdom. He moves beyond the surface to explore the facts as well as the depth of feelings beneath it. In this era of speed and change, with eternal youth as a major goal, he takes the time to find the truth and then uses it to illuminate the many facts of aging with timeless observations delivered in lively readable portions.

His writing skills have been recognized multiple times, but only a special person could acquire the respect he enjoys. He is well known throughout the state of Rhode Island for being the scribe who gives the rest of us access to real life stories. I think of the movie "An Officer and a Gentleman," and reflect on the notion that to some people, "A Journalist and a Gentleman" would be an oxymoron. They do not know Herb Weiss. He is an extraordinarily kind individual who is genuinely concerned about others and especially older people.

He is the driving force in establishing a vibrant arts & culture community in his beloved city of Pawtucket. He has the ability to see possibilities in new and exciting ways. Not for Herb is the "gotcha interview" practiced by so many in his profession. The pages of this book feature the thoughts of many people whose names are instantly recognizable. They share their real experiences and thoughts because they are confident that they will be treated accurately and fairly because Herb Weiss is trustworthy.

The insights gained in this way stand the test of time because they tell the truth. The columns were relevant when written and are still relevant today to people of all ages. An example is "Here is My Advice to the Graduating Class of 2013." He notes with wry humor, "At press time I sit with a written commencement speech, yet with no invitation from a university or college to give it." Too bad. It is a good one.

Herb's writing ranges from growing roses and taking the time to smell them to the loss of a beloved pet and finally a celebration of the famed Doolittle Raiders. He salutes the Greatest Generation with a commentary dedicated to Second Lieutenant Frank M. Weiss, his father.

This is a collection to savor for a long time—happy reading.

Kathleen S. Connell
State Director of AARP Rhode Island

PREFACE

Some people ritually read the sports or business sections, browse the stock listings, or even glance at the comics. Yet a growing number of aging baby boomers and senior readers are turning to newspapers, electronic media, and the Internet to learn more about aging issues.

With the graying of America, the *Pawtucket Times*, like many of the nation's news organizations, created an Age Beat in 2002 which continued until 2004, in which my weekly column covered a myriad of aging issues, including politics, ethics, long-term care, consumer issues, spirituality, pop culture, health care, and even economics. Ultimately I returned in July 2012 to resume writing my weekly column.

Age Beat reporting continues today. Generations Beat Online (GBONews.org, initially called Age Beat Online) is the e-newsletter of the Journalists Network on Generations, edited by San Francisco-based journalist Paul Kleyman.

Now celebrating its 22nd year, the e-newsletter, a great resource for those covering aging, is distributed to more than 1,000 journalists and authors on aging.

Kleyman, a seasoned journalist, covers a wide spectrum of issues the media must spotlight in an aging American society.

GBONews.org reaches reporters and columnists at media from *The New York Times* and *USA Today* to the *Sarasota Herald Tribune* and—Yes!—the *Pawtucket Times*. It goes to National Public Radio, Public Broadcasting Service, and commercial broadcasters as well as many online journalists and bloggers. And it reaches a growing number of reporters among the 3,000 ethnic media news outlets serving multi-cultural communities in the United States from *La Opinión* in Los Angeles to the *Irish Echo* in New York City.

Kleyman explained that coverage of the generations beat has never trickled down from media managers because they persist in believing that young people—especially the 80 million millennials — are the key to advertising sales.

In fact, in radio and television, advertisers pay significantly less for "eyeballs" of those 50-plus (and even less for those over 65) counted by the ad-rating agencies like Nielsen than for audiences in the 18 to 49 age group.

Yet those who are 50 and older (including now the first Gen-Xers) hold 75 percent of the nation's wealth. They are not only wealthier, but healthier and longer-lived than their children and grandchildren.

Still, media marketers are locked in an erroneous 1950s model that says the old are stuck in their ways on fixed incomes and can't be sold new things. And that means that media organizations, whether print or electronic, continue to produce less information about our aging society than mature consumers need or want.

But the newsbeat on aging goes on.

That's because it percolates up from the bottom of the newsroom, often with reporters and editors/producers in midlife who have experienced eldercare with their elderly parents or in-laws and discovered what a huge, untold story it is. Their personal experience gives them both the perspective and information they need to cover the issue in a balanced way, Kleyman said. One change from the past may be from new media technologies—social media, mobile, and whatever is yet to come.

For more than 36 years, with more than 600 articles written or co-written in newspapers and trade publications covering aging, health care, and medical issues, this writer has brought together the latest, most informative coverage of aging, health care, and medical issues that aging baby boomers or seniors need to know: pertinent information that will assist them in better planning that just might enhance quality of living in their later years.

In 13 chapters, this book brings together a collection of "my best of" columns, published in the *Pawtucket Times*, and later the *Woonsocket Call*, each listing the date it was published.

Opportunities to enhance our lives in our later years have never been more plentiful or accessible. This collection of columns offers insights and practical information about how people 50 and over can take charge and enjoy a full and satisfying quality of life unparalleled in our history.

Even if the column was written years ago, and the person quoted is no longer in his or her position or even deceased, the insight is still factual and valuable. While most of my sources are from Rhode Island, their stories are universal and their insights applicable anywhere in the nation.

Throughout the articles you will find experts along with people over age 50 sharing their observations and insights about a myriad of aging issues, from caregiving, retirement planning, preplanning your funeral, choosing the right nursing home, to their thoughts about spirituality and death.

Everyone has a story to tell, a personal experience that just might provide a road map for aging better and living longer.

Like my colleagues on the Age Beat, I will continue to bring the latest, most informative coverage of aging, medical, and health-care issues you need to know about.

Stay tuned.

Herb Weiss
July 2016

ACKNOWLEDGEMENTS

I acknowledge and thank my wife, Patty Zacks, for being a sounding board who critiqued my writing with her keen editorial eye. She provided sound suggestions that improved many of the articles in this book that I penned over the years and the cover design of this book.

To Kathleen S. Connell who wrote the foreword of this book, and to my reviewers, William Benson, Nancy Carriuolo, Dr. Phil Clark, Paul Kleyman, John O'Connor, Connie Goldman. I am truly honored by your participation in my book project.

Over the years J.J. Partridge, who has penned two well-crafted crime novels, and Michael Chute, who has written two well-received books on the art of growing roses, gave me their encouragement to write this book. Their insight and experiences gleaned from publishing books was key to publishing my first book.

I would like to express my gratitude to all those people who provided guidance to me, as to editorial content and graphic design, during the writing of this book —including Susan Sweet, Morris Nathanson, Scott Davis, Lori Ann Gagne, and Richard Blockson, along with seasoned writers Paul Kleyman, Michael Chute, Bianca Pavoncello, John O'Connor, Donna Kirwan, Joan Retsinas, L. Malcom Rodman, and William Spicer.

My appreciation is given to Lauren Long, who assisted in the editing, researching, and initial proofreading and to Janet Cogliano, Susan Sweet, and Mike Bilow for carefully proofreading the final draft. A very special thank you to Pawtucket-based GLAD WORKS, Inc., for the cover design and graphic and layout suggestions and publishers Steven and Dawn Porter at Stillwater River Publications for putting all these pieces together.

Mark Banuchi earns my gratitude for his assistance in organizing the content, contributing perceptive editorial suggestions, maintaining the manuscript, and making it almost painless to publish my first book.

I would like to thank the many editors and publishers with whom I have had the pleasure of working with throughout my writing career. Many of them helped to hone my writing and reporting skills. They include Michelle Garcia, Ash Gerecht, Rhodes Henderer, Jan Lamoglia, Richard Lank, Fraser Lang, John Mitchell, John O'Connor, Suzane Powell, Karen Ross, William Spicer (who published my first article in 1980), and Al Tomko.

I would like to take this opportunity to express my heartfelt thanks to Richard Fleischer, Barry Fain, and John Howell of Beacon Communications, for giving me the opportunity to become founding editor of *Senior Living* (now called *Prime Time*).

To General Manager Paul Palange at the *Pawtucket Times* and *Woonsocket Call* and to *Senior Digest*, my appreciation for giving me a bully pulpit to bring pertinent aging issues to the light of day and allowing the reprinting of my columns in this book.

To those who encouraged me during my early writing years, I acknowledge my parents Frank and Sally Weiss; my siblings Mickie, Nancy and Jim; my brother-in-law, Justin Aurbach; and family friends Fred Levy and Myron Ball.

A special thank you to my colleagues in the City of Pawtucket's Department of Planning and Redevelopment for their support and encouragement in the writing of this book.
My gratitude to Mātā Amritānandamayī Devī, known simply as Amma, a Hindu spiritual leader and guru who blessed this book project.

Most important, I thank the thousands of people I have interviewed over 36 years, who generously contributed their insights and observations about aging, health care and, medical issues to my articles and the publications I edited.

Herb Weiss

Contents

1. CAREGIVING

CAREGIVERS MUST NOT FORGET THEIR OWN NEEDS

Published June 8, 2012, in the Pawtucket Times

It seems that everywhere I turn these days, friends and colleagues are being thrust into caregiving roles for older family members or spouses. In today's hectic world, aging baby boomers and seniors who are now taking on this late-life role can find this new task demanding and stressful.

According to the National Alliance for Caregiving and AARP, most aging baby boomers will become informal caregivers at some time during their lives. There are more than 65 million Americans (29 percent of the nation's population) who provide unpaid care for a chronically ill, disabled, or older family member or relative during any given year. The caregiver spends an average of 20 hours per week providing care for their loved ones.

Statistics paint a very detailed picture of the typical family caregiver. She is a 49-year-old married woman who is employed and cares for her 69-year-old widowed mother who does not live with her. More than 66 percent of the nation's caregivers are women. More than 37 percent have children or grandchildren 18 years old or younger living with them.

The Importance of Taking Care of Yourself

Connie Goldman, award-winning radio producer and reporter whose books have given her readers insight, inspiration, and motivation for personal growth in midlife and beyond, sees a continuing need for support and services for middle-aged caregivers.

Goldman, who wrote *The Gifts of Caregiving–Stories of Hardship, Hope and Healing,* believes the secret of being a successful caregiver is to first take good care of yourself. Although her book was originally published more than a decade ago, the personal stories that family caregivers have shared continue to offer comfort, insight, and inspiration. Many will benefit from reading the compilation of 30 stories of caregivers who tell their personal stories of taking care of an ill, disabled, or aging loved one. Goldman notes all of these remarkable people cope with adversity in ways that leave us wondering: "Could I measure up to the challenge?" Most important, according to Goldman, each of their stories reveals how the hardships of caregiving can be turned into a journey of hope and self-discovery.

In her timeless book, Goldman's interviews include the late Dana Reeve (wife of the late actor Christopher Reeve), former First Lady Rosalynn Carter, Pulitzer Prize-winning author Studs Terkel and others whose lives were forever changed by their caregiving experience. There are also personal experiences told by many whose names you won't recognize, yet their stories offer personal insight that can nurture and nourish caregivers of any age.

"Taking on the commitment as a family caregiver opens the door to frustration, irritation, indecision, fear, guilt, and stress," said Goldman, so caregivers must first take care of themselves. Goldman suggests a mantra to post on your mirror or refrigerator to remind yourself that you must: *Take care of yourself so you can take care of others.* It is well known that caregivers often lose sleep, don't eat properly, don't take breaks, and don't believe they matter as much as the person for whom they are providing care. "Caregivers very often put themselves and their needs last on the list. To be the best caregiver you can be, you must care for yourself," she said.

According to Goldman, you can be a better, more efficient caregiver if you get enough sleep, eat regular meals, and make plans to get relief for some period of each day. "I know caregivers are often reluctant to ask a friend to fill in at home while you go to have your hair set, or meet a friend for lunch or go for a walk in the park. Yet an hour or two away can nourish a caregiver for the next 24 hours," she said.

Goldman suggests that caregivers can care for themselves by attending regular support groups, sharing with a friend three things that went well during a day (when everything seems to go wrong), or taking a hot bath, reading a magazine, spending time in your garden, taking a short nap, or eating a chocolate bar! It's often the little things that count in surviving each day and the challenges of being an aging baby boomer caregiver or taking on the caregiver role at any age.

Tapping into Resources

It is difficult for many caregivers to navigate the long-term-care system to find the most appropriate programs and services to keep their loved ones at home. According to the Rhode Island Department of Human Services, Division of Elderly Affairs, the National Family Caregivers Association (NFCA) might just provide that crucial information for caregivers. The Kensington, Maryland-based, clearinghouse (at **www.nfcacares.org**) offers information on a variety of topics including stress and family caregiving, caregiver advocacy, care-management techniques, support groups, and communication with health-care professionals for those who are reaching out for help and other issues. For more information on the books written by Connie Goldman, go to **www.congoldman.org**, your local bookstore, library, or **www.amazon.com**.

THE BEST OF ... KEEPING TABS ON YOUR WANDERING PARENT

Published August 20, 2008, in All Pawtucket All The Time

With the graying of Rhode Island's population, a growing number of aging baby boomers are taking care of their elderly parents who reside in their homes. Adult children are often juggling professional careers and family responsibilities while spending countless hours each week making sure their elderly parents' needs are taken care of, including getting them to doctors' appointments, taking them grocery shopping, assisting in household chores, or bringing them to family events.

In recent months this writer discovered several close friends who are dealing with parents facing these very issues, perhaps compounded with early stages of dementia or Alzheimer's disease. Often the grown children suffer in silence, balancing the daily burdens of their own lives, while steadfastly tending to their parents' care and needs, a time-consuming task especially if the older parent is frail or becomes confused and wanders.

Wandering Is a Common Occurrence

This "caregiving" life-stage experience is not uncommon, especially with approximately 25,000 Rhode Islanders afflicted with Alzheimer's. According to Elizabeth Morancy, executive director of the Alzheimer's Association, Rhode Island Chapter, about 70 percent of people with dementia reside at home or in the community. She estimated that six out of 10 people with Alzheimer's will "wander" to some degree.

Morancy noted that "wandering" occurs when a person with dementia becomes missing as when an individual becomes lost after leaving home. The restless individual may actually leave with a purpose or goal in mind. Maybe he or she might search for a lost item, look for a child, or try to fulfill a former job responsibility.

"Situations that seem harmless to us can become dangerous, even fatal, to the Alzheimer's person," Morancy noted. "Because a confused person does not panic or realize their dangerous predicament of walking on a highway or into the woods, a dangerous, even life-threatening situation, can occur," she said.

The ABCs To Reduce Wandering

According to Morancy, wandering can be reduced by following a few tips. Movement and exercise can reduce behavior, agitation and restlessness (causes for this negative behavior). Make sure all basic needs, such as toileting, nutrition, and thirst, are met. Involve the person with dementia in performing daily activities like folding laundry or making dinner. Color-matching cloth over doorknobs can effectively camouflage the hardware. A black rectangle on the floor placed inside the doorway can become a visual barrier, keeping the wanderer inside. By placing a mirror near a doorway, a reflection of the person's face will often keep the individual from opening the door and leaving the house.

"Even simple actions like rigging an alarm by hanging tin cans with string from a door or using door locks that the confused person cannot operate can work effectively," Morancy said.

Morancy added that one of the most effective ways of reducing wandering is to register the person with Alzheimer's or dementia in the Alzheimer's Association's MedicAlert + Safe Return Program. It operates through local police departments and other emergency-responder agencies working with Alzheimer's Association chapters across the country. The government-funded initiative has a national information and photo database. It operates 24 hours a day, seven days a week, with a toll-free crisis line.

Once registered, when a person with dementia wanders or becomes lost, a phone call immediately activates a community-support network that works together to reunite the lost person with his or her caregivers. Once the wandering individual is found, an identification product on the wanderer provides law officials with information to contact the caregiver. The nearest Alzheimer's Association office provides support during the rescue efforts. Medical information is immediately available if needed.

MedicAlert + Safe Return Program needs to be tweaked, said Morancy. "The initiative is not yet proactive. Although registration helps to identify the person who wears an identity bracelet or necklace or carries a wallet identity card (noting an 800-toll-free number), the identity information enables caregivers to ultimately be contacted, but this is after the fact," she said. "There is no universal system that will track down persons while they are lost."

In other states, Project Lifesaver, administered by the local sheriff's department, utilizes a tracking mechanism. However, its high cost decreases its use throughout the nation.

Initiatives like MedicAlert + Safe Return and Project Lifesaver have been instrumental in returning wanderers to safe home environments. These programs are crucial to aging baby boomers who work hard to successfully keep their confused parents at home rather than institutionalize them. The incidence of physical harm and death increases if a person is not found within a 24-hour period.

REPORT: CAREGIVERS FACE DEMANDING PERSONAL AND PROFESSIONAL CHALLENGES

Published on October 3, 2014, in the Pawtucket Times

Providing care to cognitively and complex chronically impaired family members can be hazardous to the health and mental well-being of caregivers, says a jointly issued report by the United Hospital Fund and AARP Public Policy Institute.

The researchers found that the demanding personal and professional challenges lead to high levels of self-reported challenges.

According to Family Caregivers Providing Complex Chronic Care to People with Cognitive and Behavioral Health Conditions, a publication in "Insight on the Issues" released on August 19, a majority of respondents (61 percent) reported constant stress, between their caregiving responsibilities and trying to meet other work or family obligations.

Adding to the challenge, people with cognitive and behavioral conditions (collectively termed in the 13-page report "challenging behaviors") were generally sicker than other people requiring caregiving. These persons needing care often had chronic physical health diagnoses—including cardiac disease, stroke/hypertension, musculoskeletal problems (such as arthritis or osteoporosis), and diabetes—at higher rates than those without cognitive and behavioral conditions. Further illustrating the complexity, family caregivers of people with challenging behaviors often met with resistance from the person they were trying to help. Caregivers noted that "more cooperation from their family member" would make one key medical/nursing task—managing medications—easier.

The findings are drawn from additional analysis of data based on a December 2011 national survey of 1,677 family caregivers, 22 percent of whom were caring for someone with one or more challenging behaviors. Earlier findings were published in the groundbreaking Public Policy Institute/United Hospital Fund report "Home Alone: Family Caregivers Providing Complex Chronic Care" and in earlier publications in the "Insight on the Issues" series, including "Employed Family Caregivers Providing Complex Chronic Care" and "Family Caregivers Providing Complex Chronic Care to Their Spouses."

The report concludes, "All caregivers need training and support; caregivers who are responsible for people with challenging behaviors are among those most in need of assistance."

Focused caregiver assessments were one of six recommendations outlined in the report. The others were better integration of behavioral and physical health programs, efforts to set up respite and adult day-care programs for family caregivers, training of family caregivers to better understand and respond to challenging behaviors, better training of health care providers to work more effectively with family caregivers, and revisions to most support and training materials for family caregivers to reflect care management of the whole person, rather than just the specific condition.

"Caregiving is rarely uncomplicated," said AARP State Director Kathleen Connell. "Add these issues and the stress on the caregiver grows and can feel unceasing. We need to be mindful of the circumstances caregivers face. In the larger scheme, this points to the need for a strong strategy that provides support to all caregivers."

Susan Reinhard, AARP's senior vice president for public policy, adds: "Take a hard look at this profile of today's overstretched and overstressed caregiver for someone with cognitive or behavioral issues. This is the face of caregiving's future unless we improve long-term services and support for family caregivers," she said, pointing to the expected surge in the incidence of Alzheimer's disease and the projected drop by more than half in the ratio of potential caregivers to those likely to need care.

"Caring for a family member is hard enough when the family member is on the same page," said co-author Carol Levine, director of the families and health care project for United Hospital Fund. "But when that family member has a cognitive impairment, like Alzheimer's, or a behavioral issue, such as depression—things that can interfere with daily life as well as decision-making—the burden on the caregiver is multiplied. And currently, our health care system often doesn't provide the kind of support that can make a difference."

Gearing Up

According to the Rhode Island Chapter of the Alzheimer's Association, in 2013 an estimated five million Americans age 65 and older have Alzheimer's disease. Unless more effective ways are identified and implemented to prevent or treat this devastating cognitive disorder, the prevalence may well triple, skyrocketing to almost 16 million people.

Meanwhile, with 24,000 Rhode Islanders afflicted with Alzheimer's disease, every Rhode Islander is personally touched, either caring for a family member with the cognitive disorder or knowing someone who is a caregiver or patient. As indicated by the recently released AARP/United Hospital Fund report, many of these caregivers will be doubly challenged by taking care of a loved one with chronic diseases who also has chronic and behavioral issues.

As reported in a previous column, both federal and state officials are gearing up to battle the nation's impending Alzheimer's epidemic.

Amazingly, with the November election looming, candidates for Lt. Governor may be discussing a multitude of issues, but not the Ocean State's impending Alzheimer's epidemic and its impact on caregivers. Nor are the candidates talking about how they would continue the work of Lt. Governor Elizabeth Roberts in implementing the long-term Care Coordinating Council's efforts to fully implement the state's Alzheimer's plan.

With the Lt. Governor being given the responsibility of overseeing the work of the Long-Term Care Coordinating Council, maybe aging policy issues like the state's impending Alzheimer's disease epidemic and its impact on state resources and caregivers should be thoroughly debated. It's a no-brainer.

"Family Caregivers Providing Complex Chronic Care to People with Cognitive and Behavioral Health Conditions" was produced with support from the John A. Hartford Foundation. The report is available at **www.uhfnyc.org/publications /881005**.

To review Rhode Island's Alzheimer's plan go to **http://goo.gl/rG0niF.**

TALE OF TWO CAREGIVERS

Published October 5, 2012, in the Pawtucket Times

Being a caregiver to an older parent while raising children has now become the new rite of passage for aging baby-boomers, who, by the millions, are moving into their middle-aged years and beyond. Often called the sandwich generation for having care responsibilities at both ends of the age spectrum, these individuals become emotionally challenged and physically drained in their attempts to cope with and juggle a multitude of tasks.

According to the National Alliance for Caregiving and AARP, more than 65 million persons, 29 percent of the nation's population, provide care for a chronically ill, disabled older family member or relative during any given year. The caregiver spends an average of 20 hours per week providing care for their loved one.

Taking on New Caregiving Responsibilities

Over seven years ago, Catherine Taylor, 51, the state's director of the Department of Elderly Affairs, and her husband, Rob, a practicing attorney, found themselves thrust into this new, very demanding role with huge responsibilities. Like many others, the couple took on the demanding role of being caregivers of an elderly parent while juggling the intense domestic demands of taking care of four children, whose ages ranged from 3 years old to age 15.

The Providence couple was now sharing the care of a very independent 83-year-old widow, who at that time resided in her home in Connecticut, that she had designed. The older woman still continued to practice as an architect until her health began to rapidly decline.

In 1995, "We moved her back to Rhode Island six months before she died when she became too infirm to live independently in her home," remembered Catherine.

Catherine wanted her mother-in-law to move in with her family, "but she was just too independent for that," she said. Her husband's mother would ultimately choose to live out her final days in an apartment at a senior living facility on Providence's Eastside, near the Taylor's home.

As is the case with many caregivers who relocated their loved ones to live close by, packing, scheduling the move, and getting the Connecticut house ready for sale became the first chore of being a caregiver.

According to Catherine, becoming a caregiver while working and raising a large family was incredibly hectic. "Many times we had to be in two or three places at one time," each day. Catherine adjusted her work schedule to help her mother-in-law with activities of daily living such as dressing, assistance in going to the bathroom, feeding, taking her to the emergency room, or staying with her in the hospital, while wanting to be at home cooking her family dinner and helping her children do their homework.

Tips on Coping for Caregivers

The couple juggled their roles as parents, caregivers, and employees as best they could. For instance, "our oldest child would be charged with watching his younger siblings," Catherine says. When visiting her mother-in-law to cook and assist her with eating, Catherine brought the youngest along to the senior living facility and placed him in a portable playpen next to the kitchen table. Catherine, her husband, and his sister, would divvy up cooking chores, each one taking responsibility for making either breakfast, lunch, or dinner.

Supplemental care, provided by a home health aide, was especially needed when the baby boomer couple had to be at work.

While taxing for the entire family, caregiving did have a positive impact on Catherine's children. "It really impressed on them how our family pulled together," she said, noting "that it made them feel useful because they had specific jobs to perform to keep the family running."

When asked if she got enough respite care for herself, Catherine quipped, "I never get enough!" She added, "For us being part of a large nuclear family, also having a large extended family, we were able to trade off with each other. But a lot of people don't have that option," she notes. One of the hardest things about being a primary caregiver is how alone you can feel, Catherine said. "You're living a different life from most other people. You watch other families make snap decisions to go to the movies and just hop in their car and go. For you to do the same thing, the logistics tend to be like the invasion of Normandy. You just have to go through so much organizing to have simple pleasures that other people don't think twice about."

"Most family caregivers look like they are doing fine and think they are doing fine, but family, friends and neighbors, and sometimes community agencies, need to check in and give them a break so they can recharge their batteries."

Catherine suggests that caregivers maintain their relationships with friends and colleagues as hard as that is to do so they will look in on you, stop by for coffee, bring you dinner, and help recharge you. "This will allow you to keep doing your caregiving job with love."

Double Duty as a Caregiver

Sixty-four-year old Kathy Heren, Rhode Island's Long-Term Care ombudsman, a licensed practical nurse and caregiver, and her husband, John, 63, a chef, slipped into caregiving in the mid-1990s, watching out for two elder family members at the same time, a 72-year-old mother and her 78-year-old uncle.

Both frail relatives (one had dementia and the other a heart condition) lived independently in their homes located in East Providence and on the East Side of Providence. "Being Irish, they were both very stubborn in accepting assistance," the aging advocate remembered. While professionally helping others cope with caregiving and long-term care issues, Rhode Island's ombudsman had to carve out time to personally perform chores for her two frail family members. These included shopping, paying bills, and cleaning their houses. Scheduling and transportation to doctor appointments and med management took additional time away from her very demanding job.

When dealing with her mother's finances became just too difficult, Kathy, along with her sister, filed for guardianship. "If you realize that there are some things you just can't control, then seek outside services or assistance," she recommended.

"Depending on the personality of the person you are taking care of, you may have to just step away from being a caregiver, if it impacts on your health," she says. "It may become the right time to turn to a nursing home or home care services to take care of your frail family member."

"Make sure you turn to respite care if needed because it is always available," Kathy suggests. "You need to know when to seek out this assistance and go on a trip to recharge your batteries. When taking care of your loved one, do not forget your own health, family, or nutrition," she says.

THE CHALLENGES OF CARING FOR YOUR AGING PARENT

Published July 3, 2008, in All Pawtucket All The Time

I t's not easy being a parent. Combine this with being a primary caregiver for an aging, frail relative, and you work a 48-hour day. Sixty-year-old Karen Sciolto, like many of her aging baby boomer peers, took on caregiving responsibilities in her mid-50s.

Five years earlier, the Scituate resident began her experience of taking care of frail adults by working as a Certified Nursing Assistant (CNA). "You really had to physically be able to move a person around and help to meet their emotional needs," she stated. She acknowledged she was "sort of a jack-of-all-trades" and had to "know a little bit about a lot of things."

With her CNA job, Sciolto knew that the caregiver role and responsibilities in her family would ultimately fall upon her shoulders because her parents were getting older. Very soiled long underwear discovered after a visit to an emergency room and a later inspection of the uncle's house revealed "cockroaches and filth. He just could not take care of himself," she said. Scattered piles of newspapers mingled with important papers and money hidden in holes in his mattress pushed his niece to become a caregiver in 2000 for her 87-year-old uncle, whose physical and mental health were deteriorating.

For six years, Sciolto was the solo caregiver of her uncle. She would drop him off each day at the local senior center to give him physical, emotional, and social stimulation. The aging baby boomer would also juggle a variety of daily tasks: CNA assign-ments, housework, along with raising her daughter and caring for three horses. "As a caregiver, my whole life revolved around meeting his needs," she said.

Many times she was overwhelmed with the stress of providing 24-hour-a-day care for her frail uncle. "You were lucky if you went to bed and could get a good night's sleep," she added.

A Generational Experience

According to Roberta Hawkins, executive director of the Alliance for Better Long-Term Care, Sciolto's caregiving experiences are not unique but common to thousands of aging baby boomers in Rhode Island.

Rhode Island's most visible aging advocate, who has led this nonprofit agency for more than 32 years, understands caregiving both on a personal and professional level. In her 60s, Hawkins looks back at her personal experiences. In her younger days she took care of grandparents while raising her young daughter. In recent years, Hawkins would raise her grandchildren while providing care to her disabled husband.

Hawkins warned aging baby boomers "not to take on [responsibilities] that you can't do." Know your abilities and also your limitations, she said. "You really need to think clearly if you are the right person who can provide that care."

"Often adult children will feel guilty if they do not take care of their disabled parents," observed Hawkins. "This may not be the right move due to their responsibility of raising children. They may have limited patience to deal with the changing health care needs and personality of their older parent."

"If older parent and child did not get along in their earlier years, caregiving just won't work," Hawkins said. "There won't be the patience or the connection needed to provide care in peace and harmony."

Every Day and Night

"Caregiving is a 24-hour, seven-day-a-week job," Hawkins said. "Even if you bring in outside caregivers during the day, you will still have to deal with nighttime and weekends," she said. "Nobody is happy" with household stress. This may push the older person to withdraw so they become less of a burden to their adult children.

"Sending your older parent to a senior center or day-care site might not be the most appropriate strategy," Hawkins added. "If the person was not a friendly or social person attending day-care will not be a very happy experience," she said.

Meanwhile, Hawkins said that some problems may also surface if an adult child hires an outside caregiver to keep their aging parent at home. "The older parent may be a mistrustful person and not want a stranger coming into their own home. This person may resent the fact that their children won't be there for them, and this can result in continuous complaints about the caregiver," she said.

"Before hiring an outside caregiver or becoming one yourself, always have a very frank discussion with the older person about your decision," Hawkins recommended. Conversations should begin before a health issue forces an adult child or spouse to make this decision without the wishes and desires of their older parent being known, she added.

If the time comes to consider placement in an assisted-living or nursing-home facility, it becomes crucial for the older person to be included in the decision-making process. "Give them all the pros and cons for each and every decision," Hawkins said. "Match the older person to the place they are going to live in, not the other way around."

Promises Made, Promises Broken

Finally, caregivers must give themselves some time off to recharge their batteries. "If there are siblings around, be adamant that they help take care of their older parent, too," she tells aging baby boomers shouldering the caregiving responsibilities. "Everyone promises but they tend to be too busy with their lives to give any assistance," she said.

Sadly, Hawkins brings up the old saying, "One mother can bring up five children but five children may not take care of the mom." So true, she said, noting, "I see it all the time."

WHEN IT IS TIME TO TAKE AWAY MOM'S AND DAD'S CAR KEYS

Published April 12, 2013, in the Pawtucket Times

On May 2, 2003, Rhode Island State Rep. Mabel Anderson was looking to buy her husband, George, a birthday present from one of his favorite stores, Home Depot. As she pushed a shopping carriage near the front entrance of the huge box store located in the Bristol Place Shopping Center in South Attleboro, Massachusetts, an 86-year-old driver getting ready to exit his parking space accidently shifted his vehicle into "reverse" rather than "drive" and stepped on the gas pedal.

The vehicle jolted in the wrong direction, and ran over Anderson. She was transported to a nearby hospital where she was pronounced dead hours later. Anderson's tragic death a decade ago continues to play out today in communities across the nation.

Many baby boomers, coping with a decline in their driving skills because of the aging process, keep driving well into their later years when, for safety's sake, they should retire the car keys.

Driving Skills Decline in Later Years

According to the National Highway Safety Administration, older individuals made up 17 percent of all traffic accidents and eight percent of all people injured in crashes in 2010.

Compared with 2009, fatalities among this age group increased by three percent and one percent for these older persons being injured.

Meanwhile, John Paul, manager of public affairs and traffic safety at AAA Southern New England, detailed research findings indicating that driving can be dangerous in your later years. The report, released by Carnegie Mellon University in Pittsburgh and the AAA Foundation for Traffic Safety, found the rate of deaths involving drivers 75 to 84 "is about three per million miles driven: on par with teen drivers," said Paul. Yet once they pass age 85, vehicular fatality rates jump to nearly four times that of teens, he said.

Many older motorists lose their ability to drive when the aging process kicks in. For these individuals, driving skills lessen because of poor vision caused by cataracts, glaucoma and macular degeneration, compounded with poor hearing, lack of flexibility, limited range of motion, and reduced reaction time. These aging processes make the complex tasks associated with driving more difficult. Cognitive impairments, such as Alzheimer's disease and dementias, can also impact one's ability to drive safely.

As older-driver fatalities increase and the death toll tied to older-driver accidents skyrockets, an increasing number of states are looking at licensing restrictions as a way to delicately approach this complicated issue.

Like many aging advocates, Gerry Levesque, AARP's state coordinator for the driver-safety program, said that not all seniors are equally affected as they age. "One may lose the necessary skills needed to drive safely at age 60, while another will not lose those skills until 90," stated the 66-year-old Coventry resident.

"For older adults, losing driving privileges can be translated as a loss of independence," noted Levesque. If this occurs, family or public transportation may not be available to replace the lack of transportation. "Older people may feel stranded or abandoned when they give up their keys," said Levesque, noting that driving allows an older adult to pick up prescriptions, shop for groceries, or get out to socialize at the bridge club, bingo parlor, or simply to be with family and friends.

"One thing that seniors have that the younger generation does not is a lifetime of driving. While they are losing physical abilities, they do have a wealth of experience from their years of driving," added Levesque.

Coping With an Aging Population that Drives

Over the years, states have grappled with the age-charged issue of restricting licenses of seniors, not wishing to stir up their wrath. Aging advocates oppose any "blanket" solution to this problem that calls for licensing restrictions, rather recommending that it be made on a case-by-case basis. They say age should not be used as a "predictor" of unsafe driving.

In Rhode Island, the Division of Motor Vehicles (DMV) prorates its license-renewal cycle for individuals age 71 and older. If you are 75 years of age or older, your license will be valid for two years. At license-renewal time, the older person is required to pass a vision test or provide a valid medical-examination certificate. A person's physical or mental fitness to operate a motor vehicle is reviewed by DMV's medical advisory board whenever a case is brought to its attention by law enforcement, a physician, or a family member.

With a growing aging population, Rhode Island's Department of Transportation (RIDOT) has moved to tackle senior-driving issues head-on. Two years ago, the state agency began to install a series of reflective markers, or "roadside delineators," on the sides of roads as well as mounted on small posts and on top of concrete barriers. Especially geared for older drivers, these improvements were made to assist in making nighttime driving easier and safer, while also aiding driving during adverse weather.

In addition to these improvements, RIDOT has installed cable-guard rails along narrow medians on the interstate where none previously existed. This safety feature significantly reduces the occurrence of head-on impacts with opposing traffic. State transportation officials have also made improvements to rural roads by adding rumble strips, signing, and roadside reflectors to help reduce road-departure crashes.

Sharpen Your Driving Skills

AARP, along with the AAA Southern New England, recognized the thorny issues surrounding restrictive licensing and have developed special training courses for older motorists to refresh their skills to help them drive safely, thus reducing their risk of having their license revoked by state authorities.

AAA's Senior Defense Driving Program provides information about the aging process (**www.seniordriving.aaa.com**) and its impact on a person's ability to drive. The program gives tips on how a person can compensate for these changes and drive safely for a longer period of time. In addition, a self-administered program, called "Roadwise Review," provides confidential and instant feedback on performance in key areas, allowing individuals to see how changing visual, mental, and physical conditions can impact driving. The Auto Club's "Roadwise RX" also allows older drivers to look at the interaction between medications and driving.

AARP's Safe Driving Program (**http://goo.gl/VM6BFj**) the nation's first and largest refresher course for drivers age 50 and older, has helped millions of drivers sharpen their driving skills. The four-hour program teaches defensive-driving techniques, new traffic laws, and rules of the road as well as (and more importantly) how to adjust your driving style to those age-related changes to vision, hearing, and reaction time. After successfully completing the Aging Group's Safe Driving Program held in Rhode Island, the attendee is awarded a certificate of completion. The state mandates that the insurance carrier give a discount on liability coverage to the policy holder with this certificate.

SurrenderingtheKeys

Ultimately the burden may well fall on the family or the older motorist's physician to take away the keys from the driving-challenged senior for the driver's safety as well as the safety of those sharing the road.

In the late 1990s, my mother began to exhibit signs of dementia. Yet my father could not stop my mother from driving. The only solution appeared to come from making a call to the Texas Department of Motor Vehicles (TDMV) for help.

Several times my mother got lost driving around our neighborhood, an area once familiar to her, ultimately ending up confused and miles from home on the dangerous LBJ Freeway. With her driving skills rapidly deteriorating, my siblings took on the task of making that hard decision of taking away her car keys. After several meetings with TDMV officials, the agency finally took away her driver's license.

As difficult as this decision was for my family to make, my mother, who was in the mid-to-late stages of dementia, ultimately did not realize that she had lost her driving privileges and her precious car keys.

Kristi Grigsby, vice president of Content of **www.AgingCare.com**, agreed that taking away the keys from an elderly parent is one of the most difficult decisions that family caregivers must make. "The loss of independence can be traumatic for a senior," she said, noting that some elderly parents can accept the life-altering change; others understandably cannot.

Grigsby warned that the consequences of doing nothing far outweigh the wrath of an angry parent. "Stories of tragedies that could have been avoided had those keys been taken away are sometimes all the inspiration needed to stand firm and make a painful decision with confidence," she said.

For more information about taking away the keys from an elderly parent go to **http://goo.gl/VM6BFj**.

Information on this website, **www.AgingCare.com**, connects people caring for their elderly parents with experts on aging issues. Caregivers who visit this site help family members make the best care decisions for older loved ones.

WHEN THAT TIME COMES TO LIQUIDATE YOUR CHILDHOOD HOME

Published March 29, 2013, in the Pawtucket Times

I t's a traditional rite of passage that marks a person transitioning to baby-boom-er-hood: the difficult task of cleaning out a childhood home. Like millions of aging baby boomers before her, a writer friend of mine is facing this later-life-stage milestone and the challenging chore of cleaning out 50 years' of accumulated "stuff" in her parents' home, following the recent passing of her widowed father.

The East Providence resident told me her parents, married for more than 60 years, had lived in their 1960s ranch-style house for 50 years, while the couple's household goods just kept accumulating. "Beyond basic cleaning, my parents never really 'decluttered' or even had a yard sale," she noted, where they could easily have got rid of household clutter to make some extra cash.

Overcoming Seller's Guilt, Finding Time To Sort

Never mind the emotional feelings she has experienced, especially the twinge of guilt at disposing of things that were once important to her parents and accumulated over five decades. "What about the time it takes to sift through a lifetime of accumulated household goods, clothing, and furniture," observed my overwhelmed friend. "It's just too much stuff to get rid of, especially with my very demanding full-time job and little time on the weekends to sort through things."

"Many of my parents' personal items, like a solid dark-cherrywood bedroom set, dishes, glasses, barware, and vases from the 1940s and 1950s, boxes of old coins, even hand-embroidered tablecloths and runners are just too nice to get rid of at a weekend yard sale," noted my friend. Yet these items may not be considered true antiques, she said.

"Where do you take Mom's collection of Franklin Mint plates, porcelain figurines of carousel horses and birds, even some Hummel pieces?" my friend asked, who does not want to drive around to the coin store, antique dealer, or linen store to sell each item. Selling on eBay is just too much work, she said.

Choose the Right Strategy To Liquidate

Which steps do older children take in cleaning out a lifetime of their parents' personal mementos and belongings from their childhood home? Do you rent a dumpster and begin indiscriminately tossing away loved ones' cherished possessions or hire a professional liquidator or junk hauler to have someone come and do the pitching for you? What about holding a big weekend yard sale that might just do the trick? Be warned: by choosing one of these options you might undersell an item that could be valuable due to its age, quality, or rarity.

"Making the right decision on how to liquidate your parents' personal belongings might just rest on how financially well-heeled they were," said Scott Davis, who, with his wife, Rae, operates New England's highest-volume antiques venue, the Rhode Island Antique Mall.

"Having liquidated many hundreds of estates, I can tell you that unless you come from a family of significant means or your parents were knowledgeable collectors, it's highly unlikely that the combined value of the estate's tangible assets is going to have a wholesale liquidation value of over $5,000, once the family claims the items they want to keep, which are usually the most valuable," noted the antique dealer. "Thus you have to make a decision about how much effort is really appropriate for you to spend trying to get top dollar for every object."

"If your parents' estate is known to have higher-value tangible assets, you might want to first hire an appraiser to determine the value of at least the most important items," suggested Davis, noting that "a legitimate appraiser should always charge by the hour, not by item value."

Davis stated that higher-end antique dealers or auction houses will "cherry-pick" your items, taking only the most interesting and valuable things. Antique dealers should typically pay the most for each item. Auctioneers might bring more but will never guarantee it. Many items sold at auction bring shockingly low prices, so deciding which way to go depends on your risk tolerance. Other dealers or liquidators will offer to take a larger percentage of the household goods at a lower cost per item, while junk dealers or junk-removal services may take everything in the house yet will frequently actually charge you for the service while keeping anything they can resell. "You have to determine what type of service suits your situation best," Davis said, adding that in his experience it never pays to go straight to the junk guy first.

Davis recommended that in most cases it doesn't pay to attempt to sell items yourself, noting that it can be very time-consuming to sell things one piece at a time, and buyers are hesitant to pay retail prices to inexperienced sellers. An antique dealer or private buyer can be easily found online, in local telephone books or in dealer directories that can be found in local shops. According to Davis, if you choose this option, dealers will typically offer you less than half of the anticipated retail value of the items, but they of course have a lot of risk and expense along with their entitlement to earn a profit for their efforts.

Some folks attempt to sell their items on eBay or craigslist, but Davis warned that unless you have a lot of prior experience, the results are usually disappointing or worse. Selling online yourself requires a lot of time for research, photography, copy-writing, corresponding, and shipping, while buyers tend to shy away from sellers who have little or no feedback, which can result in no takers for fixed-price sales or very low prices realized for auction sales.

While it may take longer to sell everything, consignment is another option you might consider, Davis said. However, the Pawtucket-based antique dealer warned that you'll usually pay from 35 percent to 60 percent of the item's retail selling price for this service.

Davis urged folks to always look for customer traffic, location, reputation, and fee structure if you choose to place items on consignment. Check the references of the antique dealer or liquidator you may be interested in working with, inspecting their retail establishment to determine if it is professionally run. He noted that a consigned piece usually sells in 60 days or less; otherwise the price is reduced or the item is returned to you. Antique shops or malls are the best places to consign more valuable antiques, collectibles, and vintage items, while newer or lesser-valued items will usually do best in local consignment shops that focus on useful secondhand items. Pawn shops are rarely, if ever, your best option unless you wish to borrow money using the items as collateral, he said.

When cleaning out a home, throw away old mattresses, towels, bedding, and paper-work, as these items are usually not valuable and will cost you more for others to dispose of, said Davis, who noted that often it is not easy to determine which other things should just be thrown away. "Although traditional antiques and collectibles like pottery, glassware, and china frequently have little demand in today's market, seeming-ly valueless items that include war souvenirs, political memorabilia and even nostalgic items like old telephones, light fixtures, and old linens may be quite valuable," he said.

Davis warned not to begin your housecleaning by throwing things away in a dumpster or planning your yard sale without first calling a reputable antique dealer or estate liquidator to assist you in "separating the wheat from the chaff." They are accustomed to sorting through drawers, boxes, closets, and basements, and their experience enables them to quickly identify valuable items.

"Finally, rare antiques and collectibles can be sold for top dollar at auctions," Davis noted. "The right item in the wrong auction can produce a total flop," he observed, noting that there's usually a long wait between the day you initially contact an auction house and the day an item actually sells: probably about a year. A good full-service liquidator can help you to determine when auctioning is the right option and, if so, which auctioneer will suit you best. They are usually paid by the auctioneer for this referral service, so it's a no-lose for the seller.

For more information on liquidating your childhood home, contact Scott Davis at (401) 475-3400, email him at RIAntiquesMall@cox.net, or go to **www.riantiquesmall.com.**

2. CONSUMER ISSUES

BEING VIGILANT KEEPS PHONE SCAMMERS AWAY

Published July 18, 2014, in the Pawtucket Times

When 81-year-old Cincinnati resident Roger W. answered a call in December, he thought it was his grandson on the other end of the phone. The young voice said, "Grandpa, this is your favorite grandson," he remembered, replying, "I have six grandsons and they are all my favorites." Claiming to be the oldest, the "grandson" said he had been arrested for speeding and drug possession and urgently needed money for bail. He then turned the call over to a person claiming to be a police officer. Convinced their eldest grandson needed help, Roger W. and his wife headed to a local retail store to purchase a money-order card to cover the cost of bail.

After sending a total of $7,000 to the supposed police officer, the elderly couple soon discovered they had been conned out of their hard-earned money after reaching their real grandson on his cell phone. They are among an untold number of older Americans who have fallen victim to a commonly used scam known as the "grandparent scam" that experts say is again making a comeback across the nation.

Senate Aging Hearing Puts the Spotlight on Phone Scams

Roger W., who has requested anonymity to avoid becoming a target of other con artists, testified two days ago at a hearing of the U.S. Senate Special Committee on Aging held at the Senate Dirksen building. The hearing examined the recent rise in impostor scams, particularly the grandparent scam.

Along with Roger W., witnesses at the July 16th hearing included officials from the Federal Bureau of Investigation, Federal Trade Commission (FTC), and the United States Telecom Association, who discussed potential solutions to protecting consumers and curbing phone scams.

According to the FTC, Americans lost more than $73 million to impostor scams in 2013. While the federal agency admits the figure is underreported, accounting for only a fraction of the problem because most victims fail to report the crime, instances of impostor scams have doubled between 2009 and 2013. Senators Bill Nelson (D-FL) and Susan Collins (R-ME), the committee's chairman and ranking member, called for this hearing after receiving a large number of complaints from victims through the committee's fraud hot line. The two lawmakers said they're hoping the hearing will help identify potential solutions to help law enforcement to better detect and prosecute such crimes, as well as encourage retailers and phone companies to do their part to protect consumers.

Phone Scams Commonly Reported in Rhode Island

According to the Rhode Island Office of the Attorney General, the Ocean State is not immune to the financial scam, described at the recent Senate Aging hearing by Roger W. There are slight variations of the "grandparent scam" story where con artists pretend to be a family member and claim they need money to fix a car, get out of jail, or leave a foreign country. They will beg you to wire money right away and keep the information confidential. In some cases, the scammers even know the names of family members. In other instances, the person on the other end of the line may pretend to be a police officer or friend calling on behalf of the grandchild.

In 2013, the Attorney General's Consumer Protection Unit responded to 6,229 tele-phone calls, 1,144 written complaints, 1,534 e-mail inquiries, and 74 walk-ins. While the Consumer Protection Unit does not keep statistics on each scam that is reported, the grandparent scam is no stranger to the employees.

"We see a spike in these types of scams during times when a grandchild might be on vacation, like school break or summers, making the story more believable to the person on the other end of the phone," said Attorney General Peter Kilmartin. The attorney general's office includes a Consumer Protection Unit, which, among other responsibilities, warns the public about such scams and educates consumers on how to protect themselves from being a victim of a scam, he says.

"Con artists have turned fraud into a multi-billion-dollar business. Each year, thousands of consumers lose anywhere from a few dollars to their life savings to scams. Once the money is gone, it is very difficult, if not impossible, to recover your funds."

There are big hurdles law enforcement must overcome to catch the scammer who is behind these cons. If a scam originated out of the state, or even out of the country, it is often beyond the reach of local or state law enforcement officials, adds Kilmartin. Complicating matters is technology, he says, noting that long gone are the days when people's locations could be easily identified and tracked by their phone number. With cellular technology, prepaid cell phones and "spoofing" apps, a person may be running his con from a foreign country while your caller ID shows an in-state phone number, he says.

AG's Top Priority To Protect Consumers Against Fraud and Scams

"As attorney general, it is one of my top priorities to protect all consumers from fraud and scams. Consumer protection is largely self-protection. Becoming a smart and savvy consumer does not mean changing your daily routine—it means becoming more aware of how to avoid becoming a victim. As the saying goes, knowledge is power. It is my belief that consumers and businesses can better protect themselves and their assets if they are aware of their rights and are aware of the fraudulent or deceptive practices scammers use," said Kilmartin.

Tammy Miller, director of the Consumer Protection Unit, said the reason that scamming older persons is so prevalent is because it works. "Sadly, con artists prey on older people because they tend to be more trusting. Once the money is wired, it's gone forever, and it's only then people realize they have been a victim of the scam. Because these outfits operate outside the state, and often outside the country, there is little law enforcement can do to track them down," she says.

According to Miller, Attorney General Kilmartin has made educating consumers a priority. As such, members of the Consumer Protection Unit provide approximately 150 outreach presentations each year to senior centers, community groups and organizations throughout the state in an effort to educate and protect Rhode Islanders from scam artists.

In addition, several consumer alerts/advisories are issued annually. The advisories cover a wide range of topics such as fake invoices, phishing scams, a fake jury duty and arrest scam, a "car wrap" scam, possible scams related to sporting events, consumer settlements, and holiday shopping tips.

"Although it is very difficult to measure, I believe our consumer outreach program has made a difference in lowering the number of victims of scams in Rhode Island. A good indicator is the increase in phone calls we receive from consumers alerting us whenever a scam pops up, which gives us a chance to get ahead of it, issue an alert and warn other consumers. I think that's a positive sign that we are making headway and creating confident and well-informed consumers," said Miller.

Miller says that Kilmartin has done a terrific job as attorney general in making the public aware of scams that are going around the state, which reduces the chances of someone else becoming a victim.

Quick Actions To Protect Yourself Against Phone Scams

So, what do you do if you receive a phone call from someone pretending to be a family member in need? Miller recommends that you first verify that it is your grandchild. Always ask for a phone number of the person on the other line. Before calling them back or wiring them money, contact the family member directly. If you cannot get hold of them, contact their parents or another family member to confirm their location.

Miller warns older persons to resist the intense pressure to send money quickly and secretly. Refuse to send money through wire transfer or overnight delivery. After you've thwarted the scam, Miller suggests you let your local police and the Consumer Protection Unit know about the call. Alerting the attorney general's office will allow them to alert the public that the scam is making the rounds and what to be on the lookout for.

To report a consumer-related issue, to speak with a consumer protection specialist at the attorney general's office, or to schedule a consumer protection specialist to speak before your community group or organization, call 401-274-4400, send an email at **contactus@riag.ri.gov**, or visit **http://goo.gl/5J8i1Y.**

To watch the Senate U.S. Special Committee on Aging hearing and to access witness testimony, go to **http://goo.gl/5J8i1Y.**

BEWARE OF HEALTH SCAMS

Published December 19, 2014, in the Pawtucket Times

L
ike millions of older baby boomers and seniors, some nights you just can't get to sleep. It's very late and you begin channel surfing. Does this sound familiar? Many TV viewers may ultimately find themselves, usually from 2:00 a.m. to 6:00 a.m., watching an infomercial announcer pitch a health product or service, always claiming your health will improve or that the aging process can be stopped or reversed, if you just purchase that bottle of dietary supplements, weight loss product, baldness remedies or sexual enhancement supplements, that home exercise machine or even register for a memory improvement course. The lists of products pitched on these paid commercials are endless.

The Vancouver, BC-based International Council on Active Aging (ICAA), a nonprofit group that supports professionals who develop wellness facilities, programs, and services for adults over 50, calls on older consumers to beware of false promises and products with little health benefit. "Unfortunately, as people over 50 pursue this goal, many succumb to what one industry insider calls 'graywashing' claims that chip away at older adults' retirement nest eggs with dubious promises of renewed youth and health," says Colin Milner, CEO and founder of ICAA, who coined the term *graywashing*.

There is No Fountain of Youth

According to Milner, there is no shortcut to improving your health. "Yet, people spend billions of dollars a year on products that claim there is," he observes. "Many products also say they will turn back time," he says, noting that the research shows these claims to be unsubstantiated.

Milner points to a statement by the National Institute on Aging (NIA), one of 27 institutes and centers of the National Institutes of Health, which states: "Despite claims about pills or treatments that lead to endless youth, no treatment has been proven to slow or reverse the aging process." Be aware, warns Milner, as health-fraud scams are abundant.

According to NIA's Age Page, "Beware of Health Scams," health product scams offer viable "solutions that appear to be quick and painless."

As to dietary and weight loss supplements, American consumers spend a small fortune on potions claiming to help shed pounds, many sold over the counter. Be careful.

Some supplements contain hidden illegal drugs and other chemicals that could cause serious harm.

The NIA fact sheet also says that most dietary supplements are not fully tested by the Federal Drug Administration, a federal agency charged with protecting the public's health. In 2014, FDA issued 63 warning letters to companies that cited unapproved or unsubstantiated claims, tainted products, or other health-fraud-related violations.

So think carefully before you purchase that item. It is important to talk with your physician before you begin taking a supplement or using a health product remedy.

The NIA Fact Sheet notes that arthritis remedies using magnets, copper bracelets, chemicals, special diets, and electronic devices, often unproven, can be quite expensive, potentially harmful, and unlikely to help. There is no cure for some forms of arthritis and rest, exercise, heat, and some drugs are the best ways to control the painful symptoms.

Health scams often target very sick people, especially those afflicted with cancer, in an attempt to trick people who are desperate for any remedy they can find. Buzzwords to beware of include: "quick fix," "secret ingredient," or "scientific breakthrough," states NIA's Fact Sheet.

Furthermore, weight loss, sexual enhancement and bodybuilding "supplements" are especially suspect, too, warns the NIA Fact Sheet. Some vitamins may help, but some supplements can harm people taking certain medicines or with some medical conditions. In particular, avoid those supplements claiming to shrink tumors, solve impotence, or cure Alzheimer's. There is no cure for Alzheimer's disease at this time.

Milner urges older Americans not to be swayed by personal testimonials featuring "real people" or "doctors," often played by actors who claim amazing cures. These testimonials are no substitute for real scientific studies and can tip you off to a scam. In general, never purchase or start taking a medical treatment without first talking to your health care professional, particularly if you already take other prescribed drugs, recommends Milner.

Don't Become a Victim of a Scam

Be knowledgeable about the health care products you buy, suggests Milner, noting that the NIA Fact Sheet recommends that a person question what he or she sees or hears in ads or online. Always ask your physician, nurse, pharmacist, or other health care provider about products you're thinking of buying. Most important, avoid products that "promise a quick or painless cure." Beware of claims that a health-care product is made from a "special, secret, or ancient formula" or it can "only be purchased from one company."

Also be wary if the infomercial claims the product can cure a wide variety of medical conditions or even successfully treat a devastating disease like Alzheimer's or chronic arthritis. Put your credit card away and hang up the phone if you are required to make an advance payment or there is a very limited supply of the product.

"Science may be getting closer to a Fountain of Youth," says Milner, but, "we're not there yet. The pillars of healthy aging are simple. They include a sensible diet, regular exercise, good sleep habits, meaningful relationships, and engagement in life."

A Final Note for Rhode Island's Attorney General

The Consumer Protection Unit at the office of the attorney general receives very few consumer complaints about deceptive health and beauty products, because most of these products are regulated on the federal level. The best advice they can offer con-sumers is to file a complaint with the federal Consumer Financial Protection Bureau, or CFPB. Although these types of products are not regulated by individual states, and therefore the attorney general has no jurisdiction over the sale of such products, Attorney General Peter Kilmartin reminds consumers that the age-old tip applies when considering a purchase, "If it sounds too good to be true, then it probably is."

One way consumers can protect themselves, says Kilmartin, is to "ask for medical documentation backing up the claims and to ask and understand the refund policies before making a purchase. Another way to protect yourself is to pay by credit card, not debit card. Many credit card companies will allow you to dispute payment if the product or service doesn't match up to its claims."

For more information about the National Council on Active Aging go to **www.icaa.cc**.

The FDA has created a new website(**www.fda.gov/ForConsumers/ConsumerUpdates / ucm278980.htm**) to help consumers protect themselves from fraudulent health products and schemes.

CREDIT BREACHES ARE HAZARDOUS TO YOUR FINANCIAL HEALTH

Published on October 17, 2014, in the Pawtucket Times

It seems to happen all the time. Just recently Target Corporation, Home Depot, Dairy Queen, and Neiman Marcus—followed by Michaels and more recently JPMorgan Chase and Kmart—found their data systems being breached. I thought that I had dodged the bullet from being a victim until last month when I received a letter from my local savings and loan warning me about a potential security breach affecting my credit card.

Data breaches and hacking annually affect millions of Americans, costing billions of dollars and countless hours for consumers to correct problems resulting from identity theft and fraud that results in their checks bouncing and being assessed late fees.

Data Breaches Not a Rare Occurrence

What exactly is a data breach? Simply put, a data breach occurs when a company's database, typically containing customer information, is hacked by sophisticated mal-ware programs that can infiltrate a company's network, sometimes for months before being noticed.

"Not that long ago, we were taught to always know where your wallet or purse was to ensure we didn't fall victim to a pickpocket. Yesterday's common street thief is today's computer hacker, and it is often months before you realized they've virtually picked your pocket," said Attorney General Peter Kilmartin.

According to the Rhode Island attorney general, his staff has been busy in the past year informing consumers about data breaches at some of the best-known retail and financial companies. He says there were multiple reports of massive data breaches at the nation's largest corporations. According to a recent survey, last year 43 percent of companies have suffered one data breach this past year, and 60 percent say they've been struck by multiple data breaches in the past two years.

"In today's technology-driven and paperless retail marketplace, it is inevitable that some, if not all, of your personal and financial information—credit card and banking information, email, and Social Security Number—will be compromised," warns Kilmartin.

Congressman James Langevin has been a leader on the issue of cybersecurity and is leading efforts inside the Washington Beltway. "Stories of public data breaches are becoming increasingly common, and if a Fortune 500 company is susceptible to these types of breaches, we can be sure that similar attacks are possible among other retailers and businesses," said Langevin, the co-founder and co-chair of the Congressional Cybersecurity Caucus. "I have been sounding the alarm on cybersecurity for years, and I fear the consequences if we delay any further the steps needed to strengthen our technology infrastructure," said Langevin.

The Democratic lawmaker, serving the 2nd Congressional District since 1991, says, "I am particularly concerned about the potential for cyberattack against critical infrastructure, including our power grid, wastewater management, and banking and health care systems, just to name a few. All of these essential services are tied into technology, and it is going to take both a strong commitment from government and a continued partnership between public and private industry in order to get us where we need to be on cybersecurity. Securing these networks must be a priority, and I believe it is a crucial component of our national and economic security strategies."

Kilmartin says that no doubt about it, data breaches are a crime, but law enforcement has significant hurdles to overcome when investigating cybercrimes. "Companies that have been targets of recent data breaches are working with federal law enforcement authorities to investigate how the breach happened and who is responsible," he notes, stressing that early evidence shows that most of the sophisticated criminal enterprises that commit cybercrimes operate outside of the United States, often in Eastern Europe. "The hackers are out of the reach of traditional law enforcement and U.S. courts, but that has not stopped local, state and federal authorities from investigating," he says.

Consumers Must Become Their Own Watchdog

"Consumers in today's world need to continually monitor their electronic purchases, their personal medical information as well as their banking records. Consumers can follow all the rules to protect their information, and if a business or other entity entrusted with this information is vulnerable, consumers, through no fault of their own, can still be impacted. Many times, a consumer's first contact with law enforcement may be dealing with the aftermath of a data breach or identity theft. Please know that we are there to help you and will thoroughly investigate to resolve these crimes," stated Col. Steven G. O'Donnell, superintendent of the Rhode Island State Police.

Kilmartin also confirmed that he and attorney generals in several states are looking into these data breaches and hope to get answers from the companies targeted as to how and why they took place. "There are multistate investigations by attorneys general into how these companies left consumer information vulnerable to an attack," he said, noting, "as consumer advocates, we are determined to get to the bottom of these data breaches and to work with the companies to better protect the consumer."

Kilmartin believes it is up to consumers to be their own watchdog: "While companies and law enforcement officials are trying to put an end to this trend, the only way someone can protect themselves is to be vigilant in monitoring their personal and financial information. And by that, I mean check your banking and credit card statements regularly and limit how much information you share with companies."

Keeping Credit Card Thieves at Bay

Kilmartin says, "I always tell consumers that the best way to protect yourself from scams is education. Being wary of potential scams and being a savvy consumer are the best ways to stop a scam artist in their tracks." He offers the following common-sense tips to protect your credit:

Check your credit card and debit card statements regularly, on a line-by-line basis. One may think to only look for large unauthorized charges, but thieves may place a small charge—only a few dollars—to check if the card is active. If that charge goes unnoticed, thieves will then make a large unauthorized purchase. Report all suspicious charges, no matter how small. And check your statements every day if possible. "It may be too late to recoup some or all of your money if you don't report it immediately," said Kilmartin.

If you notice an unauthorized charge, report it to your financial institution immediately, cancel the card, and have the bank issue you a new one.

Kilmartin recommends consumers take advantage of free credit monitoring many affected companies are offering. "Companies who have been impacted by a data breach don't want to lose customer loyalty. Many offer up to one free year of credit monitoring for any consumer who shopped there during the breach," he adds.

Consider adding a fraud alert to your credit report file to protect your credit information. A fraud alert can make it more difficult for someone to get credit in your name because it tells creditors to follow certain procedures, which may include contacting you directly, before authorizing the credit card, says Kilmartin, noting that while this may delay your ability to obtain credit immediately, it will protect you from someone fraudulently opening a credit card in your name.

Kilmartin urges Rhode Islanders to be suspicious of e-mails, phone calls, or text messages claiming to be from your bank or a retailer you shopped at. Hackers may not have gained access to all the information they need and will often use the information they do have, like name, date of birth, or credit card number, to convince you to part with even more sensitive information, such as passwords or Social Security numbers. When in doubt, call your financial institution directly with questions. The phone number is usually on the back of credit cards and debit cards.

Update your computer's anti-virus software. Just as hackers have wormed their way into secure databases at large-scale companies, they can worm their way into your computer.

Change your passwords. The most basic way to stop an intruder is to lock the door. Set strong passwords and don't reuse them for different accounts, especially for accounts that involve your banking or credit card information.

Go "old school" and pay with cash or check. While we have become accustomed to using credit and debit cards to make everyday purchases, every company still takes U.S. currency.

Under federal law, you are entitled to one free copy of your credit report every 12 months from each of the three nationwide credit reporting agencies. You may obtain a free copy of your credit report by going to **www.annualcreditreport.com** or by calling (877) 322-8228.

3. EMPLOYMENT SCENE

CHILDHOOD DREAM OF BECOMING A PHOTOGRAPHER BECOMES REALITY

Published December 7, 2012, in the Pawtucket Times

S ometimes an appreciation for the arts takes hold of your soul later in life and sometimes it takes place during your childhood. Briana Gallo, 39, was intrigued with photography at a very young age, which began while playing with her dad's old Nikon camera. Today with pride and excitement, she finds herself participating in her first show, selling her photographs at the 30th annual Foundry Artist's holiday sale.

Looking Back

"I could ride (a horse) before I learned to walk," remembered Gallo, who grew up on a 100-acre horse farm in Missouri. Little did the five-year-old child know that the seeds of her desire to be a professional photographer were gently planted while taking "pretend" shots of imaginary scenes. Years later, this ultimately created and shaped her photographic style as an adult.

Gallo's imagination guides her photography. "I want my photos to be full of emotion, with people becoming an integral part of the image." For those looking at her work, this Northfield, New Hampshire resident wants them to see the image she saw through the lens, hoping viewers become part of the exact moment the photograph was taken.

When Gallo turned 10 years old, the pain of her parents' divorce pushed her away from photography, taking her to Florida to live with her mother. As a sophomore at Armwood High School in her new community of Brandon, Florida, the young student again picked up a camera to join the school's yearbook staff. "I was all over the school clicking away, capturing each and every moment," she said. Gallo took on the responsibility of becoming the editor in her junior and senior years.

Snapping Pictures at College

After high school, Gallo entered Rollins College in Winter Park, Florida, where she majored in English, with two minors, teaching English as a second language and, of course, photography. The budding photographer made a few dollars on the side taking photos at sports events and sorority and fraternity parties. "Photography paid my bills," she said, yet noting that it took "absolutely no creativity."

As a college senior, Gallo traveled to attend photo workshops in Santa Fe, New Mexico, mostly focusing on landscapes and slide photography. These trips also reignited her love for riding horses. After graduating college, she ran a horseback-riding program for boys in North Carolina. Gallo trained Arabians to become "kid horses" for four years. This experience ultimately led her to meet her husband.

During her last winter in North Carolina, Gallo found her old manual camera. After wiping the dust off, she took a photograph of a white zinfandel wine bottle, which became an award-winning photo. The internal calling to become a professional photographer was reinforced when the wine company bought her photograph to use in an advertisement. "This was my sign," she said.

Relocating to New Hampshire, the couple would become directors at Interlocken, an international summer camp. Gallo fell back on her college skills of teaching English as a second language, combining it with photography, to work with the campers who came from all corners of the world. She also ultimately served as the camp's marketing and staffing director.

As a camp counselor, "I suddenly found myself back in the heart of photography," she said, " ...not taking pictures, but teaching the craft to the youngsters."

In time, the young couple bought a ranch in Northfield, New Hampshire, to establish Driftwood, their own camp and boarding facility. During the summer, they offered two three-week horseback-residential-riding programs to children.

Gallo realized that the skills she honed while training horses would also make her a better photographer as well. "Training young horses requires the eye, patience, and steadiness needed to become a professional photographer," she said. Ultimately closing her ranch allowed Gallo to bring photography back into her very hectic family life, especially with the time it takes to raise two small children.

With the purchase of a Canon 7D and learning about the digital darkroom at Rhode Island School of Design, Gallo was off and running to become a professional photographer. She traveled to Honduras with the nonprofit group, Shoulder to Shoulder, to create a photo essay of its work. This allowed Gallo to provide photos for use in the nonprofit's fund-raising, telling its story through many of her camera lenses. She also did her photo-philanthropy for City Arts and Mount Hope Youth Center located in Providence.

Last year Gallo traveled to Cuba, learning photo-taking tips from the world-renowned travel photographer Lorne Resnick, where the experience propelled her into the world of fine-art photography. Gallo reflected on her life's journey where she has found a way to do all that she loves: to be a mom, to work, to travel, to practice photography, while at the same time helping others.

Looking back over the years, Gallo has come to realize that "art is not what you see, but what you make others feel." With Gallo's attempts to become a full-time photographer, she added: "I'm definitely stepping into unknown waters. It's kind of like getting on a young horse for the first time."

Buy Local, Support Your Local Artist Community

Gallo becomes one of 65 seasoned artists who will show their work at the Foundry Artists Association's holiday sale, which is considered to be one of the top regional art sales, showcasing jewelry, glass, pottery, clothing, artwork, photography, and furni-ture. For the past 10 years, this Christmas event is held at the historic Pawtucket Armory, located on Exchange Street in Pawtucket.

The Foundry show, for Gallo, a first-time Foundry Arts Association participant, will allow her to showcase her unique photographic work (her website is **www.briana-gallo.com/**) to thousands of shoppers who want to purchase one-of-a-kind photos with the added benefit of not having to pay sales tax on their purchase.

JOB HUNTING NO EASY CHORE AS YOU GROW OLDER

Published November 29, 2013, in the Pawtucket Times

L ast Friday, the U.S. Bureau of Labor Statistics brought bad news to over 57,000 jobless Rhode Islanders. According to the federal agency, Rhode Island's unemployment rate of 9.2 percent is the nation's second highest, followed by Nevada's rate that is higher. Compare this to 7.3 percent, the national jobless rate for that month.

When hearing about the Ocean State's national distinction of having one of the highest unemployment rates among fifty states, Henry Rosenthal, an Oak Hill, Pawtucket resident who has been unemployed for 16 months, called it a "real disgrace." The dismal statistics released only confirmed what the older job hunter personally knows from sending out hundreds of resumes: it's an extremely tough job market.

Older Job Seeker Can't Find Work

But to make matters worse, 58-year-old Rosenthal and other aging baby boomers will bluntly tell you that age discrimination is derailing their efforts of finding meaningful work that pays a decent wage and benefits.

"Even if you totally believe that your age keeps you from getting a job, it is not always easy to sue because it is tough to prove," says Rosenthal.

In April 2012, his Dallas-based employer downsized, which led to Rosenthal losing his sales job of selling loan origination software to banks. Throughout his 45-year employment career, he had a very stable employment record. He recalls only two other jobs that were lost, due to his lack of seniority when corporate mergers occurred.

Rosenthal, a graduate of Temple University, had always been able to find a new position quickly when losing a job because of his "skill set and previous work experience," he says.

But today things are different.

Rhode Island's puttering economy has kept Rosenthal from landing a new position. In the few times he was able to get his foot in the door for an interview, he was told afterward that he was "perfectly qualified" for the position, in some instances even overqualified, but ultimately he received no job offer.

"I honestly believe that jobs have not been offered to me because of age," charges Rosenthal, who believes that "younger people who oversee the hiring tend to be intimidated with the older job applicants and feel threatened."

Although it is against federal law (The Age Discrimination in Employment Act of 1967) to ask applicants how old they are, "it's easy to figure out how old a person is," notes Rosenthal. "By asking when you graduated high school and college a company can figure out your age," he says.

It's About Whom You Know

During his ongoing job search, Rosenthal quickly realized that in many cases it might just take a personal relationship in a company to get an interview. With all of his previous employers based either across the nation or located all over the world, he has very few contacts with the local business community, he notes.

"Unless you get a direct reference or have a personal connection with a potential employer, they just might hire a younger applicant because they can pay less money or think they won't take time off because of health issues," he said.

"Research findings will tell you that older workers are more responsible and loyal than their younger colleagues and have a better work ethic, too," Rosenthal is quick to say. Don't believe that older workers take more time off than younger employees, he adds.

As Thanksgiving approaches, Rosenthal keeps plugging along sending out resumes hoping to reel in that full-time job. With being two years shy of age 65, he says, "I am just not interested in retiring because I don't have enough hobbies or interests to keep me busy."

Like many other long-term unemployed Rhode Islanders, Rosenthal just tries to keep the faith, realizing that "sooner or later something will turn up. To survive, you don't look backward, you just look forward."

What Some Polls Say

It seems that Rosenthal is not alone in his belief that age can make a job search more challenging to find full-time employment. According to an Associated Press-NORC poll, detailed in "Working Longer: Older Americans' Attitudes on Work and Retirement," 55 percent of those 50 and over who searched for employment in the past five years viewed their search as difficult, and 43 percent thought employers were concerned about their age.

The poll found that 69 percent of the older job seekers reported few available jobs and 63 percent say the jobs did not pay well, nor did they offer good benefits (53 percent). Around one-third of the respondents were told they were overqualified like Rosenthal.

But the October 2013 poll also revealed that some employers do value older workers. Forty-three percent of the older respondents seeking employment in the past five years say they encountered a high demand for their skills, and 31 percent say there was a high demand for their experiences.

According to the poll's findings, "unemployed people aged 45 to 54 were out of work 45 weeks on average, those 55 to 64 were jobless for 57 weeks, and those 65 and older an average of 51 weeks."

Meanwhile, an AARP poll also released last month, found age discrimination "rampant" in New York City for those age 50 and over. The researchers found that when an aging baby boomer loses a job it may take them about four months longer than younger job seekers to find another one.

Forty-eight percent of the survey respondents claim they either personally experienced age discrimination or witnessed it directed at a family member or friend who has turned 50 years old. Almost half of these respondents either personally experienced or witnessed a person not being hired because of their age.

Increasing Your Odds of Finding Work

Kathy Aguiar, principal employment and training interviewer at West Warwick-based Network Rhode Island Career Center, agrees with Rosenthal's personal observations and the above-cited poll results that indicate that older job seekers can be blocked from gaining meaningful employment by age discrimination. However, Aguiar, who has 25 years of assisting Rhode Island's unemployed in getting work, tells me that there are job-hunting skills and techniques that you can use to increase your odds in finding that job.

"It's not the 1980s, and with a 9.3 percent unemployment rate you must change with the times," urges Aguiar, stressing that the 1980s way of writing a resume is totally outdated today.

If your resume is not formatted correctly, computer systems, called Applicant Tracking Systems, won't identify you as a potential candidate, says Aguiar, who says that "75 percent of the applicants applying by Internet will be thrown out of the selection process because of this problem."

Applicant Tracking Systems will skip over employment history if you put that information under "career development" instead of "work experience," on your resume, adds Aguiar. "Always put the company's name first, followed by job title and employment dates."

Aguiar warns applicants not to save resumes as PDF files because Applicant Tracking Systems cannot read them. Save it as a Word file, she recommends. Today, one resume does not fit all, notes Aguiar. Especially in Rhode Island you have to target your resume to the position you are seeking. A well-written resume combined with using social media, including Linkedin, Facebook, and Twitter, and good networking skills can lead to a successful job search, adds Aguiar. Finally, one of the best ways to get an interview and ultimately becoming gainfully employed is by finding someone within a company to be a personal reference. "Who you know is still important, especially in Rhode Island." You may even get extra points when your resume is reviewed because of the internal reference, she says.

National polls tell us that ageism is running rampant in the employment sector. You can not deny its existence when you continue to hear stories from those age-50-and-over unemployed family members, friends, neighbors, and acquaintances, who tell you about their frustrating and very challenging experiences of seeking gainful employment.

Only in this country do we not value the wisdom and knowledge that our elders provide us. It is time for a change in our thinking and attitudes.

If an employer is worried about his bottom line, just consider hiring an older worker. You will get the bang for your buck by bringing in an aging baby boomer who is loyal, dependable, and brings a skill set and life experience that most certainly will benefit your company. To me, it's a no-brainer.

VOLUNTEERISM LEADS TO A NEW CAREER DIRECTION

Published June 15, 2012, in the Pawtucket Times

A growing number of aging baby boomers who volunteer as nonprofit-board members may find their true calling when they retire. Volunteering in your later years can lead to new, exciting careers where passion, energy and love of mission bring about opportunities to serve your community.

Fifty-two-year-old Kathy Anzeveno, who specialized in early-childhood development, taught for more than 27 years in North Providence and the Gordon School in East Providence. While raising Joe, her 21-year-old son, with her husband, Frank, the South Kingstown resident has worked for the past nine years as a volunteer for the Matty Fund. She serves as the full-time executive director of the Wakefield, R hode Island nonprofit group, whose mission is to provide family resources, promote patient safety, and improve the quality of life for children and families living with epilepsy.

Nationally, epilepsy affects more than three million people. Children United for Research in Epilepsy (CURE) estimates that more than 300,000 children with this disorder are under age 15, with up to 50,000 annual deaths from prolonged seizures as well as seizure-related accidents.

According to Anzeveno, she decided to retire in her early 50s and make a difference in another area she was passionate about: one involving lifelong friends Debra and Richard Siravo. The Siravos lost their five-year-old son, Matthew, to complications from epilepsy.

In recent years the organization had grown, prompting the founders to need an executive director to oversee the implementation of the nonprofit group's strategic plan, fundraise, and implement its programs and services. Over the years, the Siravos saw the commitment and capability when Anzeveno came around to stuff envelopes, organize fundraisers and other activities. The job offer was made and was quickly accepted.

Anzeveno explained that the Siravos needed to do something positive in Matty's memory that would allow families to connect personally with other families. "The couple felt compelled to fulfill a need for families dealing with epilepsy. For parents, there is nothing that compares to the suffering, guilt, and uncertainty when a child is diagnosed with anything, let alone a potentially disabling disorder," she said, stressing that some stigma is still attached to people with epilepsy, so parents are often reluctant to share or acknowledge their child's health issue.

With years of volunteer work under her belt and expertise as an educator in child development, Anzeveno knew that there was an extreme need for the Matty Fund's programs and services. As a volunteer, she was especially touched by the families who, besides dealing with their child experiencing regular and often severe seizures, also had to tackle the additional issues of developmental delays and physical impairments as well as medication and treatment side effects.

The Matty Fund

According to Anzeveno, from the tragedy of her longtime friends was born a foundation that truly helps families affected by epilepsy. The foundation started in the Siravo family basement. Anzeveno remembered being bruised from bumping into the foosball table while working on auction items for one of its first major fund-raisers. "We had donated items and sticky notes scattered everywhere," she said.

Five years ago, the fledgling nonprofit relocated from its basement headquarters to an office space in Wakefield, opening as a community-resource center. Anzeveno noted that one month ago, the Matty Fund moved again: down the hall to a larger space to accommodate its growing needs as a hub for support groups, meetings, and program activities. Currently there are 150 families in the nonprofit group's database, mostly Rhode Islanders.

Assisting Young Children with Epilepsy

Anzeveno and her volunteers will reach out to families and children with epilepsy, providing educational and emotional support. Monthly group meetings will be held throughout the Ocean State: in Lincoln, Warwick, and Wakefield. Lecture series in acute-care facilities will provide information to both families and health care professionals.

The Matty Fund also holds a series of events, including the Snow Angel Ball Dinner Dance and Auction, Matty's 5k Run and Walk for Epilepsy and the Matty's Memorial Golf for Epilepsy to fund the operations of the organization. Funding also supports epilepsy research at Brown University, provides scholarships for college-bound students with epilepsy, as well as funds Camp Matty, a therapeutic-riding summer day camp for youngsters with epilepsy. Friendships are forged among families and their epileptic children at the pumpkin festival, egg hunts, and at the Matty Hatty dance-a-thon held in schools around the state, which promotes epilepsy awareness.

For many aging baby boomers, their job has become a means to an end. In their later years, they are working hard to keep economically afloat, pay a mortgage, cover rising household costs, and buy groceries. Aging baby boomers know they will live a longer period of their lives in retirement then previous generations. Like Anzeveno, many will seek ways to become more fulfilled in their lives by becoming a volunteer. A new career path might even result because they volunteered at a nonprofit helping others and making their community a better place to live.

For more information about the Matty Fund, call (401) 789-7330 or go to **www. MattyFund.org.**

4. FINANCIAL ISSUES

BENEFITS OF PREPLANNING AND PREPAYING YOUR FUNERAL

Published October 19, 2012, in the Pawtucket Times

For the past six months, City Registrar Kenneth McGill juggled his increased work load preparing for the September primary and upcoming presidential elections, while taking on the role of caregiver to his elderly parents. Dividing his time between his ailing father, who was afflicted with lung cancer and a blood clot in his heart, and his frail mother, who has COPD, his new role as caregiver added up to hours per day. Both parents were recently placed in nursing facilities.

With the passing of his 76-year-old father just a little more than a week ago, McGill, 51, who had never planned a funeral, was now forced into an uncomfortable role of making final arrangements. "Dad had been seriously ill for the past six months, and we knew what he wanted, but it was never put in writing," noted the aging baby boomer, who acknowledged the stress of balancing the cost of the funeral while ensuring that his father's wishes were carried out.

Like many, McGill and his 48-year-old wife, Kristen, an employee of Memorial Hospital of Pawtucket, had never made prepaid funeral plans for their parents. While he had heard about pre-need funeral agreements, he just never thought about doing it "probably because of denial," he said. "You just never think your parents are going to die."

As a result of his father's recent death, McGill will go next week to Cheetham Funeral Home to preplan his mother's funeral. "This makes a lot of sense because it will ultimately take the stress off my family," he said.

Preplanning a Parent's Funeral

While my background is in the field of aging, I will admit I also found it stressful attempting to get my elderly parents to enter pre-need funeral arrangements. After all, my three siblings and I were only trying to give our parents the opportunity to have a say in the details of their final arrangements.

For years my elderly father took care of my mother with dementia, and after numerous conversations with him about the "what if's," and, more important, what if mother outlived him, the day finally came when my father visited the local Dallas funeral home. With my confused mother at his side, my father chose their caskets as if he was purchasing a new car. He checked under the lid, thoroughly examined the lining and the wood, trying to make the best decision. Ultimately he would not buy the cheaper model, but chose the "nicer one," a little higher up on the price list.

Of course, my father instructed the funeral director where their services should be held and who should preside over the ceremony. But what type of music, vocal or instrumental, did they want played? Would they like a visitation service or would they like to name their pallbearers? All good questions asked by the director that needed answers. These decisions might have been made right then and there on the spot, without the added stress of a loved one's death setting the tone, but rather "preplanned" with careful thought. But in the end, and, unfortunately for us, my father backed out.

My father's experience was not the norm because most aging baby boomers make it through the stressful process of preplanning and prepaying in advance.

Transient Society Creates Need for Preplanning Funerals

Ted Wynne, whose family has owned the Pawtucket-based Manning Heffern Funeral Home since 1868, sees a transient society where children are living in different states, fueling the demand for preplanning and prepayment. "Parents want to take the pressure off their children who live thousands of miles away from making the burial arrangement," Wynne said. "Thus, they pay up front or set aside money for future funeral and burial payments."

With an aging population, one or both spouses will end up in a nursing or assisted-living facility, noted Wynne, a fifth-generation funeral director. Initially the social worker will educate the prospective residents on the importance of getting an "irrevocable trust contract" to pay for the funeral in advance.

"It is pretty black and white," added Wynne. "You figure out what you want and the cost, and then determine what you want to put in the contract." For others, it may take sitting down with the funeral director to help crystallize their funeral plans, he said.

Prepaying a Funeral at Today's Prices

Bradford Bellows, funeral director of Bellows Chapel in Lincoln, agreed with Wynne that seniors in nursing facilities are also good candidates for prepaying a funeral.

"The family watches their parents' funds dwindle to a point where they are forced to go on Medicaid," he said. Prior to being eligible for Medicaid, the parents or their children should prepay the funeral costs. Assets given to the funeral home are allowed to be given under Medicaid eligibility guidelines prior to going on Medicaid.

"Consumers must understand that prearranging a funeral is not the same as prepaying for one," Bellows added, whose family has been in the funeral business in the Blackstone Valley for 191 years.

"By prepaying a funeral you are actually paying for a funeral at today's prices, not tomorrow's," Bellows said. "If the funeral occurs in the future, the funds will earn interest, which will be used to pay for the cost of the funeral at the time of death."

Bellows, a funeral director for 40 years, offers tips when prepaying your funeral:

First, make sure that your Social Security number is indicated on your savings account or insurance policy where the monies are placed to prepay your funeral. If the funeral home goes out of business or goes bankrupt, the funds are still safely yours and can easily be transferred to another funeral home.

Second, when you enroll in the Medicaid program, all the funds in your prepayment account must be used. Any excess funds will be returned by the funeral home to the State of Rhode Island, to defray health costs incurred by the Ocean State's Medicaid program.

Finally, once the funeral home opens the account or insurance policy, don't forget to get a copy of the Irrevocable Funeral Trust Agreement, which shows the bank or credit-union account number of the original insurance policy that was issued. This will give you proof that your advance payment has been set up for your funeral needs.

Make an Educated Decision

Life Insurance Agent Christine Miller, a preplanning funding specialist at Pawtucket-based Lachapelle Funeral Home and a grief counselor at Beacon Hospice, noted that preplanning and prepayment for a funeral can reduce family stress. "Knowing your loved one's final wishes and not having the financial burden of a funeral can provide relief during a very difficult time," she added.

According to Miller, it is not uncommon to have individuals call weekly to preplan their funerals. "Many people are surprised that at Lachapelle Funeral Home, they can make small monthly payments rather than one lump sum and still have their funeral guaranteed," she noted.

Miller stressed the importance of doing your homework to determine which pre-payment option is best for you. "There used to be a loyalty to funeral homes, but in these times people should shop around and talk to people with the goal of making an educated decision."

For consumer tips on planning and prepaying a funeral, go to **http://goo.gl/1WefAf.**

FINANCIALLY SURVIVING
YOUR RETIREMENT YEARS

Published August 10, 2012, in the Pawtucket Times

M oving into their mid-50s and 60s, a growing number of baby boomers wonder whether Social Security benefits in their retirement years will even pay the bills. Will they be able to survive in their "golden years?"

Federal officials say that there may be cause for alarm.

At the end of April 2012, the released 242-page Social Security Trustees report, picked up by the nation's media, gave bleak but advance warning to future retirees that the Social Security program can pay full benefits until 2033; however, it warned that probably only three-quarters of the promised benefits could be paid out beyond that time.

So it is not surprising that the Associated Press (AP), a media cooperative owned by its contributing newspapers, radio, and television stations in the United States, announced last week that the news agency will publish a four-part series to be released over four Sundays in August that will examine the long-term financial viability of the nation's Social Security program. The series plans to also take a look at policy proposals that will be debated during the upcoming election campaigns by presidential and congressional candidates that might strengthen the nation's primary retirement program.

The AP recognized that Social Security, a very politically charged issue, is a topic that must be meaningfully discussed in the upcoming November elections. Because of this, the AP has chosen to bring substantive coverage of this important policy issue to the upcoming political debates that will take place in the months ahead.

"Few things affect more Americans than the future of Social Security, and yet it is an issue most invisible during the current campaign," said AP Washington Bureau Chief Sally Buzbee, who is directing the series. "This series of stories tries to lay out complex issues in the most accessible way possible. This is part of the ongoing efforts by the Associated Press this fall to make sure issues (like Social Security) aren't absent from the campaign, but front and center," stated Buzbee.

The headline of the AP's first report, a published story on the upper fold of the August 6, 2012, issue of the Pawtucket Times, warns that "Social Security

Not Deal It Once Was." The AP wire story noted that today's retirees will be the first to have paid more in Social Security taxes during their lifetime careers than they will ultimately receive in retirement benefits. Previous retirees paid less payroll taxes, yet received more benefits.

Planning Key to Adequate Retirement Funds

If Social Security bennies are chopped, taking personal responsibility in planning your retirement may well become your financial safety net in your later years.

Economic woes fueled by the worst economic downturn since the Great Depression have left many baby boomers financially struggling to make ends meet and save ad-equately for their retirement years, according to survey findings released in July 23, 2012, by the Consumer Federation of America (CFA) and the Financial Planner Board of Standards.

According to a 60-page report, published by Princeton Survey Research Associates International (PSRAI), nearly two-fifths (38 percent) of the 1,508 household-financial decision makers surveyed said they live paycheck to paycheck, while less than one-third (30 percent) indicated they felt comfortable financially and only about one-third (34 percent) think they can afford to retire by age 65.

Survey findings indicated that only 31 percent of respondents said they had a comprehensive financial plan, while about two-thirds (65 percent) indicated they follow a plan for at least one of their savings goals. Those who have prepared a personal-savings plan feel more confident and report more success managing money, savings, and investments than those who don't.

By a margin of 50 percent to 32 percent, and for all but the lowest-income bracket (under $25,000) in which few have a comprehensive plan, those planning for retirement are more likely to feel they are on pace to meet all their financial goals, such as saving for retirement or for emergencies, stated the survey findings.

In addition, an even larger margin of 52 percent to 30 percent, and across all income brackets, those planning for their retirement years are more likely to feel "very confident" about managing money, savings, and investments.

Kevin Keller, CEO of the CFP Board, stated: "Consumers understandably are more nervous about investing their money, given recent revelations about financial fraud, manipulation, and abuse of clients. This doesn't mean that people shouldn't create a financial plan and be prepared."

Taking Personal Action Now

Unless strong political pressure is placed on Congress to act swiftly to enact policy changes to fix the nation's ailing Social Security program, expect political gridlock to continue to block any effort in both chambers to come up with bipartisan solutions.

Don't get caught up in the political spins and negative rhetoric as presidential and congressional candidates begin their debates on Social Security before the upcoming September primaries and November elections. Become an educated voter and tell the congressional candidates who seek your vote to seek bipartisan solutions to making the Social Security Trust Fund solvent once and for all.

Watch for the AP's upcoming reports on Social Security to learn more about this important policy issue. That's a good first step. Second, learn more about AARP's "You've Earned a Say" initiative, (**www.earnedasay.org**), a website that can provide aging baby boomers with both factual and straightforward information about retire-ment policies being debated by Congress inside the Beltway, ones that it is hoped will financially strengthen the nation's Social Security program.

But on a personal level, until federal lawmakers get serious about financially shoring up the nation's retirement program, developing a personal-financial plan may well become an effective short-term solution to managing your money, savings, and investments that could well supplement a shrinking Social Security check. One useful tool is the website, **www.LetsMakeaPlan.org**, which allows a person to learn more about preparing a financial plan, including working with financial-planning professionals.

GAO: REPORT SAYS OLDER PERSONS HIT HARD BY STUDENT LOAN DEBT

Published on September 19, 2014, in the Pawtucket Times

In her late 20s, Janet Lee Dupree took out a $3,000 student loan to help finance her undergraduate degree. While acknowledging that she did not pay off the student loan when she should have, even paying thousands of dollars on this debt, today the 72-year-old still owes a whopping $15,000 because of compound interest and penalties. The Ocala, Florida resident, in poor health, will never pay off this student loan especially because all she can afford to pay is the $50 the federal government takes out of her Social Security check each month.

Citing Dupree's financial problems in her golden years in his opening remarks at a Senate Panel hearing in Room 562 of the Dirksen Senate Office Building, Senator Nelson (D-FL), chairman of the Senate Special Committee on Aging, used his legislative bully pulpit to dispel the myth that student loan debt happens only to young students. "Well, as it turns out, that's increasingly not the case," he said.

Student Loan Debt Impacts Seniors Too

But last week's Senate Aging panel hearing also put the spotlight on 57-year-old Rosemary Anderson, a witness who traveled from Watsonville, California to inside Washington's Beltway, detailing her student loan debt. Anderson remarked how she had accumulated a $126,000 loan debt (initially $64,000) to pay for her bachelor's and master's degrees. A divorce and health problems combined with an underwater home mortgage kept her from paying anything on her student loan for eight years.

Anderson told Senate Aging panel members that with new terms to paying off her student loan debt, she expects to pay $526 a month for 24 years to settle the defaulted loan, settling her debt at age 81. The aging baby boomer will ultimately pay $87,487 more than her original student loan amount.

Like Anderson, a small but growing percentage of older Americans who are delinquent in paying off their student debts worry about their Social Security benefits being garnished, drastically cutting their expected retirement income.

According to a 22-page Government Accountability Office (GAO) report, "Inability to Repay Student Loans May Affect Financial Security of a Small Percentage of Retirees," released at the Sept. 10 Senate panel hearing, the amount that older Americans owe in outstanding federal student loans has increased sixfold, from $2.8 billion in 2005 to more than $18 billion last year. Student loan debt for all ages totals $1 trillion.

The GAO report noted that student loan debt reduces net worth and income, eroding the older person's retirement security.

Although the newly released GAO report acknowledged that seniors account for a small fraction of student loan debt holders, it noted that the numbers of seniors facing student loan debt between 2004 and 2010 had quadrupled to 706,000 households. Roughly 80 percent of the student loan debt held by retirement-aged Americans was for their own education, while only 20 percent of loans were taken out to help finance a child or dependent's education, the report said.

Senator Sheldon Whitehouse (D-RI), who sits on the Senate Special Committee on Aging, acknowledges that student loan debt is a burden for thousands of Rhode Islanders, including a growing number of retirement-age borrowers who either took out student loans as young adults, or when they changed careers or helped pay off a child's education. "Student debt presents unique challenges to these older borrowers, who risk garnishment of Social Security benefits, accrual of interest and additional penalties if they are forced to default," says Whitehouse, stressing that pursuing an education should not result in a lifetime of debt.

Whitehouse sees the Bank on Students Emergency Loan Refinancing Act, which would allow approximately 88,000 Rhode Islanders to refinance existing student loans at the low rates that were available in 2013-2014, as a legislative fix to help those who have defaulted on paying off their student loans. "By putting money back in the pockets of Rhode Islanders, we can help individual borrowers make important long-term financial decisions that will ultimately benefit the economy as a whole," he says.

Garnishing Social Security

The GAO reports finds that student loan debt has real consequences for those in or near retirement The need to juggle debt on a fixed income may increase the likelihood of student loan default. In 2013, the U.S. Department of the Treasury garnished the Social Security retirement and survivor benefits of 33,000 people to recoup federal student loan debt. When the government garnishes a Social Security check, multiple agencies can levy fees in addition to the amount collected for the debt, making it even more challenging for seniors to pay off their loan.

Ranking member, Susan M. Collins (R-ME) on the Senate panel warned that because of a 1998 law seniors with defaulted student loans may even see their Social Security checks slashed to $750 a month, a floor set by Congress in 1998. "This floor was not indexed for inflation and is now far below the poverty line," adds Collins, who says she plans to introduce legislation shortly to adjust this floor for inflation and index it going forward, to make sure garnishment does not force seniors into poverty.

According to an analysis of government data detailed on the CNN Money websites, "More than 150,000 older Americans had their Social Security checks docked last year for delinquent student loans."

Unlike other types of consumer debt, student loans can't be discharged in bankruptcy. Besides docking Social Security, the federal government can use a variety of ways to collect delinquent student loans, specifically docking wages or taking tax refund dollars. These strategies also include cutting the income of the older person.

Some Final Thoughts...

"It's very important that we focus on the big picture and the implications in play," said AARP Rhode Island State Director Kathleen Connell, noting that "education debt is becoming a significant factor for younger workers in preparing for retirement, delaying the ability of people to retire and threatening a middle-class standard of living, both before and after they retire."

Connell says, "It's a serious concern for some older Americans as approximately 6.9 million carry student loan debt—some dating back to their youth. But others took on new debt when they returned to school later in life and many others have cosigned for loans with their children or grandchildren to help them deal with today's skyrocketing college costs."

"It's not just a matter of federal student loan debt being garnished from Social Security payments if it has not been repaid, " Connell added. "Outstanding federal debt also will disqualify an older borrower from eligibility for a federally-insured reverse mortgage.

"Families need to know the costs and understand the long-term burden of having to repay large amounts of student loan debt," Connell concluded. "They also need information regarding the value of education, hiring rates for program graduates, and the likely earnings they may expect."

Finally, Sandy Baum, senior fellow with the Urban Institute, warns people to think before they borrow. "They should borrow federal loans, not private loans," she says, recommending that if their payments are more than they can afford, they should enroll in income-based repayment.

Addressing student loan debt issues identified by the GAO report, Baum suggests that Congress might ease the restrictions on discharging student loans in bankruptcy and end garnishment of Social Security payments for student debt. Lawmakers could also strengthen income-based repayment, making sure that they don't give huge benefits to people with student debt and relatively high incomes.

GAO STUDY REPORTS NEW TRENDS PUSH OLDER WOMEN INTO POVERTY

Published on March 7, 2014, in the Pawtucket Times

F ollowing on the heels of a Government Accountability Office (GAO) report released last week on March 5, the U.S. Senate Special Committee on Aging held a hearing to put a Congressional spotlight on the alarming increase of older Americans becoming impoverished. The GAO policy analysts concluded that a growing number of the nation's elderly, especially women and minorities, could fall into poverty due to lower incomes associated with declining marriage rates and the higher living expenses that individuals bear.

As many as 48 percent of older Americans live in or on the edge of poverty but for Social Security. "While many gains have been made over the years to reduce poverty, too many seniors still can't afford basic necessities such as food, shelter, and medicines," said Aging Committee Chairman Bill Nelson (D-FL).

Senate Aging Committee Looks at Income Security for Elders

Policy experts told Senate lawmakers on Wednesday that millions of seniors have been spared from abject poverty thanks to federal programs such as Social Security, Medicaid, Medicare, SSI, and food stamps. The testimony contrasted with the picture painted by House Budget Committee Chairman Paul Ryan (R-WI) earlier this week, who produced a report that labeled the federal government's five-decade-long war on poverty a failure.

Appearing before the U.S. Senate Special Committee on Aging, Patricia Neuman, a senior vice president at the Henry J. Kaiser Family Foundation, stressed the importance of federal anti-poverty programs.

"Between 1966 and 2011, the share of seniors living in poverty fell from more than 28 percent to about nine percent, with the steepest drop occurring in the decade immediately following the start of the Medicare program," said Neuman. "The introduction of Medicare, coupled with Social Security, played a key role in lifting seniors out of poverty."

Neuman's remarks were echoed by Joan Entmacher of the National Women's Law Center, who credited food stamps, unemployment insurance and Meals on Wheels, along with Social Security, for dramatically reducing poverty among seniors. The report was highly critical of many programs designed to help the poor and elderly saying they contribute to the "poverty trap." Ryan and other House lawmakers have long proposed capping federal spending and turning Medicaid, food stamps, and a host of other programs for the poor into state block grants.

Older Women and Pension Benefits

GAO's Barbara Bovbjerg also brought her views to the Senate Select Committee on Aging hearing. Bovbjerg, managing director of education, workforce, and income security issues, testified that the trends in marriage, work, and pension benefits have impacted the retirement incomes of older Americans.

Over the past five decades the composition of the American household has changed dramatically, stated Bovbjerg, noting that the proportion of unmarried individuals has increased steadily as couples have chosen to marry at ever-later ages and as divorce rates have risen. "This is important because Social Security is not only available to workers but also to spouses and survivors. The decline in marriage and the concomitant rise in single parenthood have been more pronounced among low-income, less-educated individuals and some minorities," she says.

As marriage and workforce patterns changed, so has the nation's retirement system, adds Bovbjerg. Since 1990, employers have increasingly turned away from traditional defined benefit pensions to defined contribution plans, such as 401(k)s, she says, thus ultimately shifting risk to individual employees and making it more likely they will receive lump sum benefits rather than annuities.

These trends have affected retirement incomes, especially for women and minorities, says Bovbjerg. Fewer women today receive Social Security spousal and survivor benefits than in the past; most qualify for benefits on their own work history. While this shift may be positive, for those women with higher incomes, unmarried elderly women with low levels of lifetime earnings are expected to get less from Social Security than any other demographic group.

According to Bovbjerg, these trends have also affected household savings. Married households are more likely to have retirement savings, but the majority of single-headed households have none. Obviously, single parents in particular tend to have fewer resources available to save for retirement during their working years. With Defined Contribution pension plans becoming the norm for most, and with significant numbers not having these benefits, older Americans may well have to rely increasingly on Social Security as their primary or perhaps only source of retirement income.

Inside the Ocean State

Although the GAO report findings acknowledge a gender-based wage gap that pushes older women into poverty, Maureen Maigret, policy consultant for the Senior Agenda Coalition of Rhode Island and Coordinator of the Rhode Island Older Woman's Policy Group, observes that this inequity has been around since the 1970s when she chaired a legislative commission studying pay equity. "Progress in closing the gender wage gap has stagnated since 2000 with the wage ratio hovering around 76.5 percent," she says.

GAO's recent findings on gender-based differences in poverty rates are consistent with what Maigret found researching the issue for the Women's Fund of Rhode Island in 2010. She found that some of the differences in the Ocean State can be attributed to the fact that older women are far less likely to be married than older men. Almost three times' as many older women are widowed when compared to men.

Maigret says that her research revealed that older women in Rhode Island are also less likely to live in family households and almost twice as likely as older men to live alone. Of those older women living alone or with non-family members, an estimated one out of five was living in poverty. For Rhode Island older women in non-family households living alone, estimated median income in 2009 was 85 percent that of male non-family householders living alone ($18,375 vs. $21,540).

Finally Maigret's report findings indicate that around 11.3 percent of older Rhode Island women were living below the federal poverty level as compared to 7.3 percent of older men in the state. Older women's average Social Security benefit was almost 30 percent less than that of older men, and their earnings were only 58 percent that of older men's earnings.

"There is no getting around peoples' fears about outliving their savings becoming a reality if they live long enough," said AARP Rhode Island State Director Kathleen Connell. "One thing that the latest statistics reveal (including the GAO report) is the critical role Social Security plays when it comes to the ability of many seniors to meet monthly expenses. Social Security keeps about 38 percent of Rhode Islanders age 65 and older out of poverty, according to a new study from the AARP Public Policy Institute."

"Nationally, figures jump off the page," Connell added. "Without Social Security benefits, 44.4 percent of elderly Americans would have incomes below the official poverty line; all else being equal; with Social Security benefits, only 9.1 percent do," she says, noting that these benefits lift 15.3 million elderly Americans-including nine million women-above the poverty line.

"Just over 50 percent of Rhode Islanders age 65 and older rely on Social Security for at least half of their family income—and nearly 24 percent rely on Social Security for 90 percent of their family income," states Connell.

"Seniors trying to meet the increasing cost of utilities, prescription drugs, and groceries would be desperate without monthly Social Security benefits they worked hard for and planned on. As buying power decreases, protecting Social Security becomes more important than ever. Older people know this; younger people should be aware of it and become more active in saving for retirement. Members of Congress need to remain aware of this as well," adds Connell.

Kate Brewster, executive director of Rhode Island's Economic Progress Institute, agrees that older women in Rhode Island are already at greater risk of poverty and economic security than older men. "This [GAO] report highlights several trends that make it increasingly important to improve women's earnings today so that they are economically secure in retirement. Among the "policy to-do list" is shrinking the wage gap, eliminating occupational segregation, and raising the minimum wage. State and federal proposals to increase the minimum wage to $10.10 would benefit more women than men, demonstrating the importance of this debate to women's economic security today and tomorrow."

House Speaker Gordon Fox is proud that the General Assembly in the last two legislation sessions voted to raise minimum wage to its current level of $8 per hour. "That puts Rhode Island at the same level as neighboring Massachusetts, and we far surpass the federal minimum wage of $7.25," he said. He says he will carefully consider legislation that has been introduced to once again boost the minimum wage.

"Bridging this gap is not only the right thing to do to ensure that women are on the same financial footing as men, but it also makes economic sense," says Congressman David N. Cicilline. At the federal level, the Democratic Congressman has supported the "When Women Succeed, America Succeeds" economic agenda that would address issues like the minimum wage, pay fairness, and access to quality and affordable child care. "Tackling these issues is a step toward helping women save and earn a secure retirement, but we also have to ensure individuals have a safety net so they can live with dignity in their retirement years," says Cicilline.

With Republican Congressman Ryan in a GOP-controlled House captured by the Tea Party leading the charge to dismantle the federal government's 50-year war on poverty, the casualties of this ideological skirmish if he succeeds will be America's seniors. Cutting the safety net that these programs created will make economic insecurity in American's older years a very common occurrence.

INVEST WISELY WITH HARD-EARNED INCOME

Published October 8, 2001, in the Pawtucket Times

With the news of the latest Federal Reserve rate cuts, stocks soared with investors showing new optimism in the stock market. The Dow Jones Industrial Average has spiraled above 9,000 for the first time since the horrific terrorist attack more than three weeks ago. With this latest rally on Wall Street, elderly investors might be more easily influenced by scam artists to invest their hard-earned income in buying stocks, bonds, and other securities.

According to the state's Securities Division of the Department of Business Regulation (DBR), charged with investigating financial scams, its staff has examined hundreds of complaints filed against stockbrokers and investment advisors.

Some complaints can be resolved quickly. Others are more complicated to tackle and take more time to resolve, stated David Briden, DBR's chief securities examiner. For instance, last April DBR entered a consent order against Alpha Telecom, Inc., and ATC, Inc.

These two companies promoted the sale of pay-telephone investments to Rhode Island residents. State regulators noted that the high risks of this investment were not fully disclosed to the 50 Rhode Islanders, some of them elderly, who had invested approximately $960,000. Under the terms of the order, the two companies paid a penalty of $50,000 to the state. This represented the largest administrative penalty in a pay-telephone case nationwide.

In addition, Alpha Telecom, Inc., and ATC, Inc., were ordered to offer a full refund to the Rhode Island investors. DBR went to Superior Court to enforce the terms of the consent order.

In August 2001, the U.S. Securities and Exchange Commission announced that the U.S. District Court of Oregon granted a temporary restraining order and froze the assets of the two companies. Meanwhile, in that month, these companies had filed for bankruptcy in the U.S. District Court for the Southern District of Florida. At press time, the investors are still waiting for their money to be returned.

So how can you protect yourself against financial scams? Don't get reeled in by a "cold call," touting an investment that is guaranteed to make you lots of money, warned Briden. Especially if you have never dealt with the caller, "simply tell them you are not interested and hang up," he said.

"Always get written information before making any investment decision," Briden said. Meet with the broker at his or her office so you get to know them and to see the firm, he suggested.

There is a problem if the caller can't produce written material. According to Briden, the old adage there is no free lunch really applies to making investments, too. Don't be conned into making a quick investment decision when high-pressure sales tactics are used, Briden said, adding that any investor should "beware of any promise made that the investment will result in quick profits or extremely high returns. Be concerned if you are told to act on it now or it will be too late," he said.

Meanwhile, a check can be a receipt of your investment. "Never invest cash," Briden added, stressing that a person should never send a check to someone at a firm you know nothing about.

Become an educated investor when considering the investment of your money. "It is important that you understand the costs (commissions, fees, and penalties) to the investment," Briden said. "Always find out the risk involved in your investment. Never make an assumption that the investment is federally insured or guaranteed."

STILL GETTING THE JOB DONE: MANY CHOOSING PART-TIME WORK IN POST RETIREMENT YEARS

Published September 13, 2015 in Woonsocket Call

I n 2010, when Michael Cassidy retired as Pawtucket's Director of Planning & Redevelopment after working for the municipality for 40 years, he had no intentions of easing himself into full-time employment. While he was retiring to "retirement" he had every intention to remain active for the rest of his life.

Cassidy instinctively knew that retirees who stay active by playing sports, traveling, or even volunteering, always seemed to live longer. His father was a good example of this belief, living to the ripe old age of 92. Before the nonagenarian died he had worked part-time as a realtor, playing softball in a Golden Oldies league, and umpired three times a week.

Part-Time Job Gives Many Bennies

With Cassidy planning to retire at age 62 from the City of Pawtucket, he went to see PawSox President, Mike Tamburro asking, "do you have a job for an old retired guy?"

Ultimately, he took the position as usher at the Pawtucket based McCoy Stadium. He says, "The job keeps me on my feet four-to-five hours." Each game he puts around 15,000 steps on his pedometer. But the job also allows him to interact with old friends and even gives him an opportunity to make new ones, too. There are additional benefits of having a part-time job, besides just getting physically active and having an opportunity to mingle with people, says Cassidy. He now has more time to spend with his six grandchildren, travel with his wife of 45 years Jane Ellen, and to just putter around his home. Now he even serves as chair of the Blackstone Valley National Heritage Corridor Organization, he says.

Work as the New Retirement Activity

Like Cassidy, according to the AARP, many older Americans are not choosing to retire but are now seeking part-time jobs in their post retirement years rather than full-time ones.

According to the findings in the 26 page "AARP Post Retirement Career Study," work seems to be the "new retirement activity." While many Americans state that they plan to retire between ages 65 and 70 (45percent), the data indicates that the typical retirement may have changed. 37 percent say they plan to work for pay in post retirement. Of these respondents, 73 percent desire a part-time job and almost half are looking to work in a new field (44 percent). 23 percent will stay in the same field, and 33 percent are undecided.

The researchers say that connecting with co-workers, interesting and challenging work, and the desire for a work-life balance are all stated as top reasons why work is enjoyable. Some are seeking to pursue their dream job or dream field in this next stage of life. Sports, hospitality, and education fields are frequently cited. Most are hoping that their new dream jobs will be part-time, flexible with work from home options, and allow time for travel and fun.

The findings also indicate the importance of job training for those who plan to work during their retirement years. Among those who plan to enter a new field training is seen as even more crucial to succeeding on the job by 46 percent, as opposed to 36 percent among those staying in the same field.

Meanwhile, when asked about what they enjoyed most about their current career, most mentioned income, benefits, and the schedule/work-life balance.

According to the AARP survey, regardless of the field, respondents are hoping to work part-time (73 percent), with over half expecting to work for someone else (57 percent) vs. being a contractor (21 percent) or starting their own business (19 percent).

Personal contacts and job listings are the primary avenues respondents say they use to find post-retirement work (49 percent and 43 percent, respectively). Professional networking is also a popular way people plan to find work, note the researchers.

When questioned about their dream job, many respondents talk about a profession, for others it may be a particular type of working lifestyle. Jobs in the sports, creative, hospitality, and education fields are mentioned frequently by the respondents, while those looking for lifestyle benefits seek flexibility, lucrative opportunities to travel, and employment with a charitable aspect to it.

"AARP's efforts to look into how people spend time in their retirement years is the first survey of this kind and there are no comparative stats from previous years," says Kim Adler, AARP's Work and Jobs Lead.

"The findings suggest that there are major implications for employers," said Adler. "Americans are living longer, healthier lives and we will see a continuation of the long term trend of working into retirement years. Nearly 19 percent of 65 and older workers are in the workplace and the percentages – as well as the actual numbers – are likely to continue to rise. This will give employers the opportunity to hire and retain experienced workers who look forward to the opportunities and challenges in the workplace," she says.

Adds Adler, "there are shortages of skilled workers in certain industries and many employers report difficulty filling jobs. For these jobs – and all others – employers and employees benefit from an inter-generational workforce that encourages mentoring and knowledge sharing."

STUDY: CITIZENS OVER AGE 50 NOT A DRAIN ON ECONOMY

Published October 10, 2014, in the Pawtucket Times

Almost one year ago, Oxford Economics in cooperation with AARP released a briefing paper, "The Longevity Economy." The national study gave the nation's largest aging-advocacy group the ammunition it needed to dispel the myth that baby boomers and seniors are a drain on the nation's economy; rather, researchers found that they are drivers of the nation's economic growth. This data should keep businesses, investors, and inventors from overlooking the wants and needs of older Americans as they develop new products and business plans.

This week the national analysis was supplemented, detailing the state level contribution of people over 50.

Shattering a Myth

According to Jody Holtzman, AARP's senior vice president of thought leadership, the nonprofit commissioned the initial "Longevity Economy" report from Oxford Economics to challenge society's and Washington's misconceptions that people over age 50 are a drain on the economy. He said, "To the contrary, the analysis shows that this population is an important driver of economic growth in key sectors of the United States economy such as technology, health care, travel, and education."

Holtzman says the formal economic impact analysis was conducted, both nationally and at the state level. The findings can shift the way federal and state policy makers will view the nation's aging population. "Not only can we 'afford' the growing population of older people, we can't do without them, as they are a key source of economic growth, jobs, salaries, and taxes that benefit people and families of all ages and generations," he says.

"The economic activity of the 'Longevity Economy' provides employment for nearly 89 million Americans with $3.8 trillion in salary and wages, contributes $1.75 trillion in federal and state and local taxes annually, and is a huge source of charitable giving, contributing nearly $100 billion annually to a variety of causes and concerns—nearly 70 percent of all charitable donations from individuals," says Holtzman.

The 19-page study notes that by 2032, it is projected that over-age-50 Americans will make up about 52 percent of the US Gross Domestic Product (GDP). The average wealth of the households of these individuals is almost three times the size of households headed by people ages 25 to 50.

As to technology, baby boomers are heavy users of the Internet and social networking, and they spend more time online when compared with either Generation X and Generation Y consumers. Boomers' average online spending over a three-month period amounts to $650, outpacing the two younger generations.

Researchers also found that those over age 50 fill nearly 100 million jobs, generating over $4.5 trillion in wages and salaries.

"The Longevity Economy" is not a passing phenomenon, observes Holtzman, noting that increased life spans will result in a "consistently large over-50 population even after the baby boomer wave has crested."

Holtzman adds, "The particular wants and needs of the 'Longevity Economy' when it comes to consumer spending, housing, health care, and employment have dramatic implications for business, society, and government." Not only does the "Longevity Economy" have a strong, net positive economic impact on the nation's economy, the nation's age 50 and over "will also continue to serve as a significant resource and safety net for their parents and children."

A Snapshot of Rhode Island

Despite being 36 percent of the state's population in 2013 (expected to reach 38 percent in 2040), the total economic contribution of the 'Longevity Economy' accounted for 46 percent of Rhode Island's GDP, or $24 billion, noted in AARP's release of its state specific analysis. The impact on the state's GDP was driven by $18 billion in consumer spending by over 50 households.

Rhode Island's $24 billion 'Longevity Economy' GDP supported 54 percent of the state's jobs (0.3 million), 47 percent of employee compensation ($14 billion) and 52 percent of state taxes ($2 billion), says the state-specific economic analysis.

Also the state-specific data noted that the greatest number of jobs supported by the "Longevity Economy" were in health care (88,000), retail trade (47,000), and accommodation and food service (33,000). Overall, people over age 50 make up 34 percent of the state's workforce. Sixty-seven percent of the workers ages 50 to 64 are employed, compared to 79 percent ages 25 to 49.

Finally, 11 percent of the state's older workers (ages 50 to 64) are self-employed entrepreneurs, compared with seven percent of people ages 25 to 49. Forty-four of these older workers work in professional occupations, compared to 47 percent of the younger workers.

"The [Rhode Island] analysis takes a closer look at something we have known for some time," said AARP Rhode Island State Director Kathleen Connell. "Rhode Islanders 50-plus are an important driver of our state's economy," she says.

Connell says the data complements findings in a paper published recently by the journal PLOS ONE, a group of international researchers at the International Institute of Applied Systems Analysis, the Max Planck Institute, and the University of Washington. "It concluded that as retirement approaches and certainly after retirement, leisure time increases. And while there are many who will gear down, relax, travel, and devote time to grandchildren (traditional retirement), baby boomers—better educated, healthier, and with greater access to information than any previous generation of retirees—will have much more time to provide the energy and intellectual capacity, as well as the capital resources to help drive innovation," she adds.

"With that in mind, AARP partners with the Small Business Administration to support 'encore entrepreneurs' 50 and older. I agree with SBA Administrator Karen Mills, who says retirees are using their decades of expertise and their contacts to start new businesses and to finally pursue that venture that has been stirring their dreams for all these years," Connell says.

"So not only do the people who make up the 'Longevity Economy' represent an economic impact," Connell added, "they are in a position to be leaders in innovation."

AARP's economic data analysis has shattered the age-old myth that a growing older population will ultimately bankrupt the federal and state budgets because of the need for increased programs and services for these individuals. Data show us that America's oldest generations can be considered the gas that revs the state's and nation's economic engine. Federal and state policy makers need to get this point.

AARP: SOCIAL SECURITY IS AN ECONOMIC GENERATOR

Published October 4, 2013, in the Pawtucket Times

For those who view Social Security bennies as just a drain on the nation's economy, adding to the nation's spiraling deficit, AARP, the nation's largest aging-advocacy group has always seen it differently. Now, according to a new report, released by AARP's Public Policy Institute on October 1, 2013, researchers found that each dollar paid to Social Security beneficiaries generates nearly two dollars in spending by individuals and businesses, adding about $1.4 trillion in total economic output to the U.S. economy in 2012. Moreover, the report's findings indicate that $762 billion paid in Social Security benefits in 2012 helped Americans keep or find more than nine million jobs.

If Congress is successful in putting Social Security on the budgetary chopping block, the economy will take a hit, warns the AARP report. According to the report's analysis, "reducing benefits by 25 percent across the board in 2012 (by $190 billion), which the Social Security Administration projects will occur around the year 2033, could cost the U.S. economy about 2.3 million jobs, $349 billion in economic output, about $194 billion in Gross Domestic Product (GDP), and about $83 billion in employee compensation."

A Multiplier Effect When Benefits Spent

The 25-page report, "Social Security's Impact on the National Economy," authored by Gary Koening, of AARP's Public Policy Institute, and Al Myles, of Mississippi State University, details the powerful multiplier effect created when Social Security recipients spend their benefits, and the companies that receive those dollars spend their profits and pay their employees, who in turn spend their wages. The report provides both national and state-level data.

The researchers use an economic modeling system known as IMPLAN to calculate the multiplier effect and trace the impact of Social Security spending through the national and state economies.

"This report tells us that any adjustments Washington makes to Social Security will have a profound effect on individuals of all ages, businesses, and our economy as a whole," said AARP Executive Vice President Nancy LeaMond. "That's why AARP is fighting the chained Consumer Price Index (CPI) and calling for a national conversation about the future of Social Security—so those who paid into the system can have a voice in the debate and so future generations get the benefits they've earned."

Social Security benefit payments in 2012 supported more than $370 billion in salaries, wages, and compensation for workers. Of the more than nine million jobs supported by Social Security spending, about four million were in just 10 industries. Nationally, the largest employment impacts were seen in the food services, real estate, health care, and retail industries.

In addition to illustrating Social Security's vital role in supporting national and local economies, jobs, and workers' incomes, this report reiterates the importance of Social Security as a vital source of income for millions of Americans. Social Security benefits keep 22 million people out of poverty, including more than 15 million older Americans, and serve as the foundation of a secure retirement for millions more.

AARP's Public Policy Institute calls the Social Security Program critical in promoting income stability among the nation's seniors, by providing a steady stream of income to replace wages lost due to retirement. "About one out of six Americans—57 million people—receive Social Security benefits, including nine out of the 10 individuals aged 65-and-older," says the Washington, D.C-based policy institute.

According to the Social Security Administration, the program is a key source of retirement income for the nation's retirees, noting that "it is the only inflation-protected, guaranteed income they have. Among the age 65-and-over recipients, 23 percent of the married couples and 46 percent of the unmarried couples rely on the program for 90 percent or more of their income. Also, 53 percent of the married couples and 74 percent of those unmarried in this age group receive 50 percent or more of their income from Social Security."

Experts Weighing In on AARP Report

According to Lisa Mensah, executive director of the Aspen Institute's Initiative on Financial Security, "The AARP study fills a key void in the debate around Social Security. Social Security is not only important for individual financial security but also it has a major impact supporting jobs and economic activity in every state. When weighing Social Security as a budget matter, the fiscal coin has two sides—what it costs and what it delivers—and too often what Social Security delivers for the broader economy is poorly understood."

Adds Dean Baker, co-director of the Center for Economic and Policy Research, "In a context where the economy is below full employment, as is clearly the case today, Social Security provides an important boost to demand. The report it released showed the importance of Social Security in each of the 50 states. When the economy is near full employment, the demand generated by Social Security may not be needed, but for now and the foreseeable future this demand will be providing an important boost to growth."

Impact on State Economies

The AARP report details the spending of Social Security checks on the economy of all 50 states. Of course California, the state with the largest economy in the nation, has the largest impact. In this state alone, Social Security benefits supported 888,000 jobs, $147.4 billion in output, and $8.7 billion in state and local revenues.

Meanwhile, for the littlest state in the nation, "People need to consider a Rhode Island economy without Social Security benefits," said AARP State Director Kathleen Connell. "Could the state live without $2.9 billion a year in federal money being spent on medications, rent, food, utilities, clothing, and services?

"When a person spends Social Security benefits, the lawn gets mowed, the driveway gets plowed, CVS sells toilet paper and the corner market sells milk. Someone gets paid and then spends that money—which means retailers and service providers are getting paid. And then they spend. It's a cycle, and each step along the way, sales tax is collected by the state—more than $280.7 million," says Connell. The AARP study shows that this spending supports 33,000 jobs in the Ocean State. Social Security makes life better for retirees and people with disabilities, it supports Rhode Island jobs, and Rhode Island taxpayers benefit significantly, she says.

"Social Security was engineered with this in mind. The money paid into the system is not doing much if it stays in the Treasury," observes Connell. "Social Security allows people to live more comfortably, improves their health and quality of life, and benefits the economy," she adds.

"Seen this way, what would we be saving if we cut Social Security benefits?" quips Connell.

Congressman David Cicilline notes this report confirms that almost 80 years after it was established, Social Security strengthens Rhode Island's economy and provides significant benefits for families across this state. Cicilline, representing the Ocean State's 1st Congressional District, states that while other lawmakers propose Social Security benefit cuts of one kind or another, he has introduced legislation to protect the program by strongly opposing the use of chained CPI to calculate cost-of-living increases.

In Conclusion

Inside the Washington, D.C. beltway, Congressional lawmakers continue to seek out ways to rein in rising Social Security program costs. Some call for a combination of reducing program benefits while raising revenues. Others support only benefit cuts, warning that raising the payroll tax or bringing other forms of additional revenue would hurt the nation's fragile economy.

After the federal shutdown, when Congress comes back to continue the people's business and begins to seriously debate policies for reforming Social Security, it becomes crucial for these lawmakers to bring the AARP Policy Institute's economic impact study findings into their discussions. Slashing benefit checks will hurt financially vulnerable seniors, but as shown by the findings of this recently released report it can also have a drastic impact on fragile state economies by slowing job growth and reducing retail and other spending, even lowering tax revenues at the local, state, and federal levels.

For a copy of the report, go to **http://googl/C91h8w.**

5. HEALTH & WELLNESS

EXPERTS: EAT LESS AND EXERCISE

Published January 2007, in the Senior Digest

As we begin a new year, many people launch promises through New Year's resolutions or take this time to reflect on overall lifestyle improvements. State aging and health care experts recommend that if your goal is to live longer, consider squeezing in time to enhance your fitness and health through ongoing exercise and better eating.

Phillip Clark, Sc.D., professor and director of the program in Gerontology and Rhode Island Geriatric Education Center, noted that exercise is key to living a healthier life. "Use it or lose it," he told *Senior Digest*. If older adults don't continue to use their capabilities, whether physical or mental, they may eventually lose those abilities. It is important for aging baby boomers and seniors to continue to be as active as they can, within the limits of any impairments or health problems they may have.

Before beginning any program, always check with your physician to be sure it is OK. "Your doctor will advise you on other special conditions or limitations you may need to address in developing your own program," Dr. Clark said.

Exercise: The Best Pill

Dr. Clark believes that exercise is the "best pill." Regular exercise for older adults is linked to many positive physical and mental-health outcomes and advantages, he said. People feel better physically and mentally, especially if they exercise properly on a regular basis.

The University of Rhode Island (URI) gerontologist compares physical activity with a savings account. Dr. Clark said: "If you 'put' deposits into your exercise savings on a regular basis, you can 'draw' on these when you are sick or have to be hospitalized to help minimize the impact of any setback on your functioning."

To exercise, expensive weight machines and bikes are not necessary, Dr. Clark said. "Keep it simple," he recommended. "For many older adults, just walking regularly can have a number of positive benefits. In the winter when the weather is bad, some folks walk inside their local senior-housing building or at the mall," he said.

Deb Riebe, Ph.D., a professor in URI's Department of Kinesiology, said that research has found resistance training is another viable option for aging baby boomers and seniors to consider staying fit.

Consider Resistance Training and Balance Exercises

The URI exercise physiologist noted that muscle strength peaks at age 30 for most people. After age 50, there is a real decline in muscle strength. By your 60s or 70s, if you don't exercise or participate in a resistance-training program, it will become more difficult to perform simple activities of daily living, like carrying the vacuum cleaner or groceries.

Strengthening your muscles can be done simply by lifting small hand weights that can be purchased in local stores, added Riebe, noting that you can use your own body weight to strengthen the muscles in your legs by sitting in your dining-room chair and then standing up. Perform this simple resistance-training exercise 10 times.

"Balance exercises are also very good to prevent a person from falling. A good example of a balance exercise is to stand up on one leg using a chair for support," she said.

Don't use lack of time as a reason not to exercise, warned Riebe. "Fit 30 or 40 minutes of exercise into your daily routine. For those who choose not to, you can always park your car far away from a store and walk a longer distance. Or you can do a few exercises during a television commercial, combining leisure with a quick workout," she said.

Even when socializing with friends or family, Riebe recommended going out and taking a walk around the neighborhood. "Everyone will benefit," she said.

Anne Marie Connolly, M.S., director of "Get Fit Rhode Island Program," oversees Governor Donald Carcieri's worksite-wellness initiative for state employees. Programs like this one in Rhode Island are being launched nationwide by state health commissioners and insurance companies attempting to reel in spiraling health care costs.

To improve health behavior, brochures, on-site lectures (controlling stress and high blood pressure), and behavior-change classes (physical exercise and smoking cessation)
are aimed at the 20,000 state workers, whose average age is 47 years old.

Good Nutrition Is Important

Connolly, a professor and research associate at URI's Kinesiology Department, stressed the importance that nutrition plays in maintaining one's good health. "Research tells us that people should eat smaller portions, increase their fruit and vegetables and decrease fat, high-calorie foods and sweets from their diet," she recommended.

For persons with high blood pressure, heart disease, or diabetes, consider asking your physician for a consult to see a nutritionist. Connolly noted that this visit is covered by most health-insurance companies. "A change in your diet can make significant improvements in many chronic conditions."

Connolly observed that some people don't buy vegetables and fruit because of the cost. "Look around for supermarkets that offer smaller packaging or portions of vegetables and fruit. Salad and fruit bars enable a person to buy a portion or quantity they need," she said. Even in senior housing, you can work with others to buy cheaply. Split a head of lettuce with a neighbor. Create a schedule to rotate the purchasing of fruit and vegetables, too.

As to exercise, Connolly suggested people start off slowly. It is important to find an exercise that you like to do. As a consultant to Club Med, she has come to believe that exercise should be fun and not a chore. "Look back and see what you did when you were younger," Connolly added. "One woman who took tap dancing in her younger years picked it up again. It does not have to be at the same intensity as when you were younger."

For persons with arthritis, go to a local senior center or YMCA and enroll in exercise programs specifically designed for that chronic condition. "Water exercise is extremely wonderful for people with arthritis," she said.

Connolly noted that some Medicare providers even give special discounts to senior citizens who join health-care-club chains. Check out your Medicare health care plan's benefits to see whether you are eligible to participate.

Experts agree that exercise benefits both young and old. "What is remarkable about the human body is that people of all ages respond to physical exercise in the same way," Connolly said.

EXPERTS OFFER SOME ADVICE ON HOW TO AGE SUCCESSFULLY

Published February 21, 2014, in the Pawtucket Times

As an aging baby boomer, the pains and aches of old age and my noticeable gray hair are obvious signs of getting closer to age 60.

Amazingly, being given a free donut with my large cup of coffee at Dunkin' Donuts, an AARP member benefit, is a clear reminder to me of how people may perceive my chronological age. When I pulled out my wallet to get my membership card, the employee said, "Don't worry, you're covered." Simply put, by having gray hair it was obvious to the young woman that I was eligible to get the free donut.

The aches and pains of getting older happen more often too. After spraining my ankle from a fall on a sheet of ice, while taking out my garbage, it took much longer for this injury to heal. Most recently, a sharp pain in my hip makes me wonder if hip replacement surgery could be in my future.

Like me, President Barack Obama has shown his age by his gray hair and is even beginning to publicly complain about his aches and pains because of living more than five decades.

The 52-year-old president told retired National Basketball Association star Charles Barkley in a recent interview that he was limiting his trips to the basketball court to once a month because "things happen."

"One is, you just get a little older and creakier. The second thing is, you've got to start thinking about elbows, and you break your nose right before a State of the Union address," said the president in the interview on the TNT network before the NBA All-Star Game.

Discussing the aging process during an exchange about his signature health care reform law, Obama said that being past 50, "you wake up and something hurts, and you don't know exactly what happened, right?"

Taking Control of the Aging Process

Of course, President Obama's complaints about getting old went viral. With two Rhode Island gerontologists and a geriatric physician, this columnist gives the middle-aged President tips on easing into his old age.

Phillip G. Clark, Sc.D., director, URI Program in Gerontology and Rhode Island Geriatric Education Center and professor, Department of Human Development and Family Studies, notes that some research has indicated that the decade between 50 and 60 is when many people start getting "messages" that they are getting older. These can be physical, psychological, familial, and social.

A lot are based on the messages that they receive from those around them, including the media. "If you're older than 50, you should be taking Centrum Silver, or you qualify for this special type of life insurance policy," adds Clark. "These messages may not reflect an accurate picture of what normal aging really is, but rather a biased and stereotypical portrait," he says, for example, supposed bodily reminders of aging, such as aches and pains, may be due more to lack of exercise rather than actual aging itself.

To successfully age, "stay physically active," says Clark, suggesting that you get an assessment from your physician. This helps both your body and your brain. A moderately brisk, 30-minute walk a day is all you need, he notes. "It's more important that you build physical activity into your daily routine and do something that you enjoy and can stick with, than spend a lot of money on a gym membership that you seldom use." Eating a diet that is high in fruits and vegetables is also important as part of a healthy lifestyle at any age.

Clark also recommends that aging baby boomers stay engaged with settings and activities that keep them involved in life through their faith community, family, and friends. Even having a sense of purpose in life that gets you outside of yourself, through volunteering, can help you age more gracefully, he adds, stressing that having a social network and people who care about and support you are essential elements of successful aging at any age.

But don't forget to "have a positive attitude and keep a sense of humor," warns Clark. According to the gerontologist, this can get you over the challenges and hurdles you may encounter. "Being resilient in the face of the challenges of life and getting older demands that we see the positive side of situations and not get bogged down in focusing on what we no longer have. We need to emphasize what we can do to keep the enjoyment in our lives."

Successful aging may not be swimming the English Channel at age 80, noted Brown University Professor of Medicine and of Health Services Richard Besdine, director of Brown's Center for Gerontology and Healthcare Research and director of the Division of Geriatrics in the Department of Medicine. However, for the general population, successful aging, that is "optimum physical cognitive functioning, rests on your genes, education, and life experiences," he says, not accomplishing great feats like swimming the English Channel.

While the Brown University geriatrician agrees with Clark about the impact of exercise and social networks on improving your health and longevity, he also sees other ways to increase the quality of your aging.

Strategies to an Improved Life-Style

According to Besdine, a majority of people with high blood pressure don't take medication to control it. This chronic condition can cause strokes. Smoking does not just cause lung cancer, but every type of cancer and chronic lung disease.

Driving safely can increase your lifespan and quality of aging. As one ages your eyesight may change, glare becomes a problem, and you lose flexibility to turn. Retraining programs, offered by AARP and AAA, can reduce the probability of having an accident, says Besdine.

Don't forget your pneumonia or influenza vaccination, warns Besdine. Having repeated occurrences of the flu can lead to heart disease and other health issues, he says.

A good nutritional diet is key to enhancing the quality of health in your later years, notes Besdine, but people living on fixed incomes may not be able to afford eating fruits, vegetables, and lean meats. Cooking for yourself may even lead to a decision not to make nutritional meals. Besdine is also a big advocate of the Mediterranean diet, a heart-healthy eating plan that emphasizes fruits, vegetables, whole grains, beans, nuts and seeds, and healthy fats. He notes that this diet reduces your chances of getting heart disease and diabetes.

Besdine also notes that there are simple things that you can do at home to increase your longevity and quality of life. Make sure your home is safe, equipped with fire and carbon-monoxide detectors. Rid your kitchen of toxic substances. He urges a "gun-free" home. "This is not a political statement. Research shows us that a person is much more likely of being shot by a gun that is kept at home," he says.

Screening for cancers (by scheduling a mammogram and/or colonoscopy) and depression, along with moderate drinking, good oral health care, and preventing osteoporosis by taking calcium and Vitamin D, even reducing adverse drug reactions and improving mobility, are simple ways to increase the chances of your successful aging, Besdine says.

Unraveling Research Findings

Rachel Filinson, Ph.D., professor of Sociology/Gerontology Coordinator at Rhode Island College, says the "devil may well be in the details," as older persons try to unravel research findings that might provide them with a clear road map to achieve successful aging. For instance, Filinson notes that while some gerontologists have long regarded "undernutrition," consuming relatively few calories to sustain oneself, as a way to increase one's longevity, others disagree with the theory.

Mental stimulation is believed by many to deter cognitive decline, Filinson says, but brain teasers and games have not been adequately proven by research findings, while reading and writing may be helpful.

Although a large social network and recreational pursuits have been lauded as essential to enhance the quality of aging, some investigations have found that solitary activities like gardening are just as effective, observes Filinson.

Filinson believes that older adults can take charge of their lives by optimizing the positives and minimizing the negatives—how we age."It's about the choices we make in life rather than the genes we were born with," she quips.

President Obama might well listen to Clark, Besdine, and Filinson's sage advice as to how he can cope with the aging process. Even small changes in his daily mundane routines, like using the stairs rather than taking an elevator in the White House or even taking Bo, the first family's dog, for a brief walk around the grounds, can result in his living longer, even reduce his noticeable aches and pains.

HEALTHY ATTITUDE, LIFESTYLE ARE LIKELY KEYS TO LIVING PAST 100

Published October 29, 2001, in the Pawtucket Times

Just a couple of days past her birthday on July 18, 2001, Henrietta Bruce, who was officially recognized as Rhode Island's oldest woman, passed away at the ripe old age of 110. Born in Barbados, West Indies, in 1891, Bruce, one of 10 children, would later move to New Jersey and finally to the Ocean State. She married in 1921, had a son who lived into his 80s, and in later life she became very active in the Evangelical Convenant Church in East Providence.

"She was cognitive right up to her 110th birthday," said Judy Riendeau, activity coordinator at Bay Tower Nursing Center in Providence, who fondly remembered Bruce's "sassy personality." As to her longevity, Bruce did not attribute it to good nutrition, regular exercise, or genetics, Rindeau noted. When asked how she had lived so long, the nursing-facility resident would respond, "Only by the grace of God."

According to the year 2000 U.S. census report released last month, there is rapid growth among America's centenarians. Bruce was one of 50,045 persons age 100 and over last year, and their ranks have increased about 35 percent from a decade ago, said Lisa Hetzel, statistician at the U.S. Census Bureau. As to Rhode Island, Hetzel noted that today there are 278 centenarians, up 43 percent from 1990.

Why are more people living past age 100? According to writer John Lauerman, who, with Drs. Thomas Perls and Margery Silver of the New England Centenarian Study at the Harvard Medical School Division on Aging, co-authored the book, "Living to 100," a picture is emerging of the typical centenarian.

Lauerman, the health care writer for the *Springfield Union-News,* said that people in the oldest age group tend to remain physically and mentally healthy as well as emotionally stable. Most important, centenarians tend to come from families in which long lives are common.

In "Living to 100," based on Perls' and Silver's New England Centenarian Study, Lauerman noted that a good attitude is one key to living longer. "Centenarians rarely consider their age as a limitation," he said, noting that they take advantage of the opportunity for longevity afforded to them by their genes.

Certain genes may be key to whether a person reaches age 100 and over, "but don't thwart them," warned Lauerman. Good health practices are key to maximizing your life, he said.

In addition, resistance-training exercise is an important factor for maintaining strength and muscle, noted Lauerman. It can also can reduce your risk of heart disease and increase your sense of well-being, he added.

Lauerman also recommended that you keep your mind active and investigate new challenges. Take advantage of opportunities like second careers, volunteering, learning to play musical instruments, writing, or even traveling. Humor, meditation, and low-impact exercise like the Chinese discipline of tai chi may also help reduce stress.

As to nutrition, increase your portions of vegetables and fruit and minimize meat, saturated and hydrogenated fats and sweets. Also eat moderately and supplement your diet with the antioxidant vitamin E, taking 400 to 800 international units (IU) daily; and selenium, taking 100 to 200 micrograms daily.

Making these changes won't necessarily guarantee becoming a centenarian, Lauerman said, but they will allow you to live longer and healthier, which is what centenarians do. Research reveals that one of the more interesting things about centenarians is that most of the unhealthy portion of their lives is packed into their last few years, he added, noting that they seldom spend many years in an unhealthy state before death.

HEALTHY LIFESTYLE KEY TO LOSING AND MAINTAINING WEIGHT LOSS

Published August 2008, in the Senior Digest

As food and gasoline prices skyrocket nationwide, a growing number of Americans with bulging waistlines who are watching their weight also steadily increase. Those who are overweight see diets as a remedy to drop the pounds. Yet to most, finding the right weight-loss strategy is at most confusing and difficult to follow.

For more than 40 years, Donald Grebien, a supply-chain manager at the Mansfield, Massachusetts-based, American Insulated Wire Corporation, has struggled with his waistline. In high school, Grebien recalled being a "chubby senior," weighing as much as 280 pounds. Even though he managed to shed 30 pounds through regular exercise, eliminating snacks, and eating healthy foods, it is still a daily struggle.

Grebien's weight would fluctuate throughout middle age because of a variety of factors. His family obligations of raising two children, combined with the pressures of being a Pawtucket city councilman, made it extremely difficult for the young man to successfully stick with a diet. It was not until this young city councilman was faced with high blood pressure that he would ultimately be forced to confront his weight issue.

"Losing weight is a daily battle for me," said Grebien, who noted that whenever his weight spiked, it was very uncomfortable to wear tight-fitting clothes.

Joining Weight Watchers with his wife, Laureen, has made a world of difference to Grebien. He has maintained his weight loss of 10.3 pounds for the past 10 weeks. "I am on track and feel a lot better," he said, even noting that his waistline seems to be shrinking a bit. His workplace even supports his dieting efforts, such as offering on-site Weight Watcher classes, a nutrition newsletter, and encouraging employees to walk during their lunch hour.

While Grebien tackles his weight problem through the support of his wife and a community weight-loss program, finding the right diet plan or strategy can be a difficult chore for many.

Tips on Losing Weight

"Get responsible and sound advice about dieting before you begin," recommended Randi Belhumeur, a registered dietitian who serves as statewide nutrition coordinator for the Rhode Island Health Department's Initiative for Healthy Weight. There is no major expense for the consultation because most health-insurance plans cover nutritional counseling so long as you have a medical diagnosis such as high cholesterol, hypertension, or diabetes, she said.

Belhumeur said that a nutritionist can provide specifics as to serving sizes, label reading, meal planning, and weight-loss goal setting. When setting your weight-loss goals, "always start with small goals that are realistic for you," she said. "Losing a pound or two a week is considered by medical experts to be a safe weight loss," she added.

"Don't forget to dovetail physical activity into your weight-loss goals," suggested Belhumeur. "If a pedometer tells you that the baseline number of steps you take a day is 2,000 steps, increase that number by 1,000 steps," she said.

"Always keep an 'activity and food journal' also," added Belhumeur, who stressed that the documentation will be critical to losing and maintaining your weight loss. "You re-ally need to be honest with yourself when you are writing the details down. Journaling will help you make better food choices and make you aware of what you are eating," she said.

Belhumeur also recommended planning to exercise each week by scheduling the time in your BlackBerry, PalmPilot, or in your schedule book. "With exercise, find something you enjoy doing. If you don't like going to the gym, you just won't go."

Social support from family and friends is also crucial in your efforts to lose weight successfully, noted Belhumeur. "Weight Watchers is one of the few responsible diet programs that offers group support and sound dieting advice," she said.

Finally Belhumeur said, "Don't forget the behavioral component of weight loss." Psychotherapy or nutritional counseling can be helpful to changing behaviors like nighttime eating or eating unhealthy foods at the workplace.

Weight Loss and Lifestyle Changes

Ray Rickman, senior consultant for Rhode Island's ShapeUp RI Program, a statewide exercise and weight-challenge program, is not a fan of dieting. The nonprofit group helps participants improve their health and lifestyle by increasing their physical-ac-tivity levels and developing smart eating habits.

Supported by Blue Cross and Blue Shield and Lifespan, more than 12,000 Rhode Islanders, in 13,000 teams, participate to see who can lose the greatest percentage of collective team weight, log the most hours of physical activity, and walk the highest number of pedometer steps over a 12-week period.

Rickman, a 55-year-old East Sider and state legislator has lost more than 20 pounds by following the nonprofit group's philosophy of reducing daily calorie intake and increasing daily exercise.

According to Rickman, people become overweight or obese because of their lifestyle and not from medical or chemical imbalances.

"On most diets you just starve yourself or you eat foods you don't like," Rickman said. "While many people can lose weight by dieting, they usually regain all the weight back within 12 months."

"We consume more food than the body can rid itself of, and portion sizes are increasing," said Rickman, noting that an "unhealthy lifestyle and poor eating" causes weight gain. Almost 50 years ago, a typical orange-juice serving was 250 calories. Today a larger glass increases the calories to 800, he added.

"In every area of our lives, we try to find ways not to exercise," Rickman noted. "Go into a four-story building, and you will see people waiting for an elevator to go to the second floor, rather than just walking up two flights of stairs. Or watch shoppers wait for a parking space close to the grocery store's entrance rather than parking farther away."

To lose weight successfully, find out how many calories you need a day, based on your height and weight, Rickman recommended. He estimated that eating 200 fewer calories, along with exercise, will help you lose 1/16 of a pound a day. In just one month, a person can lose two pounds. In one year, you can expect to lose at least 25 pounds.

"Exercise does not have to be grueling." Rickman said, "Go to the grocery store and park in the last spot on the lot where the employees park. By doing this you can lose 1/36 of a pound by choosing not to park near the entrance. Walking up three flights of stairs will also help you lose 1/36 of a pound," he said

Brown University medical student Rajiv Kumar, founder of ShapeUp RI Program, sees long-term sustained weight loss for those participating in his program. The average weight loss per person is 10 pounds and preliminary research indicates that 70 percent of the participants have kept their weight off for six months.

For chronic dieters like Grebien (or this writer) who work daily to shed pounds, the secret to successfully losing and maintaining weight loss may well be tied to healthy eating habits, exercise, and an active social network to create accountability and motivation. It's as simple as that.

KEEPING YOUR PET SAFE IN FRIGID WEATHER

Published January 11, 2013, in the Pawtucket Times

Regardless of the hot temperatures in summer or the frigid weather in winter, dog owners take those daily walks outdoors with their beloved pets. At press time, New Englanders will see unprecedented warmth this winter with temperatures rising into the 40s, but don't get complacent. This year's *Farmers' Almanac* predicts that "Old Man Winter will return with a vengeance." This annually published periodical, famous for its long-range weather predictions, wagers that the Eastern half of the nation will see plenty of cold weather and snow before spring approaches.

While those cold air temperatures and blustery winds make you shiver and bring on chills, the frigid weather has the same effect on your pets and, in some cases, can become deadly, cautioned E. J. Finocchio, D.V.M., president of the East Providence-based Rhode Island Society for the Prevention of Cruelty to Animals (RISPCA). This 141-year-old nonprofit society that advocates for the welfare of all animals also promotes being responsible pet owners, as well as advocating pet-overpopulation control.

Location, Location, Location

With Rhode Island located in the nation's "cold zone," Dr. Finocchio said that the occurrence of hypothermia is not unusual, with below-zero temperatures in winter. When the core temperature of the animal's body begins to lose heat faster than it can produce it, that is when hypothermia can set in. "Dogs that are especially prone to hypothermia are puppies under six months old, elderly dogs, short-hair breeds, small-sized dogs, dogs with health issues (arthritis, diabetes, or heart disease) and pets that are obese or underweight," he said.

"Symptoms of hypothermia in animals are similar to those found in humans, as well as in all warm-blooded animals," noted Dr. Finocchio.

According to Dr. Finocchio, mild cases in dogs might include shivering and whining while the animal begins to act lethargic or tired. For moderate cases, he added, the animal loses its ability to shiver, loses coordination, and appears to be clumsy. At this point, the dog may lose consciousness. If it gets to this point, the dog's life is in serious jeopardy. Finally he noted that for severe cases, the animal may collapse, have difficulty breathing, and its pupils will become dilated.

The dog will become unresponsive. If hypothermia reaches this point, it is critical that the animal be warmed quickly and taken to an emergency vet center. A rectal thermometer will enable you to gauge the temperature of the animal's internal organs to confirm hypothermia, noted Dr. Finocchio. A normal temperature falls between 101 degrees to 102 degrees. If the temperature falls between 96 to 99 degrees, it is considered a mild case; moderate falls between 90 to 95 degrees, and a body temperature of under 90 degrees is a sure sign of severe hypothermia.

Going to Court for Animal Cruelty

Finocchio said that if a pet's death is determined through a necropsy (autopsy performed on an animal) to be caused by hypothermia and a history of exposure, the pet's owner could be charged with a misdemeanor for animal cruelty. If the city's prosecuting officer determines that the investigative report submitted constitutes a valid case, the complaint is filed with district court. If the defendant pleads nolo contendere or is found guilty by the court, the judge can order the defendant not be allowed to live with any animal for up to five years if charged with a misdemeanor or up to 15 years for a felony conviction, said Finocchio.

Last year John Holmes, Pawtucket's animal-control officer, noted that his office responded to 44 calls to investigate alleged cases of animal cruelty, some resulting from a person leaving a pet outside in frigid weather. Although a few of the cases were unfounded, Holmes and his staff found in other instances that the pet owners needed to be educated about responsible pet-ownership practices, along with state laws and city ordinances involving animals.

Holmes asked that all concerned neighbors who notice dogs being left outside in inclement weather call his office at the City of Pawtucket's Animal Shelter. "Each and every call is taken very seriously and checked out," he warned. After an investigation, if it is found that someone knowingly abused or neglected an animal, that person will be prosecuted and held accountable for his or her actions.

"We don't in general see hypothermia in stray or feral cats," noted Finocchio, because these animals can usually seek out small places to stay warm, specifically under cars, sheds, porches, or the hoods of vehicles. "They can usually get themselves out of harm's way," he said.

Livestock animals with thick fur including cows, horses, sheep, goats, and pigs are able to withstand severe frigid temperatures, especially if they are healthy. "We often get complaints from concerned people about livestock, especially horses standing in a pasture with an inch of snow on their back," Finocchio said, noting that the caller fears that the animal is going to freeze to death. "But larger animals can handle the cold environment more than our small domestic pets."

Just Use a Little Common Sense

Finocchio advised pet owners to just use common sense when it comes to protecting their pets from the cold weather. Don't take elderly, young, or sick pets, especially small short-haired breeds, outdoors unprotected in below-zero weather. Just let them go out in the backyard for a few minutes if necessary.

If hypothermia does occur, Finocchio, one of the state's most visible animal advocates, recommended that the pet be brought inside. Do not submerge the pet in hot water. To warm a pet, wrap the ailing animal in a thermal blanket (warmed by placing in a dryer for a couple of minutes), use a heating pad or wrap a towel with a hot bottle around areas with less hair, specifically in the groin, belly areas, or arm pits. Consider placing the animal by a radiant-heat appliance or roaring fireplace. You can even take your pet and place it in the footwell of the car and turn on the vehicle's heater. If the dog will drink, give it warm water.

However, if the animal's internal temperature falls into the severe hypothermia range, go immediately to a veterinary emergency clinic, where emergency treatment will be provided, he urged.

Dog owners who own large-breed dogs (especially those with thick fur that can protect the animal from frigid weather) can get permission from a veterinarian or animal-control officer to keep the animal outside for more than 10 hours and not violate state law.

Why keep a small pet outside in extremely frigid temperatures that could result in hypothermia and lead to death?

"It only takes common sense to protect your animal from hypothermia and keep it safe, nothing else," said Finocchio.

If the weather is uncomfortable for you to be outside, even when you are wearing layers of clothing, gloves, and a hat, it becomes obvious that putting your pet outside as the temperature dips into the teens will be detrimental to the health and well-being of your pet.

PALLIATIVE CARE CAN PROVIDE COMFORT TO DYING RESIDENTS

Published May 10, 2015, in the Woonsocket Call.

A recently published study by Brown University researchers takes a look at end-of-life care in America's nursing facilities, seeking to answer the question: Is knowledge and access to information on palliative care associated with a reduced likelihood of aggressive end-of-life treatment?

The Brown researchers say when a nursing facility resident is dying, often aggressive interventions such as inserting a feeding tube or sending the patient to the emergency room can futilely worsen, rather than relieve, their distress. While palliative care can pull resources together in a facility to provide comfort at the end of a resident's life, the knowledge of it varies among nursing directors. A new large national study found that the more nursing directors knew about palliative care, the lower the likelihood that their patients would experience aggressive end-of-life care.

Research Prof. Susan C. Miller of Health Services, Policy, and Practice in the Brown University School of Public Health and lead author of the study in the *Journal of Palliative Medicine,* published March 16, 2015, worked with colleagues to survey nursing directors at more than 1,900 nursing facilities across the nation between July 2009 and June 2010. The researchers hoped to learn more about the nursing directors' knowledge of palliative care and their facilities' implementation of key palliative care practices.

Knowledge Is Power

The study, the first nationally representative sample of palliative care familiarity at nursing homes, found more than one in five of the surveyed directors had little or no basic palliative care knowledge, although 43 percent were fully versed.

"While the Institute of Medicine has called for greater access to skilled palliative care across settings, the fact that one in five U.S. nursing home directors of nursing had very limited palliative care knowledge demonstrates the magnitude of the challenge in many nursing homes," Miller said. "Improvement is needed as are efforts to facilitate this improvement, including increased Medicare/Medicaid surveyor oversight of nursing home palliative care and quality indicators reflecting provision of high-quality palliative care," she said, noting that besides quizzing the directors the researchers also analyzed Medicare data on the 58,876 residents who died during the period to identify the type of treatments they experienced when they were dying.

When researchers analyzed palliative care knowledge together with treatment at end of life, they found that the more directors knew about basic palliative care, the lower likelihood that nursing facility residents would experience feeding tube insertion, injections, restraints, suctioning, and emergency room or other hospital trips. Meanwhile, residents in higher-knowledge facilities also had a greater likelihood of having a documented six-month prognosis.

The study shows only an association between palliative care knowledge and less aggressive end-of-life care, the authors say, noting that knowledge leads to improved care, but it could also be that at nursing facilities with better care in general, there is also greater knowledge. But, if there is a causal relationship, then it could benefit thousands of nursing facilities residents every year for their nursing home caregivers to learn more about palliative care, the authors conclude.

Making Progress in Providing End-of-Life Care

Virginia M. Burke, J.D., President and CEO of the non-profit Rhode Island Health Care Association, said, "We were gratified that the authors found that most of the nursing directors who responded to their survey gave correct answers on all (43% of respondents) or most (36% of respondents) of the 'knowledge' questions on palliative care. We were also gratified to see that the number of hospitalizations during the last thirty days of life has declined significantly over the past ten years, as has the number of individuals who receive tube feedings during their last thirty days. The need for continued progress is clear."

Burke, representing three quarters of Rhode Island's skilled nursing and rehabilitation centers, adds, "It is not at all surprising that greater understanding of palliative care leads to better application of palliative care."

The state's nursing facilities are committed to providing person-centered end-of-life care, said Burke, noting that according to the National Palliative Care Research

Center, Rhode Island's hospitals are among the top performers for palliative care. "We suspect that our state's nursing facilities are as well. We would be very interested in state-specific results in order to see any areas where we can improve." Said Director Michael Raia of Rhode Island's Health & Human Services Agency, "We need to provide the right care in the right place at the right time for all patients."

When it comes to nursing facilities, Raia calls for adjusting payment incentives so that facilities are rewarded for providing better quality care and having better patient outcomes. He notes that the Reinventing Medicaid Act of 2015 reinvests nursing home reimbursement rate savings into newly created incentive pools for nursing homes and long-term care providers that reward facilities for providing better quality care, including higher quality palliative care.

SENIORS CAN FOLLOW STEPS TO AVOID HEAT-RELATED ILLNESS

Published July 5, 2002, in the Pawtucket Times

On July 3rd, it was so hot you could fry an egg on the pavement outside of McCoy Stadium.

Although more than 10,500 fans had bought tickets to watch the PawSox game against the Ottawa Lynx, which concluded with a 45-minute fireworks display, only 8,300 fans showed up, according to Ken McGill, co-chair of the Pawtucket Fireworks Committee.

There were even smaller crowds who set up chairs in the parking lots and on sidewalks in the surrounding neighborhoods around McCoy Stadium to watch the much-anticipated fireworks display, McGill said.

Yet despite the searing heat that evening, it was clear that some just like it hot.

As the PawSox game was winding down, Ray Ethier, 60, a former union electrician, chatted with his friend, George Panas, 59, of Spumoni's Restaurant.

"I don't mind the heat. I just don't like this humidity," he candidly admitted. However, Ethier acknowledged that the heat has slowed him down a bit, because "it's too hot to play golf."

Panas doesn't mind the searing outside heat either or even working in a hot kitchen.

"When people are sweating buckets in the kitchen, I feel as cool as a cucumber," he said.

Fifty-seven-year-old Stan Lachut, a retired Pawtucket schoolteacher, waited with his wife, Beverly, for darkness and the fireworks show to begin. Standing by the barbecue tent and surrounded by more than 200-plus guests of the Pawtucket Fireworks Committee, the Cumberland resident said the heat is not a problem for him.

"Being outside in summer is a time you can spend with your family and friends," he said, whereas "colder temperatures force people to stay inside buildings."

On the other hand, not everybody likes summer's hot days

Temperatures in the mid-90s, combined with high humidity, can become uncomfortable and a serious health hazard for seniors. And many are heeding the advice of experts gleaned from radio, television, and local newspaper articles about how to cope with scorching summer heat.

Patricia A. Nolan, M.D., the state's top health official, gave her advice on surviving Rhode Island's current heat wave.

Seniors, small children, and the mentally ill are the most susceptible to health problems from searing summer heat waves, said Nolan, who serves as the director of Rhode Island's Department of Health. High temperatures can be especially dangerous to individuals with cardiac and respiratory problems and to mentally-ill patients taking psychotropic medications, she said.

She noted that psychotropic medications make it harder for an individual to cool down.

According to Nolan, the early symptoms of heat-related illnesses include muscle cramps in the arms, hands, abdomen, and legs. Muscle cramps are a result of dehydration and salt loss, primary problems associated with heat stress. In addition, Nolan said that fainting in the heat is another early symptom

If someone faints because of the heat, take the person into a cool place and cool them off by using a wet, cool cloth, Nolan recommended.

"You want to sponge people down and fan them to reduce their body heat," she said.

Heat exhaustion, or heat-stroke, is a more serious problem related to dehydration caused from high temperatures, Nolan stated. "Feelings of complete exhaustion, confusion, nausea, or vomiting are real danger signs," she said, adding, "if this occurs, you must get the body temperature down by additional fluids through intravenous methods."

To successfully beat the heat, seniors should cut back on outside physical activities and drink plenty of water, Nolan recommended. While water is the best fluid to drink on a hot day, fruit juice can also be a viable substitute.

"Cooling off with a cold beer is not the best plan," Nolan said, noting that alcohol, coffee, tea, and soda are loaded with caffeine, which can increase the chances of dehydration.

"Seniors who tend to be most vulnerable to heat are those who don't have a way to get cool for part of the day," Nolan said. "One of the reasons heat waves affect the elderly more than the general population is because seniors are isolated, can't get to a cool place, don't have air-conditioning, and are afraid to open their windows at night when it finally cools down."

Nolan warned that with temperatures in the mid-90s, staying indoors in a hot house or apartment is not the best thing for seniors to do.

"Go to an air-conditioned shopping mall, see a movie, visit a restaurant, or get yourself into an air-conditioned space," she recommended. "If you can do this for an hour on a really hot day, you can protect yourself from serious health-related problems. Sometimes seniors get into trouble during days with high temperatures because they just don't realize the danger," Nolan noted.

During these days, it becomes important to monitor elderly parents or older friends. "Call on them every day to make sure they are coping with the heat. Take them out to a cool place, like a shopping mall, a library, or a restaurant to let them cool off," she said.

"In Rhode Island, some seniors tend not to adjust their behaviors to the heat because it is going to be hot for only a few days, however, adjustments are fairly easy to make," she noted, stating that not making them can be hazardous to seniors' health and perhaps even deadly.

SOME TIPS TO TAKE LYING DOWN

Published March 1, 2004, in the Pawtucket Times

Sometimes I just can't sleep. When this happens, I just lie in bed, tossing and turning and staring through the darkness at the ceiling. It is 2 a.m. All I want is a good night's sleep.

According to a publication released by the New York-based International Longevity Center-USA (ILC-USA) and the AARP Foundation, I am not alone in trying to get a good night's sleep. A whopping one-third of the nation's seniors will find themselves sleepless (and not all in Seattle). Lack of sleep can even lead to serious health disorders.

The AARP-ILC consumer publication, "Getting Your ZZZZZZZs: How Sleep Affects Health and Aging," takes a look at common sleep disorders, their effects on the brain and body and what someone who suffers from these conditions might do to get a good night's sleep.

"Not getting the right amount of sleep can become a serious health problem, and it is not a natural part of aging," stated Robert N. Butler, M.D., ILC-USA's president and CEO, in a written statement promoting the publication.

"A large number of older persons often suffer from this medical condition and go unrecognized or are not treated appropriately," he said.

According to the 12-page AARP-ILC consumer-oriented publication, sleep problems in your later years are caused by a combination of factors. Sleep problems can result from physical changes associated with growing older.

Sleep problems can also be caused by pain and discomfort associated with aging and traumatic life experiences such as the death of a spouse or the loss of a job.

Even decreased physical activity and lack of exposure to sunlight can impact a person's ability to sleep.

"Sleeplessness sets up a vicious cycle. Older people have problems that disturb their sleep, which often affect their other body systems, especially hormone production and metabolism, which cause more problems that disturb sleep even more," states the AARP-ILC publication.

"New studies highlight the significant impact of sleep on physical and mental well-being especially for older men and women," the AARP-ILC publication points out. Loss of sleep can lead to memory problems, depression, and a greater risk of falling. Lack of sleep may also cause changes in the nervous system that affect cardiovascular health.

According to the AARP-ILC publication, snoring may indicate a serious health problem, considered the most common form of sleep apnea. This sleep disorder causes sleeplessness because the sleeper frequently wakes up from the lack of oxygen caused by this labored breathing.

Findings from the Nurses' Health Study indicate that snoring is associated with hypertension as well as weight-related health problems.

Several other research studies have shown that people who suffer from sleep apnea also have high rates of automobile accidents and are at risk for diabetes.

Insomnia caused by depression, serious mental or physical illness, or unhealthy lifestyle choices is considered another major sleep disorder. Proper treatment requires a phy-sician to diagnose the cause. In addition, obesity, alcohol, smoking, nasal congestion, and menopause are also suspected of affecting a person's ability to fall asleep.

Meanwhile, the report gives tips on getting your sleep.

Tips on Getting Your ZZZZZZZZs

The AARP-ILC consumer publication notes a regular schedule of exercise and a health-ier lifestyle can help enhance the quality of your sleep.

Recent studies also indicate that taking short naps during the day of no more than 20 to 30 minutes may actually help a person sleep at night.

Although medication can be used for short-term problems, it does not seem to solve long-term sleep problems.

Always check your medications. Some actually act as stimulants. Avoid alcohol and nicotine. Both can disrupt your sleep. Also avoid overeating and drinking large quan-tities of liquids before bedtime.

Finally, create a sleep-friendly bedroom. A cool, quiet room can enhance your sleep. Make sure that your mattress is comfortable. Use the bed only for sleep or sex to strengthen the mind's association between bed and sleep.

Also, the AARP-ILC publication details two new alternative ideas, light therapy and two drugs (melatonin, a hormone, which can be taken as a supplement, and valerian, (an herbal medicine) are thought by some experts to be effective treatments for seniors with insomnia. However, the authors of the publication call for more studies to ensure that these alternative treatments are safe and effective.

"Our nation's oldest adults need not accept poor sleep as a penalty for being old," said Dr. Butler. " As researchers learn more about how the human body controls sleep, effective treatments for sleep disorders in older and younger people will become increasingly possible."

To get copies of "Getting Your ZZZZZZZs: How Sleep Affects Health and Aging." English and Spanish versions of this publication can be downloaded from the ILC-USA's website at: **my.clevelandclinic.org/ccf/media /files/Geriatrics/ gettingzs.pdf**.

TIPS ON FINDING AN AGE-FRIENDLY FITNESS CENTER

Published on November 16, 2012, in the Pawtucket Times

With cold, frigid weather approaching, that 30-minute daily walk around the block may well fall by the wayside in the winter. While this activity is just what the doctor ordered to help keep you physically fit and feeling good, many aging baby boomers and seniors "look inward" by turning to a local gym to bring their regular exercise indoors.

Seeking that Perfect Age-Friendly Fitness Facility

According to the Vancouver, British Columbia-based International Council on Active Aging (ICAA), aging baby boomers and seniors are joining health and wellness facilities at a faster rate than any other age group. Yet many of these facilities are ill-prepared or not equipped to serve those in their later years.

Older "adult-focused" small gyms like Nifty After Fifty are available. "Even the large 24-Hour fitness chains seek to attract older adults," said Patricia Ryan, ICAA's vice president of education, noting that "more than 70 percent of YMCAs had older adult programs," according to a stat cited in ICAA's "Active Aging in America, Industry Outlook 2010."

Ryan recommended that when shopping for a fitness center that caters to older baby boomers and seniors, always compare and contrast gathered information, using the following checklists created by ICAA to identify an age-friendly fitness center.

Become a savvy shopper when touring your local fitness center by making sure it gears its amenities and organizational philosophies toward the needs of those age 50-something and beyond. ICAA, the world's largest senior-fitness association, has created a checklist to help older persons to rate and compare local fitness facilities so they can choose one that meets their age-specific needs.

Some specific questions to consider can ultimately ensure that the center you choose meets your specific physical needs:

Are the locker rooms clean, accessible, and monitored by staff?

Do you feel comfortable in the atmosphere of the facility?

Are the membership contracts and marketing materials available in large print?

Are signs visible and easy to understand?

Does the facility's cardiovascular equipment have the following age-friendly features: a display panel that is easy to read, easy to change, and easy to understand?

Is the music acceptable and set at a reasonable level?

Do the facility's treadmills start slowly at 0.5 mph?

Do the recumbent bikes have a wide and comfortable seat with armrests?

Does the facility's strength-building equipment have instructional placards that have simple diagrams, easy-to-read text and font, and correct usage information?

Does the facility's strength-building equipment have a low starting resistance, such as less than five pounds?

Does the facility offer programs designed to meet the needs of those with a variety of chronic conditions (specifically osteoporosis, cardiovascular disease, diabetes, balance abnormalities, muscular weakness)?

Do the group-exercise classes have different levels of intensity, duration, and size?

Is there an extensive screening and assessment process (for balance, functional abilities, and osteoporosis)?'

Is the staff certified by a nationally recognized organization to work with people who have various health issues that may arise with age (specifically osteoporosis, hypertension, and arthritis)?

Is the staff knowledgeable about the impact that medication can have on exercise?

To download the complete checklist, visit the ICAA website, **icaa.cc/activeagingweek/support-resources/facilitytest.pdf**.

Getting Healthy and Building Close Relationships

It's no secret to Maureen Wilcox, 45, of the need to cater to an aging population. Wilcox, a certified personal trainer at the YMCA located across from the city's public library on South Main Street in Attleboro, Massachusetts, estimates that 30 percent of the nonprofit group's membership is age 50 and older. Many of these members are seeking advice on how to better manage or prevent the most common age-related health concerns: arthritis, high blood pressure, diabetes, cardiac health, and obesity.

Wilcox noted that this large constituency finds value in the Attleboro YMCA's wide variety of programs geared toward baby boomers and seniors. These programs include resistance and strength training, aqua classes, Zumba classes, chair exercises, yoga, and tai chi. "These classes will help you to manage a healthy body weight, stimulate your immune system, increase strength, improve posture, increase your flexibility and balance, and help prevent chronic illnesses," she added.

According to Wilcox, a fitness center can also be a place to build friendships among older persons. "A supportive community can enhance camaraderie among the participants, keeping them motivated and committed to meeting their exercise goals," she said, adding that commitment to an exercise regime may well be more important than pushing weights around.

Over the years, Wilcox has seen many members in their later years forge new friendships at the Attleboro YMCA. "Seeing people regularly allows them to develop meaningful relationships where they ultimately become an extended family," she said.

"Relationships developed by participating in exercise classes also build a small community among the senior-age group members," Wilcox noted, adding that they often participate in social trips and group outings outside the Attleboro YMCA. She noted that some seniors, while exercising on stationary bikes, read a large-print book, adding health and wellness to an established community literacy initiative.

Finally, in addition to personal training, various group-exercise classes including a running club, Livestrong, is also offered at the Attleboro YMCA. It is a free 12-week personal-training program that provides a place where cancer survivors can come together. Along with specially-trained staff to safely work in small groups, participating members receive one-to-one attention while working toward maintaining or regaining their independence, everyday fitness, and overall health and wellness. These participants share a bond that only cancer survivors can relate to. "This is an inspirational program and one which we are all proud to be a part of," said Wilcox.

Getting to the Bottom Line

Outdoor walking or the gym? That depends on personal preference and time availability. "Brisk walking is beneficial, emphasizing *brisk*," said ICAA's Ryan. "Faster walking to increase intensity has been reported in several studies in the ICAA research review to enhance your health, rather than the frequency," she noted.

In addition, Ryan added that scheduled classes in a fitness center help people plan physical activity into their days. There should be equipment and classes for variety. There is expertise available in many (but not all) cases, especially in gyms targeting older adults and medically-integrated fitness centers, aka hospital-wellness programs. There is recognition among most fitness clubs that older adults are not only a huge population to attract, yet also a good customer base because of expendable income.

"Exercise plays a vital role in healthy aging," said Michael Fine, M.D., director of the Rhode Island Department of Health. "Regular exercise is an important weapon in the battle against chronic diseases, such as heart disease and diabetes. Exercise also helps us maintain flexibility, balance, and mobility. It isn't necessary to join a gym or buy expensive equipment. A brisk walk around the block is a great place to start if you've been sedentary. The key is to find an activity you enjoy and to make time for it each day," he said.

Ryan strongly agreed with Dr. Fine. "The most important message for those late in life is to MOVE and to add physical activity into each day. Physical activity is the magic pill. Whether walking, raking and hauling leaves, playing soccer or even going to a fitness club, it's the right thing to do for healthy aging," she said.

TV CELEB VALERIE HARPER CALLS FOR MORE FUNDING FOR CANCER RESEARCH

Published on May 12, 2014, in the Pawtucket Times

With a growing population of aging baby boomers, the U.S. Special Committee on Aging held a hearing on Wednesday to put the spotlight on how decreased federal funding to support cancer research is derailing the nation's successful efforts on its fight against cancer and to detail treatment advances.

In Dirksen Building 562, Chairman Bill Nelson (D-Florida) addressed the packed room on how innovative cancer research has tripled the number of survivors during the past 40 years, while continued federal cuts to balance the nation's budget are having a severe impact on biomedical research.

But despite significant advances in medical treatments over the years, cancer still is a major medical condition for the nation to confront. About 1.6 million Americans—the majority of them over age 55—will receive a cancer diagnosis this year, and more than 585,000 will die from the disease.

Putting Cancer Research on the Public Agenda

In his opening statement, Nelson stated that "as a result of the sequestered cuts, Francis Collins, director of the National Institutes of Health (NIH), had to stop 700 research grants from going out the door." Federal-funding support has "accelerated the pace of new discoveries and the development of better ways to prevent, detect, diagnose, and treat cancer in all age groups," he says.

Cancer research has been put on the radar screen of the Senate Aging panel because "little is known about the impact of cancer treatments on the body as it ages," added Nelson.

Nelson notes that although many cancer survivors are in remission because of ground-breaking advances in research, there still remains a large percentage of people with cancer across the nation who are still dependent on their next clinical trial, or even the next NIH research grant to keep them alive just a little bit longer. This is why Congress must be committed in its war against cancer, he adds, noting that the best place to start is to renew the federal government's role and commitment to innovative research that is taking place at universities, oncology centers, and hospitals, where much of the federal funds are being directed by NIH.

Dr. Harold Varmus, director of the National Cancer Institute, said more research is needed to fully understand how cancer is linked to aging. "Because most types of cancer—but not all—are commonly diagnosed in older age groups, the number of people with cancer is rising (with the world's population rapidly aging) and continue to rise, here and globally."

"For people of any age, the first line of defense against cancers and their damaging consequences is prevention," states Varmus.

Dr. Thomas Sellers, director of the H. Lee Moffitt Cancer Center and Research Institute, made his views quite clear about the federal government's "irreplaceable role" in fund-ing medical research. "No other public, corporate, or charitable entity is willing or able to provide the broad and sustained funding for the cutting-edge research necessary to yield new innovations and technologies for cancer care of the future," he says.

Sellers warns, "Without increased funding now, the spectacular advancements we have witnessed in the past will not be there in the future."

Star Power To Make a Point

One of the nation's most prominent lung cancer survivors, Valerie Harper, who rose to fame on the *The Mary Tyler Moore Show* and *Rhoda*, *Valerie*, and more recently on *Dancing with the Stars*, advocated at the May 7 Senate panel for increased funding for cancer research. Harper detailed her own battle with cancer, reminiscing about her initial diagnosis with lung cancer in 2009, later finding out last year that her cancer had spread to the lining of her brain.

Through the eyes of an entertainer Harper explained her fight with cancer. "Cancer reminds me of a very bad but tenacious performer, who although no one wants to see, insists on doing an encore, having a return engagement, making a comeback and worst of all, going on tour," she said.

According to Harper, more than two-thirds of all lung cancers occur among former smokers, or those who never smoked, the majority being former smokers. Second hand smoke, air pollution and randon, a colorless, tasteless and odorless gas, can cause lung cancer. But one's genes can play a role in developing lung cancer, too, she says.

Seventy-four-year old Harper, a cancer survivor of four years, said she never smoked, but was exposed to secondhand smoke for decades. As to family, her mother developed lung cancer and later died from it. The actress believes that her lung cancer might be traced to two risk factors, secondhand smoke and genetics.

In her opening testimony, Harper claimed that 75 percent of all lung cancers are often discovered too late, in the later stages when the disease has already spread. The vocal cancer advocate called for Congress to put more funding into finding better ways for early detection of the disease.

Harper notes that research can also identify new treatment options for lung cancer when it is detected in Stages III and IV and find promising ways to personalize chemotherapy by testing genetic markers, making the treatment less toxic and more effective against specific tumors.

Others on the Witness List

In 2012, Chip Kennett, 32, a former Senate staffer, remembers passing his annual physical "with flying colors." Weeks later, a nagging, blurry spot in his right eye would lead to a PET scan that showed he had cancer "everywhere."

Looking back, he expressed to the Senate panel the shock of being diagnosed with having cancer. "There are really no words to describe what it feels like to be told you have an incurable disease that will kill you," he said.

Now 18 months post-diagnosis, Kennett, who is living with an as-yet incurable form of Stage IV lung cancer, is now in his fourth targeted treatment and the clinical trials have allowed the young man to lead a relatively normal and productive life. "Research saves lives, and I am a living example of that. The drugs that have kept me alive for the past 18 months were not available just seven years ago," he says.

Other witnesses at the hearing included Mary Dempsey, assistant director and co-founder of the Patrick Dempsey Center for Cancer Hope and Healing in Lewiston, Maine, who shared her experience of taking care of her mother, Amanda, with her brother, nationally renowned actor Patrick Dempsey seen on *Grey's Anatomy*. Over 17 years since the mother's initial diagnoses in 1997, she had a total of 12 recurrences and just recently died in March.

"My mom lived this experience, and I shared it with her as her primary caregiver," notes Dempsey. "In this role, I experienced firsthand the impact cancer had on every part of my life. For me, it really became a full-time job, navigating resources, understanding the medical world and coping with the profound changes in our lives."

A Call for Increased Cancer Funding

Hopefully the Senate Aging Panel's efforts to put medical research on the short list of the nation's policy agenda will get the attention of GOP lawmakers who, over the years, have attempted to balance the nation's budget by slashing NIH funding.

Cancer touches every family. Everyone knows a family member, colleague, or friend who has died from cancer or is a cancer survivor. Americans must send a strongmessage to their Congressional lawmakers, no more cuts to medical research. If the nation is truly at war with cancer, it is shameful not to give the nation's medical researchers the adequate funding necessary to defeat it once and for all.

AARP RESEARCH STUDY EXPLORES WHY PEOPLE ARE HAPPY

Published September 14, 2012, in the Pawtucket Times

"**G**ood conversation, meeting new people while traveling, and being in good health" brings much happiness to longtime Pawtucket resident Jean Babiec. The former Providence schoolteacher, in her eighth decade, added she would be "extremely happy" if the Rhode Island General Assembly passed legislation, signed by Governor Lincoln Chafee, to create a Pawtucket Red Sox vanity license plate.

At-Large Pawtucket City Councilor Lorenzo C. Tetreault, 65, is "happiest when he can help others." The retired Pawtucket teacher is also happy when he holds his one-year-old twin grandsons from Narragansett, Samuel and Benjamin, in his arms.

Former Pawtucket Tax Assessor, Dave Quinn, 64, who now oversees the Tax Office in the City of Providence, finds h appiness " knowing t hat h is f amily i s h ealthy a nd h is children are doing well." The Seekonk resident also feels happy by being intellectually challenged by his job.

Babiec, Tetreault, and Quinn's statements on what makes them happy are reflected by others documented in a recently released AARP study on what happiness means to aging baby boomers. The findings of this report indicate that relationships and being in control of your health and life are key factors in bringing happiness.

Defining Happiness

The new AARP study, titled "Beyond Happiness: Thriving," found that most Americans age 35 and over are happy, but compared with historical General Social Survey (GSS) data, levels of happiness are on the decline and at their lowest levels (due in part to the nation's economic downturn). In an effort to explore what happiness means to aging baby boomers and what it takes to thrive as they age, more than 4,000 adults age 35 and over were surveyed to determine what makes them happy.

"We're always looking to get a more robust understanding of the contributors and barriers to happiness in people's lives," said Steve Cone, executive vice president of Integrated Value Strategy at AARP. "Building on previous AARP research, which shows the importance of happiness and peace of mind to aging baby boomers, these new results affirm that we are on the right track—advocating to ensure basic health and financial security and making available everyday discounts that let people enjoy time with family and friends."

According to researchers, the findings of this study reveal the existence of a U-shape curve of happiness by age. The early 50s is the lowest point from which happiness builds. Thus, if you missed happiness in your 30s, there is still another chance to achieve it in your 60s.

The researchers note that as people age and eventually retire, they can devote more time to build relationships and just enjoy simple everyday pleasures. Younger people are still working hard to solidify their accomplishments.

The AARP study's results also provide four key insights about the drivers of happiness.

The Happiness Spectrum

Overall the strong majority (68 percent) of respondents say they are happy, although intensity of happiness is somewhat tempered as the largest percent report being somewhat happy (49 percent) versus very happy (19 percent). Almost half of those surveyed believe they are just as happy as others (49 percent), and the rest tend to believe they are happier than others (31 percent) as opposed to less happy than others (13 percent). Part of this may be attributed to the perceptions of people being the masters of their own happiness destiny.

More interesting, the respondents were concerned for the happiness of the next generation. Less than half believe the next generation will be as happy or more (45 percent). Most are either not sure (19 percent) or believe they will be less happy (35 percent).

Relationships: Key to Happiness

The AARP survey findings also indicate that regardless of your age, good relationships with friends, family, and even pets were found to be universally important. Activities associated with those relationships contributed most to a person's happiness. The most significant activity was kissing or hugging someone you love. Other activities included: watching your children, grandchildren, or close relative succeed; being told you are a person who can be trusted or relied upon; spending time with your family or friends for a meal or social gathering; and finally, experiencing a special moment with a child.

Researchers say that relationships with pets were especially important to women, singles, and older individuals. However, relationships did have to be real: "connecting with friends or family on a social media site like Facebook" came in 37th out of 38 activities in contributing to happiness. More important, none of the top contributors require a lot of money to achieve; they are "simple pleasures" that can be had by all.

Good Health Linked to Happiness

Without good health, it is far more difficult to achieve happiness: people in "good or excellent" health are three times more likely to report being "very" happy, the researchers say. However, one's health may be more a state of mind than objective real-ity. The findings noted that the percentage of those reporting good health is relatively stable over the ages 35 to 80, varying only seven percentage points, even as reported chronic or serious medical conditions increase 400 percent in the same age range.

Calling the Shots Brings Happiness

The majority of those surveyed believe they have control over their personal level of happiness. Interestingly, this sense of control increases with age. Moreover, people who feel in control are clearly happier—reporting that they are two-and-a-half times happier than those who believe happiness is out of their control. The study's findings indicate that a sense of control is linked to higher income and education, good health and the lack of having experienced a major life event in the past year.

Money Does Not Always Guarantee Happiness

While many will say having money can bring happiness, this research study showed that it seems that how one spends it seems to matter more. Happiness increases with income and conversely, lack of financial resources was tied to unhappiness. While less than a third of participants said money contributed to happiness, when asked how they would spend $100 on something to increase happiness, most respondents said they would spend it on their family or going out to dinner. Money is only a resource that, when applied to meaningful areas of one's life, can provide experiences that can increase happiness.

INCREASING YOUR ODDS OF LIVING TO 100 AND BEYOND

Published January 18, 2013, in the Pawtucket Times

J ust barely holding onto the record for being the nation's oldest person for about two weeks, Mamie Rearden of Edgefield, a 114-year-old South Carolina woman, died on January 2nd, just three weeks after a fall broke her hip. The amazing thing, though, is how long she was so healthy and able to live independently. According to recently published research, most people who reach the age of 110 years and beyond, spend only, on average, the last five years of their incredibly long lives with age-related diseases.

According to the Associated Press (AP), the Gerontology Research Group, an organization verifying age information for the Guinness World Records, noted that Rearden's September 7, 1898, birth was recorded and therefore verified in the 1900 U.S. Census, making her the nation's oldest living person, after last month's passing of 115-year-old Dina Manfredini of Iowa. Before Rearden died, she was more than a year younger than the world's oldest person, 115-year-old Jiroemon Kimura of Japan.

Rearden, married to her husband for 59 years until his death in 1979, raised 11 children, 10 of whom are alive. The former teacher and housewife first learned to drive a car at age 65. At this time she worked for an Edgefield County program locating children whose parents were keeping them out of school, reported the AP.

Studying the Nation's Oldest Citizens

Dr. Thomas Perls, a geriatrician who heads the Boston University-based New England Centenarian Study (NECS), considered Rearden's longevity to be a very rare occurrence. She was one of about 70 supercentenarians (people who have reached age 110) living in this country, he said.

Almost 20 years ago, when Perls' longitudinal study began, about one per 10,000 people in the United States survived to age 100. However, he noted that they are now more common at a rate of one per 5,000.

"Now most people think that getting to your 80s is expected," said Dr. Perls. Simply put, more Americans are now living longer today than in previous generations because the high childhood-mortality rates in the early 1900s have been slashed due to hugely improved public-health measures like clean water, vaccinations, and a safe food supply, combined with a more educated population and improved socioeconomic conditions, he noted.

Meanwhile, vaccinations for older people, effective antibiotics, and medications for what have become chronic rather than acute lethal diseases, as well as curative surgeries are markedly improving middle-aged people's chances of living to even older ages, added Dr. Perls.

Finding the Secrets of Longevity

Dr. Perls said his passion for working with the nation's oldest began when, at 16 years old, he worked as an orderly in a nursing home. In 1986, he received his medical degree from the University of Rochester, and later a master's degree from the Harvard School of Public Health. His specialization in geriatrics ultimately would propel him into a lifelong interest in finding the secrets as to why people successfully age well and live for more than a century.

Born in Palo Alto, California, Dr. Perls later moved to Colorado and now resides in Boston. A professor at Boston University School of Medicine, Dr. Perls, board-certified in internal medicine and geriatric medicine, has co-authored a book for the public entitled, *Living to 100*, co-edited an academic book and penned 106 juried articles. He is the author of the online "Living to 100 Life Expectancy Calculator." It uses the most current and carefully researched medical and scientific data to estimate how old you will live to be (**www.livingto100.com**) and provides some general advice according to your answers to about 40 questions that take about seven minutes to complete.

Initially at Harvard University, the NECS later relocated to Boston University School of Medicine, giving his longevity initiative "room to grow," said Perls, who is NECS' founding director. Today this demographic initiative, considered to be the world's largest study of centenarians and supercentenarians, is funded by the National Institutes of Health (NIH), private foundations, and "cherished" individual donors, he said. Study participants and their families fill out health and family-history questionnaires and provide a blood sample for studying their genes.

Along with the NECS, Dr. Perls also directs the Boston-based study center of the multicenter and international "Long Life Family Study" (LLFS), which is a study of families that have multiple members living to extreme old age. Both initiatives are enabling researchers to discover how and why centenarians and their children, who are in their 70s and 80s, live the vast majority of their lives disability-free.

As to those who participate in his NECS and LLFS initiatives, the youngest is about 45 years old (a very young child of a centenarian) and the oldest ever enrolled was 119 years old, the second-oldest person in the world ever, stated Perls. Since he began the NECS, out of 2,200 participants, 1,200 were age 100 and over. The remaining participants were children of centenarians or in the study's control group. "Because of their ages, most of these folks have now passed away," he said, adding that at any one time about 10 percent of the total centenarians in the study are alive.

Unraveling the Data

During his long career studying centenarians, the research findings indicate that it is common for centenarians to have brothers and sisters who also live to be very old. "Exceptional longevity runs strong in families," he noted.

Dr. Perls' research also debunked long-held beliefs that the longer you live, the sicker you get. But even if centenarians were afflicted by multiple age-related diseases in their 90s, on average 90 percent functioned independently at the average age of 93 years, he said. Centenarians living to age 100 were found to have avoided age-related disabilities as well as diseases until, on average, their last five years.

While a healthy lifestyle is definitely important to living into one's 80s with much of that time spent in good health, Dr. Perls stated that having the right genes becomes more crucial for living to a much older age.

Research indicates that living to your mid-80s is 70 percent to 80 percent environmental and habits, and 20 percent to 30 percent genes. Seventh-day Adventists were found to have the longest average-life expectancy in the United States, which is 88 years. Most of that longevity is likely due to their healthy habits, which include being vegetarian, regularly exercising, not smoking or drinking alcohol and also doing things that decrease the effect of stress.

However, many Americans do just the opposite, with unhealthy diets, not exercising, and many people still smoke, noted Dr. Perls. So it is not surprising that on average, Americans die eight to 10 years earlier than Seventh-day Adventists, at the average age of about 80. (According to the United Nations Department of Economic and Social Affairs, in 2010, the U.S. life expectancy was 75 years for males and 80 years for females.)

"We should take advantage of our genes and not fight them," Perls said, by adopting healthier lifestyles.

Dr. Perls said that DNA research on very old people should for now not focus on identifying genes that predict diseases. Rather the findings in the near future might just offer clues to how some genes slow the aging process and protect people from age-related diseases like Alzheimer's and heart attacks. Such discoveries could lead to the development of drugs that protect against multiple chronic diseases.

A Final Note

Make working to create a healthier lifestyle a top priority on your New Year's resolution list. This effort might just ratchet up your life expectancy into the mid-80s, and if you have longevity in your family, even longer. Why not stop smoking? Watch your drinking, too. Make exercise, weight-training, and keeping your mind active part of your daily routine. Combine these lifestyle changes with better eating habits, meditating or yoga, or even doing low-impact exercises like tai chi, and you're on your way to increased longevity.

Ultimately a healthier lifestyle along with good genes may well help you increase the odds of living to 100 and beyond.

POLL SHOWS AMERICANS UNENTHUSIASTIC ABOUT LIVING TO AGE 120

Published August 16, 2013, in the Pawtucket Times

I f new biomedical advances could slow the aging process and allow people to live into their 12th decade (to age 120), would you want to have these medical treatments? Although you might take this opportunity to keep death at bay for decades, a new research survey by the Pew Research Center's Religion and Public Life Project has found that most Americans (56 percent) say "No." They, personally, would not want treatments to enable dramatically longer life spans. Yet roughly two-thirds (68 percent) think that most other people would choose to live to 120 and beyond.

Released last week, the 10-page report, "Living to 120 and Beyond: Americans' Views on Aging, Medical Advances and Radical Life Extension," notes that "some futurists think that even more radical changes are coming, including medical treatments that could slow, stop, or reverse the aging process and allow humans to remain healthy and productive to the age of 120 or more. The possibility that extraordinary life spans could become ordinary life spans no longer seems far-fetched."

The Pew Research Center report's findings are tabulated from data compiled from a nationwide telephone survey, conducted March 21 to April 8, 2013, on cell phones and landline telephones, among a nationally representative sample of 2,012 adults. The overall margin of error for the full sample is plus or minus 2.9 percentage points.

Is Living Longer Better?

The Pew Research Center's survey explored the public's attitudes toward aging, medical advances, and what some biomedical researchers call "radical life extension" – the possibility that scientific breakthroughs someday could allow people to live much longer than is possible today. The findings indicated that overall more Americans think dramatically longer life spans would be bad (51 percent) than good (41 percent) for society.

When the researchers asked adult respondents how long they ideally would like to live, more than two-thirds (69 percent) cite an age between 79 and 100 years old. (For this writer, 89 years old is the ripe old age to shed my mortal coil in this world.) The median desired life span of the survey respondents is 90 years: about 11 years longer than the current average U.S. life expectancy, which is 78.7 years. Only nine percent of Americans say they want to live longer than 100 years.

According to the researchers, because most people say they have heard little or nothing about the possibility of radically extended lifetimes and because the scientific break-throughs are far from certain, the wording of the survey questions focused on the result—longer life spans—and are deliberately vague about how this would be achieved or how healthy an average person would be at age 120.

The survey also sought to put the forward-looking questions about radical life extension into perspective by asking the respondents about their views on aging, health care, medical advances in general, personal life satisfaction, and bioethical issues.

The study's findings indicated that the U.S. public is not particularly concerned about the gradual rise in the percentage of Americans who are 65 and older. Nearly nine-in-ten adults surveyed stated that "having more elderly people in the population" either is a good thing for society (41 percent) or doesn't make much difference (47 percent). Just 10 percent see the graying of America as a bad thing.

A Cure for Most Cancers Could Be a Possibility

The findings indicated that the public also tends to view medical advances in general as a good thing (63 percent) rather than as interfering with the natural cycle of life (32 percent). Moreover, the public is optimistic that some extraordinary breakthroughs will occur in the next few decades. For instance, about seven in ten adult Americans think that by 2050 there will be a cure for most forms of cancer (69 percent) and that artificial arms and legs will perform better than natural ones (71 percent).

Survey respondents expressed skepticism that radical life extension will be soon pos-sible. Only one-quarter think that by 2050 the average American will live to be 120 years old; nearly three-quarters (73 percent) say this either "probably" or "definitely" will not happen. And if it does happen, many Americans foresee both positive and negative consequences for society.

While 44 percent of the respondents say that radical life extension would make the economy more productive because people could work longer, 53 percent disagree. Two-thirds say they think that dramatically longer life spans "would strain our natural resources" and that medical scientists would offer life-extending treat-ments before they fully understood the health effects. And although a solid majority of respondents (79 percent) think that life-extending treatments should be available to everyone who wants them, most (66 percent) also think that, in practice, only the wealthy would have access to the new medical technology.

The researchers found that there are some differences among religious groups when it comes to their attitudes about medical treatments that would slow the aging process and extend life by decades. Black Protestants are among the most likely to say radical life extension would be a good thing for society (54 percent). In contrast, fewer white evangelical Protestants (34 percent) and white Catholics (31 percent) say the same. Hispanic Catholics (44 percent) are more likely than white Catholics (31 percent) to think these treatments would be a good thing for society.

Ideal Life Span for Some Rhode Islanders

What do Rhode Islanders think about living longer, say, into their 12th decade?

Kasey Johnson, development associate at Slater Mill Museum, will not seek advanced medical technologies to extend her life. "Aging is viewed negatively in our culture," the East Greenwich resident said, noting that those reaching very old age are often seen by many as a drain on the nation's economy and resources.

Johnson noted that Americans are not raised to honor or revere their elders as they do in other cultures. "We end up resenting them for the time and energy it takes us to care for them. I wouldn't want to live longer only to be seen as a burden by everyone else," said the 26-year-old Johnson.

Graphic designer Neville Lassotovitch, 69, who lives with her retired husband, Peter, 70, and Daisy, their 17-year-old beagle, in Barrington, would not mind extending the years of her life by decades, but only if she was surrounded by her husband, good friends, and children. "I would not want to be alone without them," she said.

Fifty-one-year-old Ken McGill, heading Pawtucket's Board of Canvassers, sees a bright prospect of living a longer life. He has much to check off his bucket list. "Nobody likes to pass on," quipped McGill, who noted that he plans to retire at age 70. "This would give me a good 40 years to do all the things I have wanted to do, like traveling to see the world, even moving to Florida," says the long time Pawtucket resident.

Finally, like McGill, Keri Ambrosino, of Design By Keri, would "love" to live to the ripe old age of 120 years, so long as her quality of life stayed "youthful" and her thinking remained sharp. "Quality of life overbears on quantity in my book," said the 33-year-old West Warwick resident.

Other Reports Released on Radical Life Extension

There is, at present, no method of slowing the aging process and extending the average life expectancy to 120 years or more. But research aimed at unlocking the secrets of aging is underway at universities and corporate labs. Religious leaders, bioethicists, and philosophers have begun to think about the morality of radical life extension. Together with the survey results, Pew Research Center is releasing two accompanying reports.

"To Count Our Days: The Scientific and Ethical Dimensions of Radical Life Extension" presents an overview of the scientific research and the emerging ethical debate.

"Religious Leaders' Views on Radical Life Extension" describes how some clergy, bioethicists, theologians, and other scholars think their religious traditions might approach the issue.

PROMINENT ONCOLOGIST'S DEATH WISH AT AGE 75

Published December 12, 2014, in the Pawtucket Timex

D r. Ezekiel Emanuel, M.D., Ph.D., a nationally-recognized oncologist and bioethicist, definitely marches to a different drummer. While millions of older Americans pop vitamins and supplements like M&M candy, regularly exercise at their local gym, religiously jog, and carefully watch what they eat to increase their life span, the chair of medical bioethics and health policy at the University of Pennsylvania says living past the ripe old age of 75 is not on his bucket list. We would be doing both society and our loved ones a favor by agreeing with this belief, he says.

When I'm 75...

Why not age 80 or even 85? Emanuel admits that his 75th birthday was just a randomly chosen number, but the year was selected because scientific studies indicate that increases in physical and mental disability occur around this age, as well as a decline in both creativity and productivity.

The renowned 57-year-old breast oncologist is at the top of his professional game. Emanuel has received dozens of awards from organizations such as the National Institutes of Health and the American Cancer Society, including being elected to the Institute of Medicine (IOM) of the National Academy of Science, the Association of American Physicians, and the Royal College of Medicine (UK). *Hippocrates Magazine* even selected him as Doctor of the Year in Ethics.

Emanuel is a prolific writer, editing nine books and penning over 200 scientific articles. He is currently a columnist for the *New York Times* and appears regularly on television shows including *Morning Joe* and *Hardball with Chris Matthews*.

The prominent physician is also considered a key designer of the Affordable Care Act (commonly called Obamacare). At a personal level, he has two well-known brothers, Chicago Mayor Rahm Emanuel, former White House chief of staff, and Hollywood agent Ari Emanuel.

With this prominence, Emanuel's death wish to die at 75 (the year 2032) before the onset of Alzheimer's disease and other dementias and decreased physical stamina (it's harder to walk a quarter of a mile, even to climb 10 stairs) is drawing the ire of critics who charge that he advocates for health care rationing and legalized euthanasia.

But Emanuel claims that these charges are not true. Setting his death at 75 is just his personal preference, for leaving his mortal coil. In his writings and media interviews he notes that setting the age when he hopes to die just drives his daughters and brothers crazy.

Last October, at the BBC Future's World-Changing Ideas Summit in Manhattan, Emanuel's prop, a full-page AARP ad from a newspaper, featured an older couple hiking above a line of text that read, "When the view goes on forever, I feel like I can, too. Go long." Reinforcing his point, Emanuel is not buying AARP's message pushing the positives of living an extended life. For him, he doesn't buy it and most definitely, 70 is not the new 50.

Sharing a Death Wish on the Airways

On December 7, on "CBC Radio Canada's Sunday Edition," Emanuel discussed his controversial October 21, 2014, article published in *The Atlantic*, "Why I Hope to Die at 75." His Sunday interview detailed his unconventional and controversial stance, especially to AARP, the nation's largest aging-advocacy group, and aging organizations who strongly oppose this type of thinking.

Throughout the 28-minute interview with Michael Enright, Emanuel warns listeners, "Don't focus on years, and focus on quality."

"A good life is not just about stacking up the years and living as long as possible. People need to focus on quality of life," says Emanuel, noting that "setting an actual date for a good time to die helps you focus on what is important in your life."

"It is really about what you are doing to contributing and enriching the world. I want people to stop focusing on just more years, focusing on quality," he says.

Emanuel says that you need to be realistic on living forever, your body and mind don't go on forever. You should just be satisfied with living a complete life, he says.

By age 75, people will have gone through all stages of life, says Emanuel. As a child you begin to develop skills and figure out your place in the world. You go to college, raise a family, work to hone your skills and talents. At the later stages of your life you give advice and mentor people, he says, noting that in your mid-seventies, physical deterioration and mental slowing along with loss of creativity begin to be felt.

During his radio interview, Emanuel claimed he is very active, recently climbing Mount Kilimanjaro with his two nephews, stressing that he is in relatively good health and doesn't have a terminal illness and has no plans to commit suicide. As a matter of fact, the physi-cian even condemned physician-assisted suicide and euthanasia in a 1997 article published in The Atlantic, a policy allowed in the states of Oregon, Vermont, and Washington. His philosophical view of ending one's life is to allow the body to age naturally, he stresses.

In 18 years, Emanuel pledges to refuse all medical procedures and treatments, including taking medications such as statins, cholesterol-lowering drugs, and antibiotics that could prevent life-threatening illnesses or extend his life. He notes that his last colonoscopy will be at 65, to screen for cancer. No more colonoscopies after 75. And he'll accept only palliative care after that milestone age, too.

"I'm not suggesting people kill themselves at 75 but, rather, let nature take its course," Emanuel says.

How Others See it

Emanuel's personal preference not to seek medical procedures or to use medications at age 75 that might lead to his death is not the same as physician-assisted suicide, says the Rev. Christopher M. Mahar, S.T.L., of the Providence Catholic Diocese, noting that this choice has always been respected by the Roman Catholic Church.

"He is not actively choosing to take his life, and as long as he is not rejecting any of the ordinary means necessary for the preservation of life, such as nutrition and hydration, and is not intentionally destroying his body, he is free to decide for himself," said Mahar.

As Emanuel says, there is a downside to aging. My 88-year-old mother died after a 14-year-battle with Alzheimer's disease. At age 89, my father, whose quality of life declined over his later years, died suddenly, by having a pulmonary embolism.

For me, 89 is the year I choose to meet my Maker, hanging up my spurs. Yes, I will let nature take its course, but I will continue to take vitamins and antibiotics, even my Lisinopril for high blood pressure. I will not turn my back on medical procedures or technology that might enhance the quality of my life, even lengthen it.

I agree with the statement of the late actress Bette Davis, "Old age ain't no place for sissies." There is no alternative, you can only hope for nature to ultimately take its course, and it will. And so, we all are inclined to pick our own magic number.

SLEEP APNEA IS HAZARDOUS TO YOUR HEALTH AND WELL BEING

Published May 25, 2012, the Pawtucket Times

In 2003, Rehoboth resident Art Warner got strong messages from his surrounding environment about his health, both during the day and at night.

At that time Warner discovered he had great difficulty staying awake at his job, often falling asleep right at his desk. Coupled with his sleepiness during work hours and his wife's constant elbowing in the middle of the night to wake him up because of his loud snoring, a very tired Warner became extremely frustrated. His worried wife would regularly watch as he stopped breathing during his sleep as he snored. The overweight, middle-aged man was finally forced to recognize he had a health condition that could not be ignored.

After an examination from Warner's primary care physician, he signed him up for a sleep lab study, which surprisingly revealed to the patient "sleep apnea." This serious sleep disorder caused hundreds of short stops of breathing each night, which kept Warner, a public relations executive, from getting a good night's sleep.

Ultimately, it was a medical treatment prescribed after the sleep lab study that would finally allow Warner to get the sleep he needed and stop his snoring. No longer falling asleep at his desk or getting sleepy behind the wheel while driving his car, instead a good night's quality sleep has resulted in Warner living "a totally different life," because he feels rested. With this newly-found lifestyle, he has more energy to work out at the gym and even stay up past midnight.

Very Observable Symptoms

According to the Sleep Apnea Association, 12 million Americans (including Warner) have sleep apnea, a common medical chronic condition in which the person has one or more pauses in breathing, or shallow breathing when asleep. The Washington, D.C.-based group estimates that another 10 million people may remain undiagnosed.

Dr. Michael A. Pomerantz, a pulmonary specialist who reads sleep lab studies for Rhode Island-based Coastal Medical, reports that untreated sleep apnea is associated with an increased risk of high blood pressure, heart disease, stroke, obesity, diabetes, in addition to traffic accidents caused by falling asleep at the wheel. "Those are all pretty good reasons to be evaluated," he says.

Snoring, night-time awakening, and day-time sleepiness are three prominent symptoms of having sleep apnea, adds Pomerantz. Frequently, a bed partner may observe heavy snoring or long pauses (lasting at least 10 seconds) in breathing during their companion's sleep, causing the sleeper to wake up periodically throughout the night, states Pomerantz.

According to the medical literature, the typical sleep apnea male patient is over age 40, and obese. Smoking and alcohol also increase the risk of this medical condition. Dr. Pomerantz, who has practiced his medical specialty for over two decades, adds that 50 percent of sleep apnea patients also complain of early-morning headaches.

Diagnosing and Effectively Treating Sleep Apnea

If sleep apnea is suspected, an overnight visit at a sleep lab is considered to be the best diagnostic test to this serious medical condition. The patient is hooked up to equipment by wires which monitor the level of sleep, in addition to the airflow to determine if the sleeper is breathing or not, the deepness of sleep, oxygen levels, chest wall movement, and pulse rate, he says.

For treating milder cases of sleep apnea, Dr. Pomerantz recommends simple 'lifestyle' changes and treatments such as shedding weight, avoiding alcohol, sleeping on your side or abdomen, or keeping nasal passages open at night by using prescribed medications. A dental device can also move a jaw forward to make breathing easier.

In moderate to severe cases, a C-PAP, or "continuous positive airway pressure" machine can deliver an increased air pressure through a mask covering the nose and mouth. The air pressure generated by this machine is somewhat greater than that of the surrounding air, just enough to keep the person's upper airway passages open, preventing the apnea and snoring.

"Compliance with sleep apnea is not always great," Pomerantz says, because patients may feel discomfort with the C-PAP machines. "For some patients it's only a matter of getting used to it and finding a more comfortable mask," he says, because their masks may feel overly confining or obstructive.

New Studies Link Sleep Apnea to Cancer

In addition to those research studies associating sleep apnea with increased risks of hypertension, cardiovascular disease, depression, and early death, the *New York Times* recently reported that two new research studies presented at the American Thoracic Society conference this week have discovered that this chronic condition has been linked to an increased risk of cancer in humans.

According to the paper, in one study Spanish researchers followed thousands of patients at sleep clinics, finding that those patients with the most severe forms of sleep apnea had a 65 percent greater risk of developing cancer of any kind. Meanwhile, lead researcher Dr. Javier Nieto, chair of the Department of Population Health Sciences at the University of Wisconsin School of Medicine and Public Health, says that his study of 1,500 government workers studied over 22 years showed nearly five times higher incidence of cancer deaths in patients with severe sleep apnea to those without the disorder, a result that echoes previous findings in animal studies.

A Personal Note...

Clearly research studies show that not being treated for sleep apnea or using your C-PAP machine, if diagnosed with this chronic disorder, is hazardous to your health and well-being.

As one afflicted with sleep apnea, this writer has experienced it all—from "denial" about the severity of my snoring to finally being sent by my partner to the couch for my very loud snoring that shook the walls of our house. Co-workers teased me about falling asleep at noon-time meetings or towards the end of my workday. Even with these severe symptoms, I denied having this medical problem for years until the urging of a friend who had a severe case of sleep apnea nudged me to "get it checked out." With my ultimate diagnosis and finally the treatment with a C-PAP machine, my snoring has virtually ceased, and I now wake up refreshed and well rested. One of my few regrets in life was losing years of "deep" sleep because I chose not to see my physician to address my sleep apnea.

For more information about sleep apnea, visit the American Sleep Apnea Association's website, **www.sleepapnea.org.** If you have sleep apnea symptoms, visit your physician.

6. LONG-TERM-CARE CONTINUUM

LITTLE THINGS COUNT WHEN DECIDING ON A NURSING HOME

Published April 23, 2001, in the Pawtucket Times

You must become a better shopper when seeking the most appropriate nursing facility in which to place your loved one.

"Until there is a health crisis, families don't often think about nursing-facility care until it's too late," stated Roberta Hawkins, executive director of the Alliance for Better Long Term Care, who serves as the state's ombudsman on the behalf of 10,000 Rhode Island nursing-home residents. "If it's possible, just plan ahead," Hawkins recommended.

"Your state health department provides a comprehensive list of nursing homes and their survey results to help you determine if the facility is reputable," stated Hawkins.

According to Hawkins, word-of-mouth or personal recommendations from family, friends, neighbors, hospital-discharge planners, and Hawkins' nonprofit advocacy group about a nursing home's care are key bits of information to determine whether the facility is well managed.

"The Alliance also offers a free phone help-line to assist matching the particular needs of a person with a specific facility," Hawkins added.

With more than 20 years of experience under her belt in assisting families in finding the right nursing facility for loved ones, Hawkins gave simple tips on selecting a facility.

Hawkins suggested that a need for upgraded services for residents requiring intensive medical care, special rehabilitation therapies and dietary requirements, along with religious and cultural needs, should also be taken into account before selecting a facility.

Location should not always be a deciding factor in selecting a nursing facility. Carefully choose a facility that meets your loved ones' personality, and medical and social needs.

In many cases, this critical decision is made only for the convenience of family members or visitors. If an elderly spouse cannot drive, make sure that the selected facility is on a bus line. Keeping a married couple close together is very important for their psychological well-being.

Always have the older person in need of skilled nursing care actively participate in choosing a facility even if they can't physically visit the site. Family members can also provide this person with brochures and admission materials.

Don't choose a facility based on a beautiful physical exterior, fancy rugs, or glittering chandeliers, Hawkins said. When visiting a nursing facility, always observe how staff members interact with residents and each other. Look for laughter, a pleasant environment, and a strong activities program.

For frail residents who are bed bound, look for a stable nursing staff.

Ask yourself if the facility's environment is cheerful and clean?

Are the bedrooms warm looking, and do they reflect the residents' individuality? Or do they all look the same, like hotel rooms?

Find out whether the residents are allowed to bring in personal belongings such as chairs, tables, lamps, or even a television into their rooms.

For those persons who have always loved nature and being outdoors, ask whether the nursing facility has an outside area for sitting or walking. Determine if this area is accessible to a wheelchair-bound person who might want to roll outside to listen to the birds. This simple amenity is very important.

When touring a facility, determine if a dining room is available for eating meals and space to allow residents to socialize with each other and participate in activities.

Is there a real working-activities room? A resident who has always been involved in crafts and enjoys participating in group activities will want to select a facility with a well-run activities program.

Also be aware of how the nursing facility smells. Sometimes you may smell strong odors of deodorants, which might be covering up unpleasant odors.

Listen for the sound of buzzers rung by residents in need of help, and observe how quickly staffers respond.

When walking the halls, say "hello" to staffers you meet. Do the staffers pleasantly respond to you? If not, consider that they may not respond well to your loved one.

Walk in and talk with residents gathered in a community room. In conversation, find out how long they have lived at the facility. Ask whether they like the facility and are respected as individuals by the staff.

If you see residents in restraints lying or sleeping in a chair or wheelchair, this may be a red flag for poor care. The facility may not have enough staff to allow the residents to lie down in bed for a nap in the afternoon.

After you locate your facility, "put your name on the waiting list," Hawkins recommended, even if the nursing-facility admission will occur months later.

For those afflicted with Alzheimer's and related dementia, it is wise for these individuals to be admitted earlier in the disease process to acclimate them to the facility and for the staff to learn more about the resident's habits, likes, and dislikes.

NEW REPORT WARNS OF NATION'S HOUSING NOT MEETING NEEDS OF OLDER ADULTS

Published on September 12, 2014, in the Pawtucket Times

I n the coming decades, America's aging population is expected to skyrocket, but the nation is not ready to confront the housing needs of those age 50 and over, warns a new report released last week by the Harvard Joint Center for Housing Studies and AARP Foundation. While it is expected that the number of adults in the U.S. aged 50 and over will to grow to 133 million by 2030, an increase of more than 70 percent since 2000, housing that is affordable, physically accessible, well-located, and coordinated with supports and services is in too short supply, says the Harvard report released on September 2nd.

According to the Harvard Report, "Housing America's Older Adults—Meeting the Needs of An Aging Population," housing stock is critical to quality of life for people of all ages, but especially for aging baby boomers and seniors. High housing costs currently force a third of adults 50 and over—including 37 percent of those 80 and over—to pay more than 30 percent of their income for homes that may or may not fit their needs, forcing them to cut back on food, health care, and, for those 50 to 64, retirement savings.

Challenges and Issues

The Harvard report also noted that much of the nation's housing stock lacks basic accessibility features (such as no-step entries, extra-wide doorways, lever-style door and faucet handles, and sufficient lighting, preventing older persons with disabilities from living safely and comfortably at home. Moreover, walkways, bike lanes, buses, subways, and other public transportation are not available to a majority of older adults who live in suburban and rural locations. They become isolated from family and friends without the ability to drive. Finally, disconnects between housing programs and the health care system put many older adults with disabilities or long-term care needs at risk of premature, costly institutionalization and readmission to hospitals.

"Recognizing the implications of this profound demographic shift and taking immediate steps to address these issues is vital to our national standard of living," says Chris Herbert, acting managing director of the Harvard Joint Center for Housing Studies. "While it is ultimately up to individuals and their families to plan for future housing needs, it is also incumbent upon policy makers at all levels of government to see that affordable, appropriate housing, as well as supports for long-term aging in the community, are available for older adults across the income spectrum."

Tackling the Challenges

"What jumped out at us from this study is that when it comes to where people want to live as they age, the 'field of view,' if you will, has very quickly widened. People today are thinking about this at a younger age with expectations that are vastly different from their parents' assumptions," observes AARP State Director Kathleen Connell.

"Most people are worried that retirement savings will not cover their long-term needs. They want housing that is affordable, physically accessible, and well-located. But they also realize that, eventually, they'll need coordination with supports and services. The challenges have never been more evident," she says.

"There are many ways to approach this, with choosing healthier lifestyles very high on the list. But the report makes it clear that where we live matters." Connell continued, "Growing older in car-dependent suburban and rural locations is a real problem because pedestrian infrastructure is generally unfriendly if you have stopped driving. That leads to isolation, which can severely compound just about any negative that comes with aging. And if access to the health care system is restricted, many older adults—especially those with disabilities—are candidates for more costly premature institutionalization. We need to preempt that cycle by building communities where people can better age in place."

The Harvard report notes that the older population in the U.S. will continue to exponentially grow with the large number of younger baby boomers who are now in their 50s. With lower incomes, wealth, home-ownership rates, and more debt than generations before them, members of this large age group may be unable to cover the costs of appropriate housing or long-term care in their retirement years.

Indeed, while a majority of people over 45 would like to stay in their current residences as long as possible, estimates indicate that 70 percent of those who reach the age of

65 will eventually need some form of long-term care. In this regard, older home-owners are in a better position than older renters when they retire. The typical home-owner age 65 and over has enough wealth to cover the costs of in-home assistance for nearly nine years or assisted living for six and a half years. The typical renter, however, can only afford two months of these supports.

"As Americans age, the need for safe and affordable housing options becomes even more critical," says Lisa Marsh Ryerson, president of the AARP Foundation. "High housing costs, aging homes, and costly repairs can greatly impact those with limited incomes. The goal in our support of this report is to address the most critical needs of these households, and it is AARP Foundation's aim to provide the tools and resources to help them meet these needs now and in the future."

To access "Housing America's Older Adults – Meeting the Needs of An Aging population," go to **http://goo.gl/Dk3fji**.

SENIOR CENTERS, NOT JUST A PLACE TO PLAY BINGO

Published February 1, 2013, in the Pawtucket Times

T oday's senior centers are not the places our parents visited to knit or play bingo. Established in the 1980s by the U.S. Administration on Aging, the centers' programming has evolved to encompass activities that encourage healthy aging and wellness, said Mary Lou Moran, who oversees Pawtucket's Leon A. Mathieu Senior Center. Established in 1980, last year more than 15,000 clients took advantage of programs and the social services offered or to eat a nutritious meal, she noted.

At Rhode Island's 47 senior centers, "we are now looking at the whole person, the body, mind, and spirit," noted Moran, a former program coordinator who serves as director of senior services. "It is very important that we encourage individuals to live independently and safely in their communities."

"At the Leon A. Mathieu Senior Center, health screenings, specifically blood-pressure readings, are performed by Rhode Island College nursing students and URI pharmacy students," noted Moran. "Proper nutritional counseling is a very big deal, too," she added, noting that a nutritionist is available to provide individual counseling.

Through the Eyes of Clients

Linda Slade discovered the Leon A. Mathieu Senior Center after retiring from work in retail for more than 38 years. Initially attending a few exercise activities in October 2010, she was forced to stop attending to take care of her terminally ill husband. After his passing, she came back four months later "to just be with people again."

Slade initially had misconceptions about Pawtucket's senior center. "I was a young 62 and not really sure what to expect," she said, expecting to be surrounded by very old people. That first visit totally changed her mind by seeing younger people. Besides knitting, playing cards or cribbage, the Pawtucket resident participates regularly in arthritis class, stretch exercises, and tai chi.

Before attending the senior center's exercise classes, Slade's son had given her a gym membership. "Basically I was intimated to go because of the younger people," she said. Now Slade is more comfortable working up a sweat with her senior-center exercise companions.

According to Slade, the city's senior center offers something (activities) for everyone. Her involvement even gave her an opportunity to develop new social bonds. "I had a work family that I truly adored, but now I adore my senior center family, too," she said. Just like at the fictional bar, *Cheers*, Slade knows everyone's name in all her activity groups.

"Going bonkers" and filling a need to get out of her home propelled Nancy Connor, 79, a former secretary to the CEO of Citizens Bank, to the doors of the Leon A. Mathieu Senior Center. Aortic-valve surgery forced the Pawtucket resident into retirement in her early 70s from a job she loved and found intellectually challenging.

Once the Pawtucket widow, who lives with her companion, Mave, a 60-pound royal standard poodle, found the Leon A. Mathieu Senior Center in the Yellow Pages directory, she went to see what it was all about. She's been going daily ever since.

The Grand Dame of the Literary Circle

Like Slade, before attending, Connor had a misconception about senior centers, thinking she would see "a bunch of old people doddering along." Now the enthusiastic participant has found out that this was not the case.

According to Connor, not as many men come to the center. "We really do outnumber them," she quipped, noting that they "usually appear out of thin air when there is a high-low-jack game."

Walking with a cane keeps Connor from exercising, yet she hopes to someday explore the Chinese practice of tai chi. However, she gets activity by being involved in other pursuits. Never published, she took up writing, participating in the book and drama clubs and considers herself the "Grandma Moses" of the senior center's literary circle.

Meanwhile Connor and a few other older participants meet monthly with third-year Brown University medical students to teach them the art of speaking to the "geriatric crowd," she said. At Friday coffee hours, invited guests come into the senior center's large activity room to entertain, teach, or educate, she said. If a cancellation happens, she's drafted to play piano for the crowd in the activity room.

As in senior centers across the Ocean State, Connor can eat lunch every day, paying only a minimal fee. "It is wonderful stuff, from soup to nuts," she remarked.

A Medical Model

Jill Anderson, executive director of Senior Services, Inc., a private nonprofit corporation established in 1975, manages the Woonsocket Senior Center. Each day, more than 100 clients (about 500 annually) participate in exercise activities and health and wellness programs at her site. A day-care program in her building handles 35 people who have limitations in their daily living.

Reflecting its medical-model philosophy, the Woonsocket Senior Center's registered nurse, who also serves as the wellness director, counsels people on how to change behaviors to maintain better health. Health screening, including blood-pressure checks, diabetic and bone-density testing are also part of a wellness program.

About 20 retired volunteers regularly help each day serving lunch and assisting staff, noted Anderson. "These individuals create a friendly atmosphere for the new clients, making sure they don't sit by themselves."

Although many of Rhode Island's senior centers have an annual membership fee or charge registration fees to participate in activities, Anderson's nonprofit does not. "We just ask people to make a voluntary weekly contribution of one dollar to fill the gap that fund-raising, grants, and memorials don't cover."

As in many other senior centers, computer courses in a computer lab are offered, said Anderson. "We would like to do more with computers. Maybe we can someday offer both intermediate and advanced computer classes, too," she added, because the older clients are interested in embracing new technology like iPads and smart phones.

"A benefits counselor also is on site to identify benefits and programs our clients are entitled to receive," stated Anderson. This ultimately helps to lower the cost of supplemental Medicare plans as well as make other economies.

Pumping Weights

Robert Rock, director of East Providence Senior Center on Waterman Avenue, provides all the typical exercise programs that senior centers offer. But through a $96,000 grant received from the U.S. Administration on Aging, his senior center houses the only fitness center in the Ocean State.

"The [fitness] program promotes attitude change and the development of appropriate exercise skills and reduces the risks of a sedentary lifestyle. It also improves the quality of life for our senior population," Rock said.

According to Rock, a client can gain privileges to use the fitness room for a minimal fee of $40 for single membership and $60 for couples. Equipment includes three treadmills, two recumbent bikes, an elliptical stepper, hand weights, and six dual-weight machines. Other features include a matted floor, mirrored walls, water, stereo, and cable television.

Rock noted that 90 percent of the 258 people, most in their 60s, are taking advantage of this fitness center room, an attachment to the senior center. "They come to work out and then leave," he said, noting that the oldest, a 91-year-old man, comes to work out three days a week. Rock said that once aging baby boomers come for the fitness room, they will choose to come back for other programs and services offered by his senior center.

Walking is also an important exercise, said Rock. Many clients take advantage of the senior center's half-mile walking track.

Finally Rock added that the East Providence Senior Center is also a Rhode Island state-certified site for diabetes education. Both classes and individual counseling are offered.

In Conclusion

Starting in church basements, many as small social clubs, senior centers were propelled into becoming key providers in the nation's long-term-care continuum by the passage of the Older Americans Act in 1965. Today, 11,000 senior centers serve one million older adults every day. In Rhode Island, 47 agencies, serving 208,000 persons, are geographically spread out from Westerly to Woonsocket and from Foster to Tiverton. Some are managed by municipalities, others by nonprofit groups. While catering to serving the state's burgeoning elderly population, some have expanded their mission to offer programs for young and middle-aged adults.

While the average age is 75, many of Rhode Island's senior centers are adjusting their programming and services to attract the state's aging baby boomers by focusing on health and wellness, recreation and lifelong learning.

According to Rhode Island's Division of Elderly Affairs (DEA), more than 14 percent of Rhode Island's population is age 65 and over. By 2030, it is projected to grow to more than 21 percent. Rhode Island's senior centers are key providers that will keep aging baby boomers healthy, independent, and at home.

Yes, today's senior centers are not your parents' bingo hall, as some mistakenly believe. Why not visit your local senior center? You may be surprised with what you find.

AARP REPORT SHEDS LIGHT ON THE NEEDS OF OLDER, DISABLED PERSONS

Published May 26, 2012, in the Pawtucket Times

AARP, a Washington, D.C.-based aging-advocacy group, has generated a new report to provide direction to the nation's policy makers on how to keep the country's age-50-and-over disabled population independent and in control of their daily lives.

According to the latest AARP study, lack of affordable services, a fragmented delivery system, and the caregiver's limited knowledge of the delivery system are barriers that keep age-50-and-over Americans with disabilities from living active and independent lives.

The AARP report, "Beyond 50.03: A Report to the Nation on Independent Living and Disability," incorporates data obtained from the first national survey of Americans age-50-plus with disabilities, documenting the gap between what they say, need, and what is available to them.

"Long-term independence for persons with disabilities is an increasingly achievable social goal," AARP Policy and Strategy Director John Rother wrote in a statement released with the report. "But it will require time and the collective creativity of the public and private sectors," he added.

"Meanwhile even minor changes can lead, at least in the short term, to important lifestyle improvements for those with disabilities today," Rother stated. On the other hand, long-term improvements will require fundamental policy changes.

"As the influx of boomers enters their 50s and 60s, they will bring their attitudes of competitive consumerism to health care delivery and will demand greater choice and control of available services," explained Rother. "The good news is that there is time to prepare for those demands," he said. "Along with improvements in medicine and health, we are seeing some declines in disability. New technologies are also extending Americans' years of independence."

According to the AARP report, 46 percent of the over-50 respondents with disabilities (including nearly 60 percent of those between the ages of 50 and 64) believe that having more control over decisions about services and the help they need would bring a major improvement in the quality of their lives. However, they report that their greatest fear is loss of independence and mobility.

The AARP report, the third in a series of comprehensive studies on the status of Americans over age 50, found that 51 percent of older persons with disabilities are managing independently, while 49 percent are not receiving any regular help with daily activities, such as cooking, bathing, and shopping. More than half of those with disabilities (53 percent) tell researchers that they were unable to do something they needed or wanted to do in the past month, quite often basic tasks such as household chores or exercise.

Most (88 percent) of the assistance the older, disabled persons reported receiving is volunteer assistance from family or other informal caregivers. Sixty-one percent strongly prefer this type of assistance with everyday tasks, while only one of three uses any community-based service.

The AARP report found that independence for older, disabled persons can be easily enhanced by using assistive equipment (such as walkers and wheelchairs) and new technologies that are more widely available. However, caregiver assistance with daily activities will take more time and resources. The researchers estimated that as many as three million persons over age 50 with disabilities (almost 25 percent) need more assistance than they receive now with daily activities.

Furthermore, the report said that persons 50 and older with disabilities place inadequate health insurance on the top of their list of issues that are not being adequately addressed. Basic Medicare coverage still does not pay for prescription drugs, and assistive equipment is not covered by some health insurance plans.

Rhode Island AARP Director Kathleen Connell added that many of the issues addressed in the AARP report are not just about today's persons with disabilities, but about all of us, who, if we live long lives (and longevity is increasing) are likely to face disability.

"This is about long-term independence and not long-term care, which refers not just to what we need during the most vulnerable and frailest stages of our disability, as 'long-term care' suggests, but to what we want during what, in most cases, is a longer, more functional stage of disability," stated Connell.

While minor fixes would make a difference, other improvements will require long-term fundamental changes and more public dollars. Based on the "Beyond 50" findings, AARP has outlined a number of policy changes for making critical long-term improvements:

Older persons with disabilities must be insured against the high costs of accessing long-term supportive services. Ways must be found to share the risk of these unpre-dictable costs more widely among public and private sources.

Public funding for long-term supportive services needs to be reoriented toward more options for home and community-based care. The nation also must provide more options for "consumer-direction" in publicly funded programs.

Communities need to be made more physically accessible for more people with disabilities.

Information and services need to be more navigable for those who are trying to learn about available long-term services and whether or not they are eligible.

The U.S. health care system must adjust its focus to enhance functioning and health-related quality of life, not just provide acute and curative care.

The "Beyond 50" report found that people 50 and older with disabilities gave their community poor grades (between C-plus and B-minus) in their efforts to make it possible for them to live independently. In many communities, the researchers said, public transportation is often poorly rated.

The researchers said that the troubling findings reveal the nation is ill-prepared to meet the needs of age-50-and-over persons with disabilities for more control and independence in their lives.

AARP's report is a wake-up call for state and national policy makers, who will be charged with making sound policy decisions for a graying nation with disabilities. If policy makers heed the recommendations of AARP's report, systemic changes may well give dignity to millions of older persons with disabilities who want only to remain independent and in control of their daily lives. Just like the rest of us.

7. MENTAL HEALTH

ALZHEIMER'S DISEASE ALSO TAKES A TOLL ON MIDDLE-AGED ADULTS

Published May 10, 2013, in the Pawtucket Times

While many view Alzheimer's disease as a devastating illness afflicting persons well into their late retirement years, Jacob ("Jake") Vinton knows better. The 57-year-old is one of an estimated 200,000 persons (out of five million Americans) who have been diagnosed with early-onset Alzheimer's.

Discovering the Truth

Jake's physical deterioration derailed any plans to re-enter the workforce, forcing him into early retirement. Because of his age, he will not be eligible for the full range of federal retirement and pension benefits that he could be eligible to receive if he had waited to retire at age 65.

The middle-aged man experienced early signs of cognitive impairment that included memory loss, specifically not remembering conversations, previous events, or the names of people and things. As the disease progressed, Jake gave up his car keys.

In 2006, Jake chose to become a stay-at-home father, taking care of his two teenage sons, while his wife, Karen, a clinical psychologist, became the family breadwinner, working as a public-health researcher for a national nonprofit consulting firm.

Before making this decision, Jake, an electrical engineer who graduated from Trinity College in Hartford, Connecticut, had decided not to re-enter the job market or even to apply for graduate school. Looking back, his wife believes that his declining "planning and organizational" skills played a key role in his decision.

Karen, 54, never attributed her husband's occasional loss of words to be due to a serious, devastating cognitive condition. Warning signs became obvious to her when Jake could not remember a conversation that had taken place 15 minutes earlier.

For Jake, a daily walk with the family's rescue golden doodle down a very familiar walking path, gave him a startling "wake-up call," that something was definitely wrong. He broke down crying when he realized he was lost and did not recognize his surrounding neighborhood. The emotionally distraught man would ultimately get home through the assistance of others in the neighborhood.

Being a professional researcher, Karen tirelessly sought answers to explain her husband's cognitive decline through professional contacts in the medical field. After a year of medical appointments that included multiple diagnostic tests (there is no one definitive test) by a neuropsychologist and a neurologist who specializes in Alzheimer's disease, his wife's worst fears were confirmed: Jake had early-onset Alzheimer's disease.

Karen was not shocked by the medical findings. Alzheimer's disease has limited pharmacological treatments that slow but do not stop the disease's progression. Although Jake was not happy with his medical diagnosis, he felt relieved knowing the cause of his memory slips and why he was so "loopy," as he put it.

Following the 2011 medical diagnosis, the Foxboro, Massachusetts, couple made a joint decision to relocate to the City of Providence. "Providence offered more medical and support services and also allowed him to walk to his volunteer activities and classes," Karen said.

Loving Friends at Hamilton House

Jake also began taking Aricept and Namenda, prescription medications used to treat mild, moderate, and even severe Alzheimer's disease. Over time, with adjustments to the dose, "it has made a big difference in my thinking," Jake remarked.

Yet every morning has become time-consuming, when Jake needs to be oriented to the day's activities, reported his wife. "He can be told that he has an art class at Hamilton House, but he'll forget it," she said, adding that even if you write it down, he might lose the piece of paper.

Even before his symptoms of Alzheimer's intensified, Jake did a little carpentry and painting at Hamilton House, a center for active adults age 55 and over on Providence's East Side, located close to his home. Today, he still does his maintenance chores, but attends art classes and other activities at the French Chateau-style home.

"I am just the kid here," joked Jake, noting that "everyone keeps an eye on me" during his three weekly visits.

Director Jessica Haley of Hamilton House said that Jake is the only person with early-onset Alzheimer's among its 300 members. "He's comfortable here because we're not a senior center, but an adult-learning exchange," she said.

"People love his sense of humor, and he just hugs everybody," added Haley.

When not at Hamilton House, Jake also spends time at the Eastside Mount Hope YMCA. "It's like playtime," he said, a place where he can lift weights and exercise. He also regularly attends Live & Learn, a weekly social-engagement program held at this YMCA, run by the Alzheimer's Association, Rhode Island Chapter. Yet as the disease progresses, forgetting details and names continues to frustrate Jake. As to coping:

"He rolls with the punches and goes with the flow," said his supportive wife, noting that "he really is an easygoing person." However, Jake believes his daily walking helps him to think more clearly. "I try to do the best I can, not wanting to be a burden on my wife and family," he said

So far he seems not to be a burden to anyone.

Finding Needed Support and Resources

Karen keeps tabs on her spouse, making sure he does not get lost when he walks their dog. "This has not happened in a long time," he said. She has also taken over the household finances and has power of attorney over his legal issues. All these changes took an enormous amount of time and effort.

She has turned to a large network of friends who could help. "You should be not shy in asking for assistance when you need it," she added.

According to Annie Murphy, outreach coordinator for the "Live & Learn" Program at the Alzheimer's Association, RI Chapter, out of 24,000 people in the Ocean State with Alzheimer's disease, there are about 900 diagnosed under age 65.

Early intervention is extremely important for those afflicted with early-onset Alzheimer's, said Annie, noting that a formal diagnosis can allow for earlier treatment.

"We know that medications approved to manage the symptoms of Alzheimer's are more effective if they are given in the earlier stages of the disease," she said.

Once diagnosed, a person has an opportunity to participate in their future care planning, stated Annie. "This gives them an opportunity to be able to learn what they are living with and to personally manage this disease along with their care partners," she added.

A "healthy, active lifestyle combined with proper nutrition and appropriate medication treatment" is important for those living with this disease, noted Annie. "It won't slow down the progression, but improves the quality of life."

The Alzheimer's Association, Rhode Island Chapter, offers a new education series, "Living with Alzheimer's," geared to persons who are in the early stages of this disease and their care partners. The nonprofit's website (**www.alz.org/ri/**) also provides information about the debilitating Alzheimer's and other related dementias as well as available resources, services, and support groups, which are offered free to persons with Alzheimer's and their families.

In addition, she noted a new support group for people in the early stages of Alzheimer's at her office is available in Providence.

Annie also said that information related to the nonprofit's annual caregivers' conference at the Crowne Plaza in Warwick is also posted on the nonprofit's website. There is no registration fee, and one of the workshops specifically addresses early-onset Alzheimer's issues.

COMIC ROBIN WILLIAMS' DEATH PUTS SPOTLIGHT ON DEPRESSION, SUICIDE

Published August 15, 2014, in the Pawtucket Times

Last Monday evening, millions of Americans were shocked to hear that 63-year-old Robin Williams died from an apparent suicide. While it was well-known that he had a history of severe depression and years of alcohol and drug addiction, we were stunned by the unexpected tragic news. Williams had it all: fame, fortune, loyal friends and fans in every corner of the globe. But like millions of Americans he suffered in silence trying to slay his personal demons when he went into substance abuse treatment.

The sudden death of this Oscar-winning actor, recognized as America's comic genius, squarely puts the spotlight on depression, a mental illness that commonly afflicts tens of millions of Americans.

Depression Becomes a Public Conversation

Within the first 48 hours of Williams' suicide, The Samaritans of Rhode Island saw an increase in calls from people concerned about loved ones and friends, says Executive Director Denise Panichas, who expects to also see an increase in visits to her Pawtucket-based nonprofit's web site. Last year, its website received more than 50,000 visitors.

Panichas says, "Williams' death reinforces the fact that suicide knows no boundaries, it being a relentless demon afflicting both rich or poor and those having access to therapy or medical care and those not having it."

According to the Woonsocket resident, Williams' suicide has raised the awareness of suicide prevention in a way that millions of dollars in public health announcements could never have done. "Williams' movies as well as his dedication to community service resonate with multiple generations," says Panichas, stressing that his six-plus decades had value "which will live on."

Williams' substance abuse problems also highlight the need for more awareness as to how addictions can be a risk factor for depression and suicide. Throughout the country, in every city and town, budgets for substance abuse treatment are being cut, she adds.

"Promoting wellness and preventing addictions will always be a big challenge but we must do more if we want to see a decrease in suicides," says Panichas.

Panichas expects the death of Williams, an internationally acclaimed movie star, will have an impact on fund raising for suicide prevention or addiction and depression prevention programs. She has seen an increase in donations from Rhode Islanders as well as from around the country.

"One donor gave a donation in memory of 'Mork.' The donations coming in may be small but every one counts toward keeping our programs available to the public," says Panichas, noting that over the years public funding has "been drying up." The Samaritans of RI is using more creative fund raising structures, like crowdfunding (**www.crowdrise.com/samaritansri2014**) and other social venture sites to create new revenue streams for her nonprofit, she adds.

An Illness That Can Affect Anyone

Lisa B. Shea, M.D., medical director of Providence-based Butler Hospital, Providence, learned of Williams' suicide by a CNN alert on her iPhone. To the board-certified psychiatrist who serves as a clinical associate professor at Brown University's Alpert Medical School, "it was tragic but preventable."

Shea, a practicing psychiatrist for 20 years, notes that people who have suicidal thoughts, like Williams, are struggling with mental health disorders. "Their thinking can get very dark and narrow, and they believe they have no options," she says, often feeling like a burden to others. "It does not matter who you are, mental illness can strike anyone regardless of their wealth and fame," she says.

According to Shea, the public's interest in Williams' tragic death sheds light on the fact that people can get help, and it begins with taking a positive first step. "People with suicidal thoughts, who feel intensely tortured and cannot see any way out of their situation, can benefit from supportive therapeutic relationships, medications, and getting support from family and friends who can push them into getting professional help," she says.

Shea calls on Congress and Rhode Island state lawmakers to positively respond to Williams' suicide by providing increased funding for access to treatment and prevention programs and to support mental health research.

Finally, Shea says that there are a number of telltale signs of a person expressing hopelessness who may be thinking of ending his or life. They include statements made by someone that others would be better off if he or she were not around; excessive use of alcohol and/or drugs; not taking care of themselves, and giving away personal items. When these occur, talk to the person, telling them that you care about them and are concerned for their well-being.

Adds Melinda Kulish, Ph.D., a clinical psychologist/clinical neuropsychologist and instructor of psychology at Harvard Medical School, "There are also times when depression is not easily recognizable. Some people who are depressed experience it most acutely when by themselves but can appear fine, even quite happy, when they are with other people."

Kulish explains that, for various reasons, some people feel the need to make others happy. Cheering up others or making others laugh makes them also feel happy.

"But if that person is suffering from depression, the happiness is fleeting—the laughter ends, and they once again feel empty and sad. The cheering up of others is a fix that is OUTSIDE, not inside of them.

"And drugs and alcohol can make them feel better for a time. The high always ends, and when alone, they feel empty and even more depressed," says Kulish. "There's really good research to suggest that talking about traumatic and upsetting events leads to much healthier responses. The old idea: 'I'm just not going to talk about it so it'll go away' doesn't work."

"It's a myth that if you ask a person if he or she is suicidal, you will put that idea in their heads," says Shea.

Feeling Low, a Place to Call

When this happens, "feeling low with nowhere to turn" as noted singer songwriter Bill Withers once said in a public service announcement, there is a place to call– The Samaritans of Rhode Island–where trained volunteers "are there to listen." Incorporated in 1977, the Pawtucket-based nonprofit program is dedicated to reducing the occurrence of suicide by befriending the desperate and lonely throughout the state's 39 cities and towns.

Since the inception, The Samaritans has received more than 500,000 calls and trained more than 1,380 volunteers to answer its confidential and anonymous Hotline/Listening Lines.

While the first Samaritan branch started in England in 1953, chapters can now be found in more than 40 countries of the world. "Samaritans, can I help you?" is quietly spoken into phones across the world in a multilingual chorus of voices," notes its website.

Executive Director Panichas notes that the communication-based program teaches volunteers to effectively listen to people who are in crisis. Conversations are free, confidential, and, most important, anonymous.

A rigorous 21-hour training program teaches volunteers to listen to callers without expressing personal judgments or opinions. Panichas said that the listening techniques, called "befriending," calls for 90 percent listening and 10 percent talking. Panichas noted The Samaritans of Rhode Island Listening Line is also a much-needed resource for caregivers and older Rhode Islanders.

Other services include a peer-to-peer grief Safe Place Support Group for those left behind by suicide as well as community education programs.

In 2014, The Samaritans of Rhode Island received more than 4,000 calls and hosted more than 50,000 visitors to its website.

The Samaritans of Rhode Island can be the gateway to care or a "compassionate non-judgmental voice on the other end of the line," Panichas notes. "It doesn't matter what your problem is, be it depression, suicidal thoughts, seeking resources for mental health services in the community, or being lonely or just needing to talk, our volunteers are there to listen."

For persons interested in more information about suicide emergencies, The Samaritans website, **www.samaritansri.org,** has an emergency checklist as well as information by city and town including Blackstone Valley communities from Pawtucket to Woonsocket.

For those seeking to financially support the programs of The Samaritans of Rhode Island, its Art Gallery and Education Center is available to rent for special events, meetings, and other types of occasions. For information on gallery rental, call The Samaritans business line at (401)721-5220; or go to **www.samaritansri.org**.

Need to Talk? Call a volunteer at The Samaritans. Call (401)272-4044 or toll-free in RI (1-800) 365-4044.

For mental health resources, go to **www.butler.org**.

DECIPHERING THE EFFECTIVENESS OF ALZHEIMER'S RESEARCH FINDINGS

Published July 6, 2012, in the Pawtucket Times

For more than a decade, my mother was afflicted with the devastating medical disorder Alzheimer's disease. Over the years with this affliction, her physician would update our family on the effectiveness of pharmaceutical research on medications that could put the brakes on this disorder, one that would ultimately erase her short- and long-term memory, making her husband of 60 years and adult children virtual strangers to her.

My family, like hundreds of thousands of baby boomers and seniors, sought information from newspapers, senior publications, and national magazines like *Time* or *Newsweek* to unravel the medical mysteries of Alzheimer's disease. Occasionally, I, like many shoppers at the grocery store, would sneak a peek to read the *National Enquirer* while waiting in line, looking for a little bit more information on new, effective treatments for Alzheimer's disease.

Unraveling the Mysteries of Alzheimer's Disease

Often it becomes very confusing for caregivers to determine which profiled treatments are promising ones and which ones are not, due to the diversity of opinions in the research community. Some articles might detail the effectiveness of taking Vitamin E while others stress the effectiveness of ginkgo biloba, noting how it just might improve your memory. Others describe studies that indicate that estrogen-replacement therapy is not really an effective treatment for Alzheimer's disease for some women. Or some might even issue a warning to readers "not to eat off aluminum plates" because some research findings indicate that an accumulation of heavy metals, such as aluminum, in the brain might cause the devastating disorder of Alzheimer's.

Years ago I provided the following helpful tips to readers of my column that might unravel the mysteries of findings in Alzheimer's research that are reported by the nation's media. These tips are just as relevant 11 years later.

Always beware of catchy headlines. Time limitations keep people from reading every word in articles that appear in their daily, weekly, or monthly newspapers. As a result, many readers choose to quickly scan the headlines for their information. Don't judge an article by its cute headline. The content of an article is much more balanced than the headline, which is often composed of catchy words, crafted to draw readers in.

Look for authoritative commentary. You can consider an article to be more credible when it provides multiple quotes on the indications of an Alzheimer's treatment. Consider the report to have done a good job if there is an authoritative expert commentary on the significance of the study. Two likely sources might come from staffers employed by either the National Alzheimer's Association or the National Institutes of Health, a major federal government agency that funds Alzheimer's research studies. One might consider the National Alzheimer's Association's point of view to be a less-biased, more reliable opinion than those researchers who have ties to a pharmaceutical company that issued a press release.

Determine whether there are disputes in research findings. Keep in mind that even if a research study is reported, there might be those persons who believe the study is not well designed or contains major research flaws. On the other hand, the study might just be accepted by the scientific community as a solid study. However, there might still be serious disagreements about how to interpret the results or how to classify it. Some researchers might consider it a major study while others will not. A well-researched article will include the quotes of those who oppose the study.

Seeking Out Reliable Expert Sources

Are you still confused by how to cull articles for tips to learn about safe, effective treatments for Alzheimer's? Where do we go from here? Caregivers should view any article written about new Alzheimer's treatments as informational in nature. The article can open the door to the nation's research community, and it now becomes your responsibility to do your homework by seeking out more details about what the research findings indicate.

If the article describes the results of an actual published research study, obtain the scientific journal with the published study at your local library or search for it on the Internet. Carefully read it. If the findings are reported from a presentation at a conference, attempt to track down the researchers for more information. Finally cruise the Internet and check out the official websites of the Alzheimer's Association or the National Institute on Aging to determine if you can locate more information about a reported new treatment.

Finally don't hesitate to call Donna McGowan, executive director of the Alzheimer's Association, Rhode Island Chapter, at (401) 421-0008, or email **Donna.McGowan@alz.org**, to solicit the organization's comments on research findings reported by the media. Remember that federal agencies, along with national and state Alzheimer's organizations, monitor research studies and their implications for treatment.

KEEPING YOUR MEMORY SHARP IN YOUR LATER YEARS

Published July 14, 2012, in the Pawtucket Times

In her 20s, while attending nursing school, Donna Policastro discovered she had a photographic memory. Even in her middle years, the Providence resident's memory was still pretty good. She had no need for appointment books or PDAs to keep up with her busy work schedule as a registered nurse. Like an elephant, she never forgot, always remembering minute details and never missing an appointment or meeting.

Approaching age 50, missing meetings and even some appointments forced Policastro, executive director of the Rhode Island State Nurses Association (RISNA), to keep a to-do list and use her computer's calendar program. Policastro, now age 59, speculated that being overwhelmed at work because she had no support staff combined with not being able to reject new duties and responsibilities took a toll on her memory.

Sometimes the aging baby boomer would forget a colleague's or patient's name altogether or not remember a first or last moniker. She became physically exhausted trying to remember their full name or details of their initial meeting. It even bothered Policastro "to no end" when she could not remember an actor's name she saw on a television program. She became obsessed in her attempts to remember his name.

As Policastro would ultimately discover when reading *Aging With Grace*, a book that described a longitudinal health study of an order of nuns, she was not losing her mind or becoming afflicted with dementia or devastating Alzheimer's disease. Her memory loss was due to normal aging.

Memory Gradually Declines with Age

Laurence Hirshberg, Ph.D., director of the Providence-based Neuro Development Center, would agree with Policastro's self-assessment as to why her memory was not as sharp or clear as in her earlier years. "Advancing age seems to cause gradual declines in some aspects of memory and thinking, brain structure and brain functioning, while sparing others," he said. The clinical psychologist noted research findings indicate that up to half of people over age 50 have mild forgetfulness linked to age-associated memory impairment.

According to Dr. Hirshberg, who serves as clinical assistant professor in the Department of Psychiatry and Human Behavior at Brown University Medical School, as a person ages, there is often a decline in one's ability to encode new memories of events or facts, as well as the ability to hold the information you need to perform a simple task (for example, to dial a telephone number). "Studies also show declines in memory of events, times, places, associated emotions, certain forms of reasoning, and numeric and verbal ability. Procedural memory, or remembering how to perform a process, for example, playing the piano, is less affected by aging, as is memory of words and memory of emotional experience, both of which are enhanced with age," Hirshberg said.

"All of us show some forgetfulness at times," noted Dr. Hirshberg, especially when we forget where the car is parked, forget a person's name (yet remember it later), forget events from the distant past or forget parts of an experience. He noted that signs of more serious memory problems include forgetting an experience or recent events, forgetting how to drive a car or read a clock, forgetting ever having known a particular person or loss of function, confusion, or decreased alertness.

Memory loss can be caused by a variety of factors, Dr. Hirshberg said, from lack of physical or mental activity, boredom, social isolation, stress, drug or alcohol use, smoking, or poor nutrition, to an array of medical conditions that includes sleep disorders, head trauma, depression, diabetes, impairment to vision and hearing, head trauma, and even high blood pressure and cholesterol.

Living with Memory Loss

Preventing memory loss in your later years can be as simple as staying socially active, learning and staying mentally active, eating nutritious meals, reducing stress, and seeking help for medical conditions, Dr. Hirshberg suggested. "Making lists and creating schedules can be effective strategies to increase memory skills. Many people use technological aids such as PalmPilots," he said.

Even brain exercises can be helpful in keeping your memory sharp, Hirshberg said, specifically working crossword puzzles and soduko, playing chess, checkers, bridge and other card games. Reading, attending lectures, or learning new skills are also beneficial, along with using formal brain-exercise programs for the computer (such as Mental Fitness, Brain Power, Captain's Log, and Sharper Brain). Some examples of computerized brain-exercise games can be seen at **www.youcanstaysharp.com.**

Many aging baby boomers wonder when is the appropriate time to see a physician about memory loss. Dr. Hirshberg said the rule of thumb that clinicians often use is: If you are worried about your memory, it is probably not that serious. Yet if your friends and relatives are worried about it, then it probably is more serious.

MUSIC REDUCES AGITATION IN ALZHEIMER'S PATIENTS

Published August 19, 2002, in the Pawtucket Times

After not being at my parents' home for two years, I traveled to Dallas to visit my family and celebrate my 88-year-old father's birthday last week.

My trip was a bittersweet experience for me as I reconnected with my parents and siblings. It was great to spend time and catch up with everyone, but I saw firsthand how Alzheimer's disease had ravaged, both physically and mentally, my 80-year-old mother. I saw the impact the disease had on my family.

My mother, who is in the mid-to-late stages of Alzheimer's, was largely unaware of recent events or even who I was.

There was no recognition of my brother or sisters, and many times she did not even recognize my father, who has been her husband for the past 60 years.

My mother could not tell time on her watch, was not aware of what day it was, or even where she lived.

Moreover the staff warned me about her frequent mood swings and said that she could get agitated very quickly.

However some say "music soothes the savage breast."

That may be true, and it's most certainly true for victims of Alzheimer's disease. Soothing music can reduce agitation. While Alzheimer's robs individuals of their memory or cognitive abilities, a timeless tune can reduce agitation and have calming, positive effects on Alzheimer's patients. This point was driven home to me following my visit to my mother's 28-bed Alzheimer's unit at the Dallas-based Marriott Brighton Gardens.

On Friday afternoon, Carrie A. Johns, of Blue Rose Entertainment, kept things hopping in the Alzheimer's unit's television room with her music-therapy program.

Popping CDs into a compact-disc player, Johns played a continual string of popular tunes from the early 1900s to the 1960s. On that day, about 20 songs were played, ranging from golden oldies to country and western and Broadway tunes.

Johns chose from 8,000 songs in her CD collection, and she often selected songs during her one-and-a-half-hour program that reflected memorable, happy periods in the residents' lives.

Johns, who raises Arabian horses on a 12-acre ranch in Mabank, Texas, has a client list of more than 500 nursing facilities, assisted-living facilities, and senior centers in the Dallas-Fort Worth metroplex region.

Swaying, Johns sings the Andrews Sisters' 1942 hit "The Boogie Woogie Bugle Boy of Company B" into her microphone, as residents Rose Grimes, Helen Webb, and Francis Donathan dance up a storm with Ashina Jackson, a personal-care assistant, big smiles lighting up all their faces.

"It is a joy to make these residents happy when their families are not here," Jackson told me. "I like to see their expressions when they remember the tunes. It's like I'm going back to their time."

To the beat of the 1920s tune, "Ain't She Sweet," Activity Director Dave Mandt dances with my mother.

She belts out the song, remembering all the words, not even missing a beat.

Jane Atobajeun, special-care manager, said music helps to calm the residents. Residents with Alzheimer's disease don't remember recent events: what they ate for lunch, for instance. Yet they will remember songs that were once popular in distant eras, because they can retain long-term memory.

"Music makes them laugh," added Atobajeun, noting that it "touches their very being and also triggers memories and emotions."

According to Atobajeun, throughout the day residents can get frustrated if they can't remember things.

Yet singing makes them very happy because they remember the words. Dancing can also get the residents up and moving, she added, noting that even wheelchair-bound residents are assisted to stand and move.

Throughout the program, my father and I traded off dancing with my mother. Several times, my smiling mother goes up to the microphone and dances with Johns.

You guessed it. She automatically knows every word of the song. When the music ends, I say good-bye to my mother.

Knowing the challenges she faces with Alzheimer's, I at least know that there are brief periods of pleasure in her life: at least twice a week when she attends the Alzheimer's unit's music program.

REPORT: ALZHEIMER'S POSES GREATER RISK FOR OLDER WOMEN THAN MEN

Published May 11, 2014, in the Pawtucket Times

According to the Alzheimer's Association 2014 "Facts and Figures" report released last month, a woman's estimated lifetime risk of developing Alzheimer's at age 65 is one in six, compared with nearly one in 11 for a man. As real a concern as breast cancer is to women's health, women age 60 and over are about twice as likely to develop Alzheimer's over the rest of their lives as they are to develop breast cancer, says this year's report.

The "Facts and Figures" report, an annual report of the Alzheimer's Association, the world's leading voluntary health organization in Alzheimer's care, support, and research, is a comprehensive compilation of national statistics and information on Alzheimer's disease and related dementias. The 75-page report conveys the impact of Alzheimer's on individuals, families, government, and the nation's health care system. Since its 2007 inaugural release, the detailed report has become the most-cited source covering the broad spectrum of Alzheimer's issues.

"Through our role in the development of 'The Shriver Report: A Woman's Nation Takes on Alzheimer's in 2010,' in conjunction with Maria Shriver, we know that women are the epicenter of Alzheimer's disease, representing the majority of both people with the disease and Alzheimer's caregivers. The recently released Alzheimer's Association's 'Facts and Figures' examines the impact of this unbalanced burden," said Angela Geiger, chief strategy officer of the Alzheimer's Association. "Well-deserved investments in breast cancer and other leading causes of death such as heart disease, stroke, and HIV/AIDS have resulted in substantial decreases in death." Geiger calls for comparable investments in research to reach the same levels of successfully preventing and treating Alzheimer's as the other leading causes of death.

Adding to women's Alzheimer's burden, there are two-and-a-half times as many women as men providing intensive "on-duty" care 24 hours for someone living with Alzheimer's disease, says the report, also noting that among caregivers who feel isolated, women are much more likely than men to link isolation with feeling depressed (17 percent of women versus 2 percent of men).

Also noted in the 2014 Alzheimer's "Facts and Figures" report released on March 19, 2014, the strain of caring for someone with Alzheimer's is also felt in the nation's workplace, too. Among caregivers who have been employed while they were also caregiving, 20 percent of women versus three percent of men went from working full-time to working part-time while acting as a caregiver. The report also noted that 18 percent of women versus 11 percent of men took a leave of absence while 11 percent of women versus five percent of men gave up work entirely. Finally, 10 percent of women versus five percent of men lost job benefits.

Far-Reaching Fiscal Human Impact of Alzheimer's

Meanwhile the Alzheimer's Association "Facts and Figures" report noted that there are more than five million Americans living with this devastating disorder, including 3.2 million women and 200,000 people under the age of 65 with younger-onset Alzheimer's disease. However, Alzheimer's has far-reaching effects by impacting entire families. Also, it was reported that there are currently 15.5 million caregivers providing 17.7 billion hours of unpaid care throughout the nation, often severely impacting their own health. The physical and emotional impact of dementia caregiving resulted in an estimated $9.3 billion in increased health care costs for Alzheimer's caregivers in 2013.

The total national cost of caring for people with Alzheimer's and other dementias is projected to reach $214 billion this year, says the 2014 "Facts and Figures" report, not including unpaid care given by family and friends valued at more than $220 billion. In 2014, the cost to Medicare and Medicaid of caring for those with Alzheimer's and other dementias will reach a combined $150 billion with Medicare spending nearly one dollar of every five dollars on people with Alzheimer's or another dementia.

The "Facts and Figures" report predicts the cost numbers to soar as the baby boomers continue to enter the age of greatest risk for Alzheimer's disease. Unless something is done to change the course of the devastating disorder, there could be as many as 16 million Americans living with Alzheimer's in 2050, at a cost of $1.2 trillion (in current dollars) to the nation. This dramatic rise includes a 500 percent increase in combined Medicare and Medicaid spending and a 400 percent increase in out-of-pocket spending.

The country's first-ever National Plan to Address Alzheimer's disease has a goal of preventing and effectively treating Alzheimer's disease by 2025. Ensuring strong implementation of the National Alzheimer's Plan, including adequately funding Alzheimer's research, is the best way to avoid these staggering human and financial tolls.

Lack of Understanding of Alzheimer's Disease

"Despite being the nation's biggest health threat, Alzheimer's disease is still largely misunderstood. Everyone with a brain—male or female, family history or not,—is at risk for Alzheimer's," said Geiger. "Age is the greatest risk factor for Alzheimer's, and America is aging. As a nation, we must band together to protect our greatest asset, our brains."

In 2010, the Alzheimer's Association in partnership with Maria Shriver and The Shriver Report conducted a groundbreaking poll with the goal of exploring the compelling connection between Alzheimer's disease and women. Data from that poll were published in "The Shriver Report: A Woman's Nation Takes on Alzheimer's," which also included essays and reflections that gave personal perspectives to the poll's numbers. For the first time, that report revealed not only the striking impact of the disease on individual lives, but also its especially strong effects on women—women living with the disease, as well as women who are caregivers, relatives, friends, and loved ones of those directly affected.

Realizing the impact Alzheimer's has on women—and the impact women can have when they work together—the Alzheimer's Association is launching a national initiative this spring highlighting the power of women in the fight against this disease. To join the movement, visit **www.alz.org/mybrain**.

Maureen Maigret, policy consultant for the Senior Agenda Coalition of Rhode Island and coordinator of the Rhode Island Older Woman's Policy Group, concurs with the findings of the Alzheimer's disease "Facts and Figures" report. She calls for the education of elected officials on the facts about Alzheimer's disease and its greater prevalence among women. "It is clearly a tragedy for the women affected with the disease and can be devastating for their caregivers, mostly daughters, trying to keep them at home," she says.

Maigret says that Alzheimer's disease and other dementias at the state level have tremendous implications for this state's budget. "Data show that in Rhode Island, about three-quarters of persons in nursing homes paid for by Medicaid are older women. An overwhelming number of them have some cognitive decline or dementia," she notes.

"We must do more to ensure that quality long-term care is available for persons with dementia and that robust caregiver support services are in place for the many families dealing with parents, spouses, and other loved ones suffering from this disease," says Maigret, stressing that government funding on research must also be greatly increased in the hopes of finding a cure or ways to prevent its onset.

Director Catherine Taylor, of the state's Division of Elderly Affairs, believes that the Alzheimer's Association's released 2014 "Facts and Figures" report, about a woman's lifetime risk of developing the devastating cognitive disorder versus breast cancer "really helps us understand, in stark terms, what a public health crisis Alzheimer's disease is, especially for women."

Taylor notes that the Ocean State is in the implementation phase of its state plan on Alzheimer's Disease and Related Dementias (see my November 13, 2013 commentary), where state officials are working to improve information, care, and supports for every family that confronts Alzheimer's disease. "The work will continue until there's a cure," she says.

"It's important to note that new research findings also indicate that up to half of the cases of Alzheimer's disease may be linked to risk factors, within our control," states Taylor, adding that reducing the risk of developing Alzheimer's disease may be as simple as eating a healthy diet, staying active, learning new skills, and maintaining strong connections with family, friends, and community.

For those concerned about their risk of developing Alzheimer's disease, join Prevent AD, Rhode Island's Alzheimer's Disease Prevention Registry. Prevent AD volunteers will learn about prevention studies for which they may be qualified to participate in as well as the latest news on brain health. For more information, call (401) 444-0789.

The full text of the Alzheimer's Association 2014 "Facts and Figures" can be viewed at **www.alz.org/downloads/facts_figures_2014.pdf**. The full report also appeared in the March 2014 issue of *Alzheimer's & Dementia: the Journal of the Alzheimer's Association* (Volume 10, Issue 2).

RI'S STATE ALZHEIMER'S PLAN WON'T SIT ON DUSTY SHELF

Published on November 3, 2013, in the Pawtucket Times

S eeing a huge rise in Alzheimer's disease over the past two years, federal and state officials are gearing up to strategize a battle to fight the impending epidemic.

According to the Rhode Island Chapter of the Alzheimer's Association, in 2013 an estimated five million Americans age 65 and older have Alzheimer's disease. Unless more effective ways are identified and implemented to prevent or treat this devastating cognitive disorder, the prevalence may well triple, skyrocketing to almost 16 million people.

Furthermore, national health care costs are spiraling out of control, says the nonprofit group's Facts Sheet. By 2050, it's estimated that the total cost of care nationwide for persons with Alzheimer's disease is expected to reach more than $1 trillion dollars (in today's dollars), up from $172 billion in 2010.

Meanwhile, with 24,000 Rhode Islanders afflicted with Alzheimer's disease, every Rhode Islander is personally touched, either caring for a family member with the cognitive disorder or knowing someone who is a caregiver or patient.

In February 2012, the U.S. Department of Health and Human Services released its draft National Plan, detailing goals to prevent or treat the devastating disease by 2025. Almost six months later, in May 2012, the Rhode Island General Assembly passed a joint resolution (the same month that the final National Plan was released), signed by Governor Lincoln Chafee, directing the state's Long Term Care Coordinating Council to lead an effort to create a statewide strategy to react to Rhode Island's growing Alzheimer's population. Almost one year later, a 122-page document, "the Rhode Island State Plan for Alzheimer's Disease and Related Disorders," was released to address the growing incidence in the Ocean State.

In July 2013, with the graying of the nation's population and a skyrocketing incident rate of persons afflicted with Alzheimer's disease, the Chicago-based Alzheimer's Association and the U.S. Centers for Disease Control (CDC) and Prevention released a 56-page report that called for public health officials to quickly act to stem the growing Alzheimer's crisis.

Battle Plan Against Alzheimer's Disease

The state's plan to battle Alzheimer's disease is the culmination of a yearlong effort co-chaired by Lt. Governor Elizabeth Roberts and Division of Elderly Affairs Director Catherine Taylor, in partnership with the state chapter of the Alzheimer's Association.

Much of the research and writing was conducted by six subgroups (Caregivers, Access, Legal, Workforce, Long-Term Care, and Care Delivery and Research) formed to identify and tackle the many challenges that Alzheimer's disease poses to individuals, their families, and to the health care delivery system.

At their meetings, the subgroups drew upon the expertise of staff at the Geriatric Education Center at the University of Rhode Island, the Brown University Center for Gerontology and Health Care Research, the Brown Brain Bank, the Norman Price Neurosciences Institute, and the Alzheimer's Prevention Registry.

Public input was crucial in the development of the state plan. Eight listening sessions were held across the Ocean State, two of them with Spanish translators, at public libraries and local YMCAs to get the opinions of those with the cognitive disorder, caregivers, and health care professionals. The Probate Judges' Association, law enforcement, and other groups with unique perspectives on Alzheimer's disease were invited to listening sessions, too. Finally, the draft plan was made available for a 10-day public comment as part of the extensive outreach process.

The narrative in each section, nicely pulled together by Lindsay McAllister, the lieutenant governor's director of health policy, reflected many of the concerns and challenges identified by many presentations and discussions in each of the subgroup meetings over several months. The state plan details 30 pages of recommendations outlining solutions and specific steps to be taken for preventing and caring for persons with Alzheimer's disease for six identified areas.

A Sampling of Recommendations

The plan encourages the development of social media networks as resources for caregivers, also calling on utilizing existing caregiver newsletters to detail more information about the Ocean State's specific programs and services. It also calls for better training and education opportunities (for young children) to help them understand the devastating disorder and the creation of a two-week certification program offered by local colleges and universities with input from the state's Alzheimer's Association.

In addition, the plan recommends the timely dissemination of research findings and best practices in nursing facilities, dementia care units, and home care to providers and families. Meanwhile, recommendations note the need to standardize dementia training and educational programs as well as the certification of facilities that offer dementia-specific care so that individuals and families impacted by Alzheimer's disease can rely upon high-quality "dementia-capable" care that they can find more easily.

The plan pushes for all Employee Assistance Programs (EAPs) to receive information about referral resources for employees requiring more intensive or long-term mental health services. EAPs might also provide educational and informational resources on caregiver support for families dealing with Alzheimer's disease.

Another key recommendation is the development of an Internet resource referred to as the Rhode Island Alzheimer's Disease (RIAD) web site. The site would enable better coordination among researchers and clinicians and assist them in recruiting participants for clinical trials and research studies. It would also provide consistent centralized support to individuals living with Alzheimer's and their families by making practical caregiving information readily and easily available.

"AARP has a long history of supporting Alzheimer's patients and their families," said AARP Rhode Island Advocacy Director Deanna Casey. "We applaud the effort in Rhode Island and Lt. Gov. Roberts' efforts on behalf of those who suffer from the disease," she says.

Casey says "far too many of our nonprofit's 130,000 Rhode Island members are painfully familiar with Alzheimer's, and the work of the many stakeholders in this effort is further indication of the great need to recognize our collective responsibility to help families through what is a most challenging journey."

"Rhode Island has a tremendous opportunity to be a national leader in response to this disease," she believes.

Briefing by Key Supporters

Two days ago, the full Alzheimer's work group kicked off the implementation phase of the "Rhode Island State Plan on Alzheimer's Disease and Related Disorders," discussing how to move forward with the goal of getting the recommendations up and running.

In Room 116 at the State House, Lt. Governor Elizabeth Roberts and Director Catherine Taylor of the Division of Elderly Affairs were clearly pleased to see their yearlong initiative moving into its implementation phase to assist the state to handle a growing number of persons with Alzheimer's disease.

On the heels of a nationally released plan to address the Alzheimer's epidemic, Taylor tells me that it was "great timing" for the Rhode Island General Assembly to enact a joint resolution to create a state plan to "respond to Rhode Island's specific needs and gaps of service." She credits the Rhode Island Chapter of the Alzheimer's Association with getting the ball rolling on this major health care policy initiative.

According to Lt. Governor Roberts, public sessions where caregivers and people with Alzheimer's disease told their stories allowed the subgroups to understand the personal impact of the devastating disease on both the afflicted and caregivers. For instance, the listening sessions made it very clear that the specific care needs of middle-aged adults with early onset Alzheimer's disease is quite different from those who are decades older, she said. Taylor agreed, citing adult day-care eligibility requirements, which keep those under age 60 from participating in this program, one that provides respite care to caregivers.

Lt. Governor Roberts states "younger people cannot relate to programs that are developed for older people." The patient must become the center of the treatment rather than the treatment geared to age, she says.

Both Lt. Governor Roberts and Taylor do not want to see the state plan sit on a dusty shelf, noting that it now becomes important to implement the written plan's recommendations. "Let's get the ball rolling now," says Taylor.

While many of the state plan's recommendations may take time to implement, some are easy to implement like a Spanish-language support group, says the lieutenant governor. Taylor states that Rhode Island has already requested a modification to the Medicaid waiver to expand Adult Day Health Center eligibility to individuals younger than 60 who have a diagnosis of Alzheimer's.

"Senior police and fire advocates need to be trained in every Rhode Island community about Alzheimer's disease and resources available for caregivers," states Taylor.

"These individuals know those who need programs and services in the community," she notes, adding that an information conference is scheduled this week to train these individuals.

Lt. Governor Roberts believes that the state plan is a "living document," and it will be around as long as there is one person with Alzheimer's disease.

To review the State plan go to **http://ltgov.ri.gov/assets/documents/StatePlan.pdf.**

8. POP CULTURE & MUSIC

CULTURAL ICONS, CELEBRITIES GIVE US CAUSE TO REFLECT ON OUR LIVES

Published September 7, 2012, in the Pawtucket Times

The deaths of celebrities and cultural icons who were familiar to us growing up give us cause to reflect on their lives and our own, as well as one's contributions to society.

Astronaut Neil Armstrong traveled 250,000 miles from the Earth to the lunar surface and was the first man to walk on the moon. At age 82, he died last month in Cincinnati, Ohio, from complications resulting from cardiovascular procedures.

With his death on August 25, 2012, hundreds of tributes would come in from all over the world: from world leaders, former astronauts, and his family, which called him modest and humble, a "reluctant American hero," an explorer, an exceptional test pilot, and recognized him as a war veteran who flew 78 combat missions during the Korean conflict.

Not unexpectedly, even President Barack Obama, commander in chief, recognized Armstrong's impact on the cultural fabric of the nation. "When he and his fellow crew members lifted off aboard *Apollo 11* in 1969, they carried with them the aspirations of an entire nation," said Obama in a written statement released by the White House. "They set out to show the world that the American spirit can see beyond what seems unimaginable; that with enough drive and ingenuity, anything is possible. And when Neil stepped foot on the surface of the moon for the first time, he delivered a moment of human achievement that will never be forgotten."

Man on the Moon

In July 1969, one month after my 15th birthday, I was riveted to our television as my family watched the *CBS News with Walter Cronkite*, as he told a captivated nation that American astronaut Neil Armstrong and lunar module pilot Buzz Aldrin, along with command module pilot Mike Collins, had reached the moon four days after being launched from Kennedy Space Center. Cronkite, America's most trusted newscaster, detailed the landing, noting how the lunar module *Eagle* separated from the command module and made its descent to the moon's surface.

When making that lunar contact, the 38-year-old Armstrong would say, "Tranquility Base here, the *Eagle* has landed." No aging baby boomer will ever forget the memorable quote of the young commander of *Apollo 11* as he climbed down *Eagle's* ladder and stepped onto the lunar soil on July 20, 1969, at 10:56 p.m. "That's one small step for [a] man, one giant leap for mankind."

According to NASA, Armstrong would prance around on the lunar surface for two hours and 32 minutes, while Aldrin, who followed him, spent about 15 minutes less than that.

For years, a small, framed replica of the front page of the *Dallas Morning News*, featuring Armstrong's voyage, sat on my old dresser, which served as an inspirational reminder: a piece of history I had witnessed and now recorded into the nation's history books.

Longtime Comedienne Passes Away

Phyllis Diller, a high-profile stand-up comedienne who, during a 50- year career served as a role model to younger women (including Roseanne Barr, Ellen DeGeneres, Whoopi Goldberg, and Joan Rivers, among others) trying to make a career out of telling jokes, died on August 20, 2012, at the age of 95. She was one of the first women to break into the male-dominated stand-up comedy profession, even giving them a run for their money.

Over her long career, she made dozens of movies, appeared in specials, situational-comedy shows on television, recorded comedy LP records, and even performed on Broadway, as well as breathing life into animated characters on films and television shows with voice-overs.

Keeping my mother company on the couch while watching Johnny Carson after the late-night news, as a young child I would lay my head on Mom's lap, watching *The Tonight Show Starring Johnny Carson* in the early 1960s. Diller appeared on this show as well as variety shows hosted by Jack Benny, Dean Martin, Red Skelton, and Ed Sullivan. She captivated the nation with her quirky sense of humor and signature laugh.

As I grew up watching Diller on television, I can remember the self-deprecating professional jokester wearing an unkempt wig, wrist-length gloves, and cloth-covered ankle boots, while carrying a long, fake, jeweled cigarette holder (even though she never smoked) and taking lob-sharp barbs at her fictional husband, Fang, and her home life during her routines. She was confident and proud of her place in the world, despite the trials and tribulations of "family life."

At age 37, Diller, a mother and homemaker, got her first break in 1955, playing San Francisco's Purple Onion nightclub. The two-week engagement ultimately ended a year and half later.

Diller, a longtime resident of the Brentwood area of Los Angeles, appeared regularly as a special guest on many television programs throughout her career, including *What's My Line?* She also made cameo appearances, bringing her unique humor to *Rowan and Martin's Laugh-In*, *Love Boat*, *Chips*, *Love, American Style*, the *Drew Carey Show* and even appeared on ABC's *Boston Legal*.

Diller underwent 15 different plastic surgeries (this noted in her 2005 autobiography) and surprisingly was recognized as an accomplished pianist as well as a painter.

Archie Bunker's chair went to the Smithsonian. So did Diller's jokes, so to speak. From August 12 to October 28, 2011, the Albert H. Small Documents Gallery at the National Museum of American History displayed Diller's gag file, a steel cabinet consisting of 48 file drawers holding more than 50,000 jokes penned on index cards and costumes that had become part of her "comedic persona."

The Passing of Cultural Icons and Celebrities

When we are young, we feel invulnerable and that we will live forever. Unrealistically, we see death as no match for us. In our later years as aging baby boomers, we begin to see death close-up through the passing of our parents, siblings, co-workers, friends, and sometimes even our children. Health conditions continually remind us of our impending mortality.

As we look at the passing of Neil Armstrong and Phyllis Diller, their impressive life stories should give us confirmation of their major impact on our culture. Their deaths become "mortality markers," subtly giving us the gentle message that "generations come and go" and that we, like them, will not live forever. Time becomes the most valuable commodity that we carry throughout our lives.

If we use time wisely, we can better spend our remaining days to make a positive difference in our communities, whether it be through the profession we chose or simply our outlook on life to those around us. Armstrong, to take mankind to where we had never been, and Diller to make us laugh and forget the pains of life.

PAULA DEEN AND FORGIVENESS

Published June 28, 2013, in the Pawtucket Times

This week nobody could escape the 24-hour-news cycle reporting of how American celebrity chef Paula Deen, a product of her Southern upbringing, admitted that she had spoken the racially charged "N-word" decades ago. Once the dust settles, the nation will get to see whether one of Savannah, Georgia's most prominent residents can rehabilitate herself. Will she personally and professionally survive the swift backlash of the racial-slur controversy? Or will the pubic respond to her tearful pleas for forgiveness and give her one last chance for redemption?

The Ugly "N-Word"

Deen joins actors Mel Gibson, Charlie Sheen, Michael Richards (aka Kramer), real-ity-television stars, Dog the Bounty Hunter and hotel heiress Paris Hilton, along with musicians John Lennon and Yoko Ono, Jennifer Lopez, John Mayer, Eminem, even radio-show host Laura Schlessinger, who all stirred public wrath by uttering the "N-word."

The 66-year-old former Food Network host, restaurateur, writer of cookbooks, actress and Emmy Award-winning television personality suddenly finds her career unraveling, like many who have uttered the racially charged "N-word," one of the more offensive words in the English language, a word that invokes ugly racial stereotypes.

Media details of a deposition on May 17, resulting from a $1.2 million lawsuit filed by a former restaurant manager at the Uncle Bubba's Oyster House, a Savannah, Georgia-based restaurant owned by Deen and her brother, created a public firestorm over her use of a very ugly word. Deen stated that she had used the "N-word" at times, decades ago. She even detailed her plans to dress waiters at a 2007 wedding as slaves, "wearing long-sleeved white shirts, black shorts, and black bow ties."

The Food Network quickly responded to news reports by announcing the dropping of her show, "Paula's Home Cooking," then announcing Deen's contract would not be renewed next month. Later the Smithfield Foods, Inc., retail giant Wal-Mart, and Caesars Entertainment followed suit, severing ties with Paula Deen Entertainment.

Many of her business partners and sponsors including Shopping Network CVC, which sells a line of her cookware, and Random House, publisher of her cookbooks, are monitoring the situation closely to determine their actions.

Trying to control an issue spiraling out of control, a teary Deen created two YouTube apology videos to offer her mea culpa for using racial slurs last week, also making a 13-minute appearance on the *Today Show* with Matt Lauer on June 16 to address the controversy.

Public-relations experts gave mixed reviews as to how effective she was in reducing the negative impact on her brand and celebrity image. Deen's salvation may well rest on the public's short attention span and their desire to forgive, say experts.

Circling the Wagons

Although Deen cannot shake the financial impact of being politically incorrect, her fans are rallying behind her.

This week, thousands of irate Deen fans are rallying to support her by leaving their comments on the Food Network's Facebook page to support the besieged celebrity chef, saying that the network moved too fast to oust her and even overreacted. Many viewed her sacking as political correctness run amuck and called for her to be given a pass for the use of the "N-word."

Just two days ago, a newly created "We Support Paula Deen" Facebook page already has 418,452 Likes with many loyal fan comments urging Deen's sponsors to give her a second chance. Many noted that people make mistakes in life, and ask who hasn't told an inappropriate or off-color joke or used inappropriate words in private or with family?

According to The Associated Press, the Rev. Jesse Jackson, the civil-rights leader, has agreed to help Deen try to make amends for her past use of the "N-word," saying she shouldn't become a "sacrificial lamb" over the issue of racial intolerance. Dean had called him to seek his guidance as to how to recover, noted The Associated Press.

Bravo for Jackson, who said in this press report that if Deen is willing to acknowledge mistakes and make changes, "she should be reclaimed rather than destroyed."

Jackson, a Baptist minister, who was a candidate for the Democratic presidential nomination in 1984 and 1988 and served as a shadow U.S. Senator for the District of Columbia from 1991 to 1997, said he's more troubled by racial disparities in employment, lending, health care, business opportunities, and the criminal-justice system.

Anne Rice, author of Gothic fiction, Christian literature, and erotica, best known for her popular and influential series of novels, *The Vampire Chronicles*, joined Jackson in defending Deen.

On her Facebook page, Rice says what is happening to Deen is "unjust," comparing it with a "High Tech Execution," a witch hunt and a public burning that is a "horrible thing to witness."

Furthermore, best-selling author Rice, who has written 33 books, all novels except one personal memoir, quips, "It is all too easy to 'hate' a witch and join in the 'fun' of a public execution and to feel smug and superior and righteous for doing it. And that is what we are seeing now with Paula Deen. Pure ugliness. This is the very opposite of respect for the dignity of all persons."

Finally, even liberal Bill Maher goes to bat for Deen on *Real Time with Bill Maher* in a recent episode on HBO.

The Power of Forgiveness

For those like Deen, who have made terrible mistakes through their misjudgments and use of inappropriate slurs (like the "N-word"), many rarely survive the backlash of political correctness, even when they plead for forgiveness as their lives are destroyed.

Deen's racial controversy can positively impact our society by allowing more dialogue to confront both personal and institutional racism. Rather than allowing a single mistake to ruin a person's life, give the individual an opportunity to take responsibility and learn from inappropriate behavior and actions. Give them a second chance. What a great celebrity spokesperson Deen could become to bring the races together.

It is so important for individuals to learn to forgive family and friends who have hurt or disappointed them. So too must society do this.

Former South African President Nelson Mandela is an international role model as to how forgiveness can become the perfect way to heal a nation's racist tendencies. At press time, the former president remains in critical condition in a hospital in Pretoria, South Africa, kept on life support, where he is being treated for a lung infection.

Writer Simon Kent, in a June 10, 2013 post on the *Toronto Sun*'s web site, stated that the frail 94-year-old leader's legacy to the world is to teach us "forgiveness."

When Mandela's African National Party won the election that would end apartheid in South Africa, he forgave his white political foes, said Kent, noting that the power of forgiveness kept the black majority-ruling party from seeking revenge.

Kent said: "He didn't hate the political system that had barred him from voting. Mandela didn't hate the rest of the world that for years had turned its back on non-white South Africans."

Mandela "offered mercy both to his tormentors and foes and urged fellow South Africans to do the same," added Kent. Yes, forgiveness.

According to Kent, at Mandela's 1994 inauguration, former Prisoner 46664, Nelson Mandela, kept a seat set aside for a special guest he wanted to witness his swearing-in as president. This person was one of his former jailers from Robben Island, where he was held for 18 years of hard labor, he said.

If Mandela can easily forgive his former jailer and a white society that kept his black brothers and sisters enslaved for centuries, why can't we just forgive Paula Deen for saying the "N-word" decades ago? Simply put, it just seems like the right thing to do.

ROCKERS HENDRIX AND JOPLIN HONORED WITH USPS STAMP

Published on February 28, 2014, in the Pawtucket Times

Miriam R. Plitt, like many of the baby boomer generation, was ecstatic with the announcement by the United States Postal Service (USPS) of its unveiling of a new line of commemorative stamps, including music culture icons. These stamps will be sold as Forever stamps and are good for mailing first-class letters at that price anytime in the future even if stamp prices increase, she says.

The longtime Oak Hill resident was elated that two of her '60s favorites, Jimi Hendrix, one of the most celebrated guitarists in the 20th century, and legendary singer and songwriter Janis Joplin, who pushed their way into the public psyche at the Woodstock festival at Max Yasgur's 600-acre dairy farm in the Catskills near the hamlet of White Lake in the town of Bethel, New York, made the cut.

"Janis Joplin and Jimi Hendrix reach my soul, they speak to me," notes Plitt, who chairs Pawtucket's Advisory Commission on Arts and Culture, and grew up loving rock 'n' roll when this musical style became entrenched in her generation. "Any time I hear these musicians, I just go into my own world and dance," she says.

"Joplin and Hendrix are not artists that came onto the nation's musical scene and left," she observed, but they have had an impact on preceding generations, even setting high standards for other musicians who came after them.

Now in her mid-60s, Plitt notes that this is a terrific honor for her generation, having musicians that her contemporaries listened to growing up to be placed on first-class postage stamps.

Pushing the Musical Boundaries with His Guitar

According to Mark Saunders, USPS spokesman, this month, the Jimi Hendrix stamp will be released on March 13 at the South By Southwest Concert in Austin, Texas, and available nationwide that day. It's a natural venue for Jimi Hendrix fans to purchase the stamp, he says.

According to the USPS' bio on Hendrix (1942–1970), the musician was considered to be one of the most influential electric guitarists in the history of popular music, this being a key factor for the honor of being selected by the USPS.

Combining influences from rock, modern jazz, soul, and the blues with his own innovations, the legendary Hendrix created a unique style that influenced musical guitarists of his era and continues to inspire musicians well into the 21st century.

As shown at Woodstock, Hendrix pushed the boundaries of what his guitar could do, manipulating various devices to produce sounds that could be loud—the quintessential psychedelic music—or melodic and gentle. A master at the controlled use of distortion and feedback, he expanded the instrument's vocabulary in a way that had never been heard before—or since.

While Hendrix is remembered as one of the most innovative guitar players of all time, he was also a gifted songwriter, combining visionary, sometimes haunting imagery, with deft pop hooks.

Rolling Stone ranked Hendrix No.1 on its list of the 100 greatest guitarists of all time, and No.6 on its list of the 100 greatest artists of all time. His band, the Jimi Hendrix Experience, was inducted into the Rock and Roll Hall of Fame in 1992 and the U.K. Music Hall of Fame in 2005. The band's first album, *Are You Experienced*, is considered by many critics to be one of the best rock albums of all time, and in 2005, the Library of Congress selected it for permanent preservation in the National Recording Registry, a list of sound recordings that "are culturally, historically, or aesthetically important, and/or inform or reflect life in the United States."

In 1993, Hendrix was awarded a posthumous Grammy for lifetime achievement.

Through Hendrix's mastery of the guitar and use of controlled feedback as a melodic element, he revolutionized and redefined popular music. His music sounds as innovative and fresh today as when it was first released, winning legions of new fans who just might buy commemorative stamps with his image.

Bluesy Voice Propelled Her to the Top

Joplin (1943-1970), an icon of the 1960s whose bluesy voice propelled her to the pinnacle of rock stardom, gets her image on a stamp, too. Her stamp will be issued later in 2014.

When announcing the issuance of the Joplin stamp, the USPS detailed her musical track record, too. Joplin broke onto the national music scene with an explosive performance at the Monterey Pop Festival in 1967. Known for her rebellious public persona, Joplin roared and wailed her way through uninhibited, soulful performances.

Her time at the top, however, was very brief. She recorded only two hit albums and performed at the Woodstock concert, but in October 1970, just three years after she became a star, she died at the age of 27 of a drug overdose. The album she was recording at the time of her death, "Pearl," went on to cement her reputation as one of the premier white blues singers of all time. "Me and Bobby McGee," written by Kris Kristofferson, became a number-one hit.

As the years passed, Joplin's legacy was increasingly recognized by critics. She was inducted into the Cleveland, Ohio-based Rock and Roll Hall of Fame in 1995 and received a Grammy Lifetime Achievement Award in 2005. *Rolling Stone* included Joplin on its list of 100 Greatest Artists. Some of her most popular songs include "Piece of My Heart," "Ball and Chain," and "Cry Baby."

Washington Post Reporter Lisa Rein reported in a February 21 article that while stamp designs for both Hendrix and Joplin were scheduled for 2014, other pop and music icons were selected for 2015 and beyond. Specifically, Rein's commemorative stamp listing also included Beatle John Lennon, NBA Basketball player Wilt Chamberlain, celebrity chefs, recording artist and musician James Brown, and late night talk-show host Johnny Carson. She noted that the USPS even was considering the reissuing of an Elvis Presley stamp.

However, USPS Spokesperson Saunders stated that while Hendrix and Joplin are confirmed for release this year, the others cited by Rein are only being considered at this time, subject to change and most certainly not finalized. "We may or may not move forward with these stamps," he says.

Yes, there is controversy even in the world of stamps. When hearing that Beatle John Lennon might be honored by having his image on a stamp, collectors voiced their opposition and concerns. Traditionally, only American subjects have been selected, they say. But Saunders explains that the USPS has the discretion to select subjects that have made a significant impact on American society and culture, citing examples of Mother Teresa and Winston Churchill. This opens the door to John Lennon's consideration, he says.

Bringing more relevant stamps reflecting pop culture icons to market is a way to attract younger buyers and increase USPS revenues, notes Saunders. "With 300 million customers across the nation, our diverse stamp program has something to offer everybody," he adds.

Saunders notes that "We receive over 40,000 suggestions of subjects on stamps each year." Many people suggest the inclusion of rock stars on stamps. Most certainly, "Joplin and Hendrix will appeal to fans of rock music from the '60s and '70s," he says.

Will Joplin and Hendrix's commemorative stamps be a big hit with the American public? It's a mixed bag, says Ken Martin, Executive Director of the American Philatelic Society, a nonprofit group representing 34,000 stamp collectors, educators and postal historians in 110 countries. "Some collectors feel that people commemorated on stamps should be without flaws," he says, noting that some might just not agree with Hendrix or Joplin's music style or the way they lived. However, others might just love them.

But Martin concedes that "a little bit of controversy adds to promotion of the released stamp and may well increase sales." He recognizes that the USPS is broadening the scope of the diverse stamp program to reach out to a broader section of the population.

Countering the concerns of collectors who may well frown upon the USPS issuing stamps of people with nontraditional or controversial lifestyles, like Hendrix and Joplin, Rick Bellaire, Vice Chair of the Rhode Island Music Hall of Fame, has another take on it.

Bellaire says that the sudden deaths of Hendrix and Joplin, especially coming as they did (from drug overdoses), one after the other in the fall of 1970, "were a great blow to the music world." These musicians were "such giants that there could never be anyone to replace them nor carry on their work," he says, noting that their "highly original styles promoted deep rhythm & blues to the young, white masses in the guise of psychedelic rock 'n' roll while always making sure the audience knew the source material."

"I am proud of the U.S. Postal Service for honoring these two masters, judging them not by their personal lives and lifestyles, but by their groundbreaking work as musicians and their generosity of spirit," says Bellaire.

For more information on submitting to the USPS your suggestion for a stamp design, go to **about.usps.com/who-we-are/leadership/stamp-advisory-committee. htm**.

WHO WAS HARRY WEATHERSBY STAMPS?

Published March 22, 2013, in the Pawtucket Times

Once upon a time, the *New York Times* was reputed to publish the best and most colorful obituaries, which wove resume-like facts and personal stories together to concisely sum up a person's life and death. Now the legendary daily newspaper has competition. With the passing of Harry Weathersby Stamps on March 9, 2013, his obituary was printed in the *Sun Herald*, his hometown newspaper. The daily paper, covering southern Mississippi, called it "the best obit ever."

I totally agree. More interesting to me is that the obituary, written by his daughter, has gone viral on Twitter, Facebook, and email, receiving rave reviews from around the world.

During a long drive to Long Beach, Mississippi, where Stamps had died at home surrounded by family, daughter Amanda Lewis, an attorney at Irving, Texas-based TRT Holdings, penned the obituary (edited by her sister, Alison Stamps) of their 80-year-old father, a former educator at Mississippi Gulf Coast Community College at the Jefferson Davis Campus.

Lewis' colorful, lighthearted, and humorous 841-word obituary, detailing her father's extremely quirky likes and dislikes, has caught the attention of the nation through the news media, even the entire world via the World Wide Web.

So Who Was Harry Stamps?

According to Lewis, her father was a "ladies' man," "foodie," "natty dresser," and even an "accomplished traveler." He disliked phonies, she noted, especially "know-it-all Yankees, Southerners who used the words 'veranda' and 'porte-cochere' to put on airs, eating grape leaves, *Law and Order* (all franchises), cats, and even Martha Stewart." These are in reverse order, she quipped.

He did love his 1969 Volvo.

As to the important women throughout his eight decades, there were many, Lewis revealed in the published obituary. Almost 50 years ago, her father married his "main squeeze," Ann Moore, a home-economics teacher, and raised two girls, Amanda and Alison.

Lewis fondly remembered that her father taught her and her sister how "to fish, to select a quality hammer, to love nature, and to just be thankful," taking "great pride in stocking their toolboxes."

The obituary noted that Stamps' beloved mother, the late Wilma Hatzog, raised him in his teenage years with the help of her sisters and cousins in New Hebron. "He worshipped his older sister, Lynn Stamps Garner (deceased), a character in her own right, and her daughter, Lynda Lightsey of Hattiesburg," Lewis said.

Moreover, Lewis said that her father loved his grandchildren. "He took extreme pride in his two grandchildren, 8-year-old Harper Lewis and 6-year-old William Stamps Lewis of Dallas, for whom the grandfather would crow like a rooster on their phone calls."

Who Says Politics and Religion Don't Mix?

As to politics, "One of his regrets was not seeing his girl Hillary Clinton elected president," added Lewis, who noted that her father was a former government and sociology professor. She wrote that Stamps, with an interest in both politics and religion, "enjoyed watching politicians act like preachers, and preachers act like politicians."

Lewis remembered him often saying, "I am not running for political office or trying to get married" when he was "speaking the truth."

The obituary noted that over Stamps' lifetime, he had developed culinary tastes for particular delicacies. Her father made his "signature" bacon-and-tomato sandwich with "100 percent all-white Bunny Bread from Georgia, Blue Plate mayonnaise from New Orleans, Sauer's black pepper from Virginia, homegrown tomatoes from outside Oxford and Tennessee's Benton bacon from his bacon-of-the-month subscription."

He even openly had "a lifelong love affair with deviled eggs, Lane cakes, boiled peanuts, Vienna (pronounced: Vi-e-na) sausages on saltines, his homemade canned-fig preserves, pork chops, turnip greens and buttermilk served in Martini glasses garnished with cornbread," she admitted.

Juggling Many Hobbies in Retirement

What does Stamps' obituary say about his many hobbies and leisure activities?

Her father, who had green thumbs, "excelled at growing camellias," said Lewis. His knack for carpentry was just the skill needed for "rebuilding houses after hurricanes (like Katrina)," she noted.

Because history was important to Stamps, he would read any history book he could get his hands on, Lewis said. As for his love of cable programming, the history buff "loved to use his oversized 'old man' remote control, which he was thankful had survived

Hurricane Katrina, to flip between watching *The Barefoot Contessa* and anything on the History Channel," she added.

"Rocking," "eradicating mole crickets from his front yard," "composting pine needles," "living within his means," and even "outsmarting squirrels, and never losing a game of competitive sickness," also tweaked his interest in his later years, Lewis observed.

As to military service, "he also took pride in his service during the Korean conflict, serving the rank of corporal—just like Napoleon, as he would say," Lewis wrote in the obituary.

Lewis acknowledged that her father "took fashion cues from no one." Usually his daily dress was a "plain-pocketed T-shirt designed by the fashion house of Fruit of the Loom. Black-label elastic-waist shorts were worn above the navel and sold exclusively at Sam's on Highway 49. He sported a pair of old-school Wallabees. Yet most will remember his wearing a grass-stained MSU baseball cap," she said.

On his many family vacations, Lewis remembered her father "only stayed in the finest-quality AAA-rated campgrounds, his favorite being Indian Creek outside Cherokee, North Carolina." The avid outdoorsman always upgraded his tent rental to have a creek view. Later in life he would purchase a used pop-up camper for "his family to travel in style, which spoiled his daughters for life," she said.

The obituary concluded by noting that a private, family-only service would be held, because of Stamps' "irrational fear that his family would throw him a golf-themed funeral despite his hatred for the sport." A theme-free funeral was held.

The family urged friends, and colleagues of Stamps to "write your congressman and ask for the repeal of daylight-savings time." Why? Stamps wanted "everyone to get back on the Lord's Time."

Stamps' Obituary Goes Viral

On a very slow news day, the "finely crafted words of this loving tribute" published in the *Sun Herald* quickly spread from one person to another by Facebook postings, tweets, and email, sending the heartwarming obituary viral from Long Beach to all corners of the world, noted Vice President and Executive Editor Stan Tiner in his March 14th column touching on Lewis' "seamless" obituary.

"In the days that followed, the tsunami-like power of the Harry Stamps' obituary washed away records on our website, with only Hurricane Katrina remaining above this viral surge of page views," wrote an amazed Tiner in his column, who noted within days that the company's website recorded a whopping 530,000 page views, with the obituary drawing a considerable part of that traffic. Even the following day, visits exceeded 500,000 page views, he said.

Meanwhile a front-page story in the *Sun Herald* about the previously printed "well-crafted" obituary attracted reader interest in the next days, becoming the newspaper's "all-time single-story record-holder with more than 100,000 page views," added Tiner.

"Untold thousands heralded the late college dean and the perfect obituary. One tweet called him 'the most interesting man in the world,'" stated Tiner in his column, noting that Stamps' "everyman common sense, taste, and humor brought to mind a modern-day Will Rogers."

Yes, Lewis' colorfully-written obituary clearly detailed her father's persona, his spirit and, most certainly, his uniqueness. In life, he chose to march to a different drummer. His family knew this and accepted it. In death, his life story told by his obituary keeps his memory alive in the hearts of his wife, Ann, daughters Amanda and Alison, and to the millions of people, including this columnist, who now know him.

To see the original obituary, go to: **http://goo.gl/9yc3Oy.**

LEGENDARY COWSILLS COME HOME TO BE RECOGNIZED BY THEIR OWN

Published January 25, 2013, in the Pawtucket Times

B ob Cowsill, of Rhode Island's legendary Cowsills, has come full circle in his 40-year musical career. Now living on the West Coast, the nationally-acclaimed musician and his band-member siblings are planning a trip back to their childhood home. On Sunday, April 28th, at the Hope Artiste Village complex in Pawtucket, they will be inducted into the Rhode Island Music Hall of Fame (RIMHOF).

Beginning a Musical Journey

The Cowsills, who play pop and rock 'n' roll, are one of the successful family-musical acts of the 1960s. They grew up just an hour's drive from Pawtucket on Aquidneck Island, where their names are still carved into a tree on the family homestead. The band was founded by four of the Cowsill brothers (Bob, Bill, Barry, and John) in 1965. Within two years, it encompassed nearly the entire family with the addition of brother Paul, sister Susan, and their mother Barbara ("Mini-Mom"). Their father, Bud, became their manager. (Bob's twin brother, Richard, is the only sibling who never joined the band.) The Cowsills later became the creative inspiration for the 1970s television show, *The Partridge Family*, which is still in syndication today.

The Cowsills were the first of the family rock groups, who opened the door for others, said Bob, the eldest of the musical clan. Those following in their footsteps included The Jackson 5 and the Osmonds, who made the switch to rock following the Cowsills' success.

"The family angle just evolved," said Cowsill, stressing that it should not be considered "premeditated." When it became difficult to interest musicians on Aquidneck Island to join the fledgling band, Cowsill noted that it was obvious the younger siblings were the answer to filling the empty slots.

In the mid-1960s, the Cowsills were hired as a regular act on Bannister's Wharf, playing weekly at Dorians in Newport, "at that time a rough Navy town," said Bob.

He noted that the group's first big career break in 1965 came after playing in the basement disco of the MK Hotel at 38 Bellevue Avenue in Newport. From this performance came an invitation to play on the *Today Show*. Their 20-minute performance caught the attention of singer Johnny Nash, and the group signed their first recording contract with his JODA Records label, releasing their first single, "All I Really Want To Be Is Me," in 1965.

America's Musical Family

Cowsill recalled how that first single was pitted against "The Sound of Silence" on a WPRO radio contest. When the votes were tabulated, the Newport band had "won by a landside." To this day, he chuckled when remembering the Cowsills' victory over America's most recognizable musical duo, Simon and Garfunkel.

From the late 1960s into the early 1970s, the Cowsills appeared on many popular television shows, among them: *The Ed Sullivan Show, American Bandstand, The Tonight Show Starring Johnny Carson,* the *Mike Douglas Show,* and the *Johnny Cash Show.* They even hosted their own NBC-TV special called *A Family Thing.*

"Bewilderment," said Cowsill, thinking about their two performances on *The Ed Sullivan Show.* The group had contracted to appear 10 times, which would have put them on Sunday's popular show more times than The Beatles. But a fiasco over a microphone, which was accidentally turned off between Sullivan's son-in-law and Bud Cowsill, resulted in the cancellation of their remaining eight shows, he said.

Before the young Cowsills had their first hit record, they were hired as one of the headliners, along with Ray Charles, Stevie Wonder, The Byrds, and The Beach Boys (all Rock and Roll Hall of Fame inductees) for Soundblast '66 at Yankee Stadium in New York. "We were in pop wonderland. It was just unbelievable. Somehow my father worked magic and got us to Yankee Stadium for this show. We were not famous at the time but apparently good enough to play for the crowd."

Bringing Home the Gold

In 1967, the Cowsills' first MGM release, "The Rain, The Park & Other Things," sold more than one million copies and was awarded a gold record. This song would ultimately reach No. 2 on the "Billboard Hot 100" and No. 1 in *Cash Box* and *Record World.* One year later, the band scored another near-million-selling hit with the song "Indian Lake," reaching No. 10 on the charts. In 1968, the band hit No. 1 again with their version of "Hair," a three-million seller, which brought them a nomination for *16 Magazine*'s Best Group of 1970. "Hair" was banned from Armed Forces Radio Network in Vietnam for being too controversial, noted Cowsill, who stated that, "We were amused at the time because our brother, Richard, who was in Vietnam, reported back that they were playing it everywhere!"

Baby boomers may remember the Cowsills being spokespersons for the American Dairy Association with their "Milk Song," appearing in commercials and their images in print ads promoting milk. Cowsill also noted that his group has been referenced in trivia-game questions and twice was on David Letterman's "Top Ten List."

In 1969, the Cowsills became the first rock group to record a theme for a television show, *Love, American Style*. Their melodic sound has also been featured in movies such as *The Impossible Years* and *Dumb and Dumber*, and other television shows including *The Wonder Years* and *The Simpsons*.

A feature-length film, *Family Band–The Story of The Cowsills*, which documents the rise and fall of the group, is coming to cable television in March. "It will show what really happened in our family band," said Cowsill.

The Cowsills disbanded in the early 1970s, yet most of them have never fully retired from the music business, and various members have regrouped throughout the years.

Cowsill and his siblings John, Susan, and Paul, plus two of the band members' sons, continue to play concerts across the country at casinos, fairs, and music festivals.

Today Cowsill has come full circle in his career. For more than 27 years, the sixty-three-year-old musician played at Pickwick's Pub in Woodland Hills, California, every Friday night, once again performing the songs of The Beatles and The Byrds. During the day, Cowsill coordinates medical conferences across the country, provides medical-coding services to emergency departments, and assists in developing and installing software for use in emergency rooms.

On April 28th, 2013, the Cowsills will be inducted into The Rhode Island Music Hall of Fame along with Steve Smith & The Nakeds, Bobby Hackett, Paul Geremia, Jimmie Crane, Eddie Zack, Sissieretta Jones, George M. Cohan, and Bill Flanagan.

Reflecting on this upcoming recognition, Bob said, "The fact that we are being inducted into RIMHOF and not the Rock and Roll Hall of Fame is more special to us. There is more meaning to us because we are Rhode Islanders to be recognized by our own. It is very cool to go to Pawtucket rather than Cleveland!"

For more information about the Cowsills, to leave a message on the group's guest book or sign a petition to get them inducted into the Rock and Roll Hall of Fame, visit: **www.cowsill.com/home.html**.

LIKE THE ENERGIZER BUNNY, STEVE SMITH & THE NAKEDS KEEP GOING, GOING & GOING

Published April 5, 2013, in the Pawtucket Times

Following months of speculation, The Rolling Stones have announced their upcoming 50th-anniversary tour, leaving many fans in awe of their continued energy, stamina, and staying power. And like the venerable British rockers, Rhode Island's own Steve Smith & The Nakeds, currently celebrating their 40th anniversary, have also proven their staying power as they continue to enjoy a full touring schedule and an ever-growing fan base.

Fondly called simply "The Nakeds" by their legion of fans, this band of middle-aged musicians operate just like the Energizer Bunny; They keep going, and going, and going...

The band began in 1973 as Naked Truth and Steve Smith, and the 62 other guys who have passed through the band's ranks are among just a handful of Rhode Island musicians who can claim that milestone. (They became The Nakeds in 1981 to avoid confusion with a Long Island band also called Naked Truth; the word "truth" remains with them to this day "hidden" within their logo.)

In recognition of their success and their impact on the Rhode Island music scene, on Sunday, April 28, 2013, Steve Smith & The Nakeds will be among the nine new inductees into the Rhode Island Music Hall of Fame (RIMHOF).

The Younger Years

Looking back, Smith clearly remembers a Saturday-night tradition in his family—a musical talent show—when he and others would perform in front of the refrigerator. The 61-year-old's singing career began at his family-built seaside retreat on Carpenter's Beach in scenic Matunuck, Rhode Island, where as a 4 year old, he would sing Pat Boone's "Love Letters in the Sand" to his family and friends.

At the tender age of 7, Smith's father, recognizing his son's growing vocal range, enrolled him in classical voice training. In 1964, the elder Smith, a traveling salesman who loved to listen to the radio while on the road, knew talent when he heard it and gave his teenage son a newly released album, *Meet the Beatles*, and told him,

"These guys are gonna be great, and I want you to listen to them." His father's sage advice ultimately led young Smith to form his first band with his cousin John Cafferty. The newly formed rock group of junior high students, The Nightcrawlers, would go on to win a Battle of the Bands contest held in Smithfield area in the late 1960s, beating out several established and seasoned college-age bands. (Steve's cousin John would find fame in the 1980s with his band Beaver Brown's score for the motion picture *Eddie and The Cruisers*.)

The Long Journey

Looking back, Smith, a 1973 graduate of Providence College, never thought he would still be performing in his 60s. As the group's band leader recently noted, "We figured we would keep playing as long as the phone kept ringing." And that it did!

During the band's early years, Smith remarks that business was booming. He had a jam-packed calendar of bookings at concerts, clubs, and special events. However, in 1984, lawmakers reinstated the 21-year-old drinking age, and the band saw its bookings dwindle. "We went from playing seven days a week to only performing on weekends," he said.

But Smith would put his hard-earned college education in graphic design to very good use, a career that would ultimately help him to survive the lean economic times.

According to the lifelong Smithfield resident, his band's longevity and success was tied to the "high caliber of the musicians who played in the group" throughout its four decades. Smith's strong vocals, combined with a five-piece horn section and a guitar, keyboards, bass and drums rhythm section, gave The Nakeds their own unique style of rock 'n' roll and rhythm & blues.

The Nakeds fame began to spread after the release of their first album in 1984, *Coming To A Theatre Near You*, and they appeared on MTV's "Basement Tapes." They signed on with Miller Beer's "Rock Network" promotion as one of the best unsigned bands in the country and were featured on a RCA Records compilation album.

Over the years, Smith and the band often shared the stage with Bruce Springsteen's saxophonist, the late Clarence Clemons, mounting a series of critically acclaimed national tours which included a 1994 appearance with President Bill Clinton at his health rally at Liberty State Park in New Jersey. Clarence and another E Street band member, Nils Lofgren, contributed heavily to the band's best-selling 2000 album, *Never Say Never*.

In 2009, the band's 1984 indie hit, "I'm Huge (and the Babes Go Wild)" was featured on the DVD for the sixth season of *The Family Guy*. The often-controversial Fox Network cartoon, which takes place in the fictitious town of Quahog, Rhode Island, would immortalize the group when a YouTube posting of the video went viral and the group was offered a Sony Records deal. The *I'm Huge* album, a best-of compilation from their earlier releases, became the biggest-selling album of their career. The video remains a fan favorite and is approaching 400,000 views.

Steve Smith & The Nakeds will take their place among Rhode Island's musical greats when they are inducted on April 28th into the Rhode Island Music Hall of Fame as members of the Class of 2013. RIMHOF Vice Chair and Archive Director Rick Bellaire has this to say about the band: "With a new album, *Under The Covers*, just out and a full schedule of shows on the horizon, there's no doubt in my mind that The Nakeds will be around to help us celebrate the Class of 2023 during their 50th anniversary tour! We are extremely proud to honor them with this induction, and they are stoked to pull out all the stops for their induction concert on the 28th."

Introducing the Other 2013 Inductees:

In announcing RIMHOF's Class of 2013, Bellaire notes that "sometimes it's easy to forget, and it may be hard to believe, that such world-acclaimed artists actually have roots right here in Rhode Island just like the rest of us."

Bellaire says, "For the smallest state, Rhode island has produced an inordinately large number of truly great, successful, and important artists," and that their devoted local fans helped to place them on the world stage.

Bellaire adds some of his thoughts about the other new RIMHOF inductees:

Cowsills—A family band in the truest sense of the term – six siblings and their mom! They sang their way out of Newport all the way to the top of the charts.

George M. Cohan—The pivotal figure in the development of the modern Broadway theater tradition grew up in Fox Point.

Sissieretta Jones—One of the greatest sopranos in the history of modern opera head-quartered and managed her career from Pratt Street on the East Side of Providence.

Bill Flanagan—A guy from Warwick who went from writing about music in all of our local papers to editing Musician Magazine and then became the vice-president of MTV and VH-1, but continued to promote and advocate for Rhode Island music along the way.

Jimmie Crane—From the 1950s through the '70s, he wrote a long string of huge hit songs for such stars as Eddie Fisher, Doris Day, and Elvis Presley, all the while maintaining a successful jewelry manufacturing business in his hometown of Providence and assisting dozens of up-and-coming musicians.

Bobby Hacket—Bobby was born on Federal Hill, but spent most of his youth in Olneyville where the action really was: Jake E. Conn's Olympia Theatre and Petteruti's

Twin City Music store. He became one of the greatest—and most acclaimed—improvisors in the history of jazz.

Eddie Zack & The Hayloft Jamboree—The Zackarian family of Providence virtually introduced country & western music into Rhode Island and the Northeast at large, recording for Decca and Columbia Records and broadcasting nationwide on the NBC radio network, but always maintained their home and headquarters right here in Rhode Island.

Paul Geremia—The world-acclaimed acoustic artist, who has not only helped keep the folk-blues tradition alive, but has brought it into the modern era with his unique guitar style and voice, grew up in Silver Lake!

"As the organization grows," RIMHOF Chair Robert Billington says, "the Hall of Fame will be committed to developing programs and services aimed at promoting and strengthening Rhode Island's musical heritage and ensuring that music continues to play an important role in the lives of all Rhode Islanders."

9. RELATIONSHIPS

DOCUMENTARY TAKES A LOOK AT SPEED DATING FOR SENIORS

Published August 9, 2014, in the Pawtucket Times

Three years ago, a personal story would lead filmmaker Steven Loring to zero in on a topic for his MFA thesis film while studying at the Social Documentary Film Program in the NYU's School of Visual Arts. His thesis ultimately grew into a 78-minute documentary, "The Age of Love," which follows the adventures of 30 seniors who sign up for a speed-dating event exclusively for 70- to 90-year-olds. The film premieres at the Rhode Island International Film Festival, Sunday, August 10, at 12:15 p.m. at the Paff Theatre at URI, 80 Washington Street, Providence. And there's a special offer for anyone who comes to the box office with a date: When you buy one ticket, your date gets in FREE! Any date! Any age!

The story took shape after the passing away of Loring's father in 2008 left his still-vibrant mother alone after being married to her soul mate for nearly half a century. At that same time, his 80-year-old uncle, who'd never even dated, to Loring's amazement suddenly fell madly in love with an 80-year-old woman, both acting like love-struck teenagers.

"It was like they were in high school again," Loring says, noting that the couple walked around holding hands and that he even found their bedroom door shut when he visited.

These events pushed the Brooklyn-based filmmaker to take a look at relationships in one's later years. His research efforts revealed that the nation's media had neglected issues involving seniors' emotional and intimate needs. On the Internet, he found that speed dating for seniors was a newly emerging trend, which had occurred in a few communities in Florida and Colorado. Ultimately, a speed-dating event in Rochester, New York, would give him the perfect place to explore, document, and come away with new insights into the issue.

Loring's efforts to reconcile two dynamically opposite life experiences, losing a long-term intimate relationship and suddenly finding one at an advanced age, led the graduate student to finally formulate this thesis question, "Do decades of life and loss constrict our hearts, or might time develop them in unexpected ways?" That's the question the 51-year-old filmmaker attempts to answer in his film project.

Speed Dating for Seniors

Loring's documentary, a winner of the 2013 Paley Center DocFest Pitch Competition and recently awarded a prestigious Fledgling Fund social engagement grant, follows the amusing and emotional adventures of the seniors who signed up for the Rochester speed-dating event, which was organized by a "healthy aging" coalition to bring new social opportunities to the older community. The trendy matchmaking process allowed these individuals to meet for a brief five minutes. When the time was up the organizer sounded a bell, signaling participants to move on to the next table. Each kept a tally of those they would like to contact later. If both parties were interested in each other, a follow-up date would occur.

According to Loring, as a result of the heavy promotion of this unique event, combined with the intense local media buzz, "dozens of area seniors called to register, all willing to put themselves out there, to take stock of their aging bodies and still-hopeful hearts."

"The film takes viewers where no documentary has gone before – directly into the lives of older singles who still yearn to be seen and understood, who still desire another's touch, who seek a new chance of love," says Loring. Unlike other recent documentaries exploring issues of aging, the filmmaker saw an " opportunity to break social and generational barriers by looking at the older participants not in terms of singular talents or specific communities, but through shared human desires."

For three months, Loring filmed without a crew. He was able to easily develop personal relationships with the senior speed daters "allowing candid stories to emerge by following their everyday routines," he says.

Looking To Find That Perfect Match

Loring notes that some participants came seeking simple companionship, while others came looking for that special mate. Among the speed daters who appear in the film: An 81-year-old bodybuilding champ, divorced since his 50s, who still believes new love is possible; a widow who skydives and dulls her loss by pursuing younger men; a grandmother and online-dating addict searching the web for Mr. Right; a romantic 79-year-old who discards his portable oxygen for a sunset tango on the beach; a 1940s movie fanatic who escaped an abusive marriage, yet still seeks her "Fred and Ginger" romance.

Janice Ledtke, 78, a resident of Webster, New York, a suburb of Rochester, remembers making the decision to participate in speed dating. After 38 years of being single following her divorce in 1976, she jumped at the chance to meet new people. "What did I have to lose?" says Ledtke, a former property management employee, who met dates over the years at singles groups or through being fixed up by friends.

"You never know who you just might meet," remembers Ledtke noting when her friends found out about her participation in the speed-dating event and documentary, "they thought I was crazy, but it's just another one of my adventures."

Ledtke says she met a variety of personalities at the speed-dating event. But her follow-up dates with a filmmaker, a retired professor, and an owner of a small insurance company went nowhere. "I was not necessarily looking to find the love of my life, but if it happened, it happened," she adds, stressing that it was not the end of the world because she came away with a number of new friends.

Linda Sorrendino, 72, had many long-term relationships since her 1973 divorce. "I have many diamonds to prove this," quips the resident of Victor, New York. Over the years, like Ledtke, she would meet people by attending singles groups or through friends.

Learning from a friend about the speed-dating event, Sorrendino, a retired office clerk, immediately signed up. "You just never know." As to landing a relationship, "you just go with the flow," she remarks.

As Sorrendino reflects on her speed-dating experience and her late-life relationships, she notes, "I don't want to be with a decrepit old man, but I also don't want to be with somebody a lot younger who looks better than I do and feels like he's with an old lady."

A Final Thought...

"The film's message is so positive and encouraging," said AARP Rhode Island State Director Kathleen Connell. "Watching these folks surely will make it easier for others to re-enter the dating scene. At the same time, there is a subtext that is very important: No one featured in the documentary seems desperate. Each has found a way to move on from divorce or loss of a spouse or partner. Will they find their storybook ending? I think the film makes it clear that there are no promises. But there's a strong message that giving love another chance is not so intimidating – especially if you find an organized group that puts you among people of similar age and circumstance."

"The documentary also will reveal to its broader audience that the desire for companionship and intimacy does not evaporate at some advanced specific age," Connell added. "These feelings are not always easy for people to discuss with their children or grandchildren. It's great people get to see these folks take part in the speed-dating experience because in the accompanying interviews they reveal hopes and fears many hold inside. But I love the takeaway: 'If something happens, that's great. If not, I'll still be okay.'"

Loring plans to work with AARP and other "healthy aging" organizations across the country to bring older adults together in 25 cities next year at senior speed-dating events. For more information go to **theageoflovemovie.com/story/** or email **steven@theAgeofLoveMovie.com**

INTERNET SEX SURVEY SHEDS LIGHT ON WHAT'S "NORMAL" IN RELATIONSHIPS

Published February 8, 2013, in the Pawtucket Times

J ust after the little blue tablet, Viagra, endorsed in television commercials by former Senate majority leader and U.S. presidential contender Bob Dole in the late 1990s, the prescription wonder drug for those with erectile dysfunction in later life literally became the talk of the town.

We began to talk more openly about our sexuality, joking about the miraculous powers of drugs like Viagra, Cialis, and Levitra, probably with the intent to relieve our personal discomfort on the taboo topic of sex.

Yet even today, this columnist still hears snickers from those who believe that older persons are asexual and that sex is of no interest to them in their twilight years. It's a myth, experts say, their observations supported by a recently published book and a decade's worth of AARP studies on sexual attitudes and practices.

Creating a New Normal for Your Relationship

Based on data obtained on the Internet from nearly 70,000 respondents from the United States and around the world (with significant numbers of returns from China, Spain, Italy, France, England, Australia, Philippines, Hungary, Brazil, and Canada), last Wednesday Random House released *The Normal Bar: The Surprising Secrets of Happy Couples and What They Reveal About Creating a New Normal in Your Relationship.*

Pepper Schwartz, Ph.D., the "love and relationship ambassador" for AARP and a sociologist who teaches at University of Washington, and her co-authors, wellness entrepreneur Christiane Northrup, M.D., and James Witte, Ph.D., a sociologist who serves as director of the Center for Social Science Research at George Mason University, teamed up to design a unique interactive Internet survey that would draw relationship data from around the world.

The researchers partnered with AARP, America Online, the *Huffington Post*, and *Reader's Digest*, who encouraged tens of thousands to take the project's innovative Internet survey.

Dr. Schwartz and her co-researchers took a look at what constitutes "normal" behavior among happy couples and outlined which steps you should take if that "normal" is one you want to strive for. They believe their study gives the "clearest picture yet of how well couples are communicating, romancing each other, satisfying each other in the bedroom, sharing financial responsibilities, and staying faithful," she said.

Because *The Normal Bar* survey methodology sorts for age, gender, racial, and geographic differences as well as sexual preferences, the authors were able to reveal, for example, what happens to passion as we grow older, which gender wants what when it comes to sex, the factors that spur marital combat, how children figure in, how being gay or bisexual turns out to be both different and the same and, regardless of background, those tiny habits that drive partners absolutely batty.

The book provides revelations to the reader, from the unexpected popularity of certain sexual positions to the average number of times happy and unhappy couples kiss, to the prevalence of lying, to the surprising loyalty most men and women feel for their partner (even in a deteriorating relationship) to the vivid and idiosyncratic ways individuals of different ages, genders, and nationalities describe their "ideal romantic evening."

Much more than a peek behind the relationship curtain, *The Normal Bar* offers readers an array of prescriptive tools that will help them establish a "new normal" in their relationship. Mindful of what keeps couples stuck in ruts, the book's authors suggest practical and life-changing ways for couples to break cycles of disappointment and frustration.

AARP Article Zeroes In on Older Couples

The Normal Bar survey findings in this recently released book, drawn from responses of 8,000 survey respondents who are over age 50, were published in the February/March issue of *AARP The Magazine,* in an article by Northrup, Schwartz, and Witte, entitled "Sex at 50+: What's Normal?" Among the findings reported in this AARP article:

Thirty-two percent of men and 48 percent of women do not hug their partner in public. The researchers believe that public displays of affection (PDA) positively impact relationships. Sixty-eight percent who show PDA are unhappy or slightly happy with their partner. A whopping 73 percent of the happiest couples can't keep their hands off each other in public and do so at least once a month.

Meanwhile, 78 percent of the couples admit they hold hands at least some of the time. However, it seems to be the younger pairs, because among all the couples who have been together for more than 10 years, more than half say they no longer hold hands.

"I love you," just three little words said often may just spice up your relationship. The researchers found that among the happiest couples, 85 percent of both men and woman said those words at least once a week. It's a male thing: More than 90 percent of men regularly tell their partner "I love you," while only 58 percent of the women do so.

The researchers found that 74 percent of the happiest couples will give their partner a passionate smooch. Thirty-eight percent of all age-50-plus couples do not passionately kiss. Kissing can be the connector between each partner, noted the researchers.

Thirty-one percent of the aging baby-boomer couples have sex several times a week while only 28 percent have sex a couple of times a month. About eight percent have sex just once a month.

Forty-seven percent of women regularly praise their partner's appearance in comparison with 55 percent of men. The study's findings reveal that praise is important for a couple's happiness.

Thirty-two percent of the couples give a thumbs-down to date nights. Eighty-eight percent of the happiest couples spend time alone together. The researchers recommended that you go out twice a month to "maintain the sense of closeness."

Thirty-three percent of the respondents report they rarely or never have sex. However, even among the happiest couples, a whopping one-quarter doesn't do it.

Dr. Schwartz believes the most important observation made from the study is that sexuality is important throughout one's life span. "People have to take care of their relationship and not put it on automatic pilot," she said.

Bringing Sexuality Out of the Closet

With the graying of America's population, it is time to bring senior sexuality out of the closet. We must accept the fact that sexuality continues throughout the human life span and encompasses more than just intimate sexual intercourse. It also includes cuddling, a tender kiss, a light touch on the shoulder or holding hands, as noted in *The Normal Bar*.

A well-known song, "As Time Goes By," reminds us sexuality is to be experienced by both young and old. "You must remember this, a kiss is just a kiss, a sigh is just a sigh, the fundamental things apply, as time goes by."

For more info about *The Normal Bar*, to take the survey or to purchase the book, go to **www.thenormalbar.com**.

REAL ROLE MODELS
FLY UNDER THE RADAR SCREEN

Published August 24, 2012, in the Pawtucket Times

A s we go through our life stages, we are attracted to "role models" or people we look up to—"mentors" as they are commonly referred to. They are the individuals who possess the correct attributes and specific traits we hope to emulate—a person we admire and respect.

Children growing up or those having reached their middle years may look up to and view their parents as that "perfect" role model. Others may see redeeming qualities they try to imitate in entertainment celebrities, professional athletes, successful business entrepreneurs, or religious and ethical figures.

I found myself stumped when I was recently asked who my role model was as I responded to a "Power Player" questionnaire by **www.Golocalprov.com**. I never looked up to any individual in the celebrity, sports, or even political cultures.

Influential People in My Life

As I pondered this question, there were a few people that came to mind.

Of course I thought of my father, Frank Weiss, who had a great impact on my life. He taught me the importance of using a business network in my profession. While the Dallas businessman raised money to fund cancer-research projects and other worthy causes, I, as economic and cultural affairs officer, try to do the same, such as working to support the city's annual Pawtucket Arts Festival.

Then there was Fred Levy, a former U.S. Army intelligence officer during World War II, who was also a fabric salesman and writer. When I was a young man, Levy was my neighbor and a man for whom I had great respect. He might be a likely candidate for my role model. Levy gave me advice on how to become a better writer during my early professional years. He juggled his job, writing, and was also a full-time caregiver to his adult daughter, Faye, who was bedridden with multiple sclerosis. He was an inspiration to me. He read my published articles and encouraged me to continue writing.

More recently in my present work, I thought of my former boss, Planning Director Michael Cassidy. He was a role model to me—teaching me the value of tenaciousness. He looked at all the bureaucratic and political angles to accomplish his planning goals.

While it took him 10 years to get the city's skateboard park up and running, it took me seven years to see my project, the Pawtucket Dog Park, come to fruition. Yet it happened.

While my father, my neighbor, and former boss all taught me valuable lessons in life, I realized that the most influential person in my life was an 82-year-old, semi-retired man right here in my Pawtucket community.

Being an Advocate for the Voiceless

Like the "Energizer Bunny" with gray whiskers and a plump belly, Pawtucket businessman Paul Audette has always been an advocate for the "voiceless" in the City of Pawtucket and the surrounding communities.

Watching out for the elderly, he became a volunteer "ombudsman" for the Alliance for Better Long-Term Care. Paul even served as chairman of the Pawtucket Affirmative Action Committee to ensure that everyone had equal opportunities in municipal government. He has worked for decades assisting those who are down-and-out, even providing them financial assistance out of his pocket, to help them navigate the state's regulatory process.

Paul has long ties to many of the city's nonprofit groups including the Pawtucket Arts Collaborative, the Pawtucket Armory Association, the Foundry Artists, the Pawtucket Fireworks Committee, the Pawtucket Preservation Society and the Pawtucket Arts Festival, just to name a few groups. He has even been active bringing his expertise as a property manager and developer to assist the Pawtucket Planning Department to streamline the city's building-permit process.

Paul cofounded a nonprofit group called Helping Hands and has provided financial assistance to local organizations that help youth at risk, the helpless and homeless. Since 2006, Helping Hands has given donations to 37 organizations including Crossroads, Pawtucket Boys and Girls Club, Dana Farber Cancer Institute, Pawtucket Salvation Army, and the American Cancer Society.

Paul did not learn the ropes about business by attending any of the Ivy League schools, but instead learned the tricks of the trade by working. For more than 50 years, his hard work landed him senior-level positions for major corporations including Dunkin' Donuts, in addition to serving as "special assistant" to the president of Providence Metalizing, working in the personnel department as well as managing its properties and taking on special projects as assigned.

This local businessman even ran one of the larger catering companies in Rhode Island, catering more than 300 weddings and 10,000 functions over the years. His corporate and nonprofit clients include widely recognized organizations in the Ocean State, including Hasbro, Hospital Trust, La Salle Academy, Bay View Academy, and Swank.

Exemplifying the Rotary International's motto "Service Above Self," Paul has been a member of the Pawtucket Rotary Club since 1999 and was recognized and awarded the prestigious Paul Harris Award, the highest recognition that the national civic group bestows upon an individual.

Throughout one's lifetime you might have many role models who inspire, teach, and give you a road map to overcome obstacles in your personal life and professional career. Yet sometimes the more important ones are those individuals who are not so visible or obvious, like those reported in surveys reported by the nation's media—the celebrities, professional athletes, or beloved religious figures, yet rather that person in your community whose mere existence quietly impacts you as well as a community.

The most important role model in your life may well be that person flying under the radar screen, seeking to help others—one person at a time—giving of himself or herself without seeking public notice.

For me, my mentor is Paul Audette.

WHEN DEATH COMETH TO MAN'S BEST FRIEND

Published November 23, 2012, in the Pawtucket Times

Like many of my fellow aging baby boomers who are childless or empty nesters, I am a pet owner. Over the years, my pets have evolved into pampered little "children" and have become my "faithful companions." However, when death comes to our furry, four-legged friends, coping with the death can make even the most Spock-like "intellectual" person shed rivers of tears and become emotionally unraveled.

The End Is Near

The early-Sunday-morning call from our Seekonk-based veterinary clinic delivered a message we were not prepared to hear. We were told that "Murray's temperature had soared to 105 degrees, and his system was beginning to shut down." It was no longer regulating the insulin for our 13-year-old diabetic chocolate labrador, or trying to find a cure for the sudden onset of arthritis that reduced his movements to a painful crawl. The doctor recommended we come down to the office as soon as possible to end Murray's suffering.

Just two days earlier, concern with Murray's declining health led us to take him to our longtime veterinarian for a blood-glucose check. Maybe our diabetic dog's blood sugar was not under control. We suspected that his sugar was off. Adjusting the amount of insulin he received twice a day would be an easy fix to these sudden medical problems. Or perhaps the new medicine prescribed to reduce his arthritic pain would finally kick in and make it easier for him to walk again. Our faithful, frail pet was blind from cataracts and was well into his 90s, if you calculated his age in terms of human years.

Saying good-bye to the beings in your life that you love does not come easily.

Traveling to the vet's office, we drove in silence. Tears flowed as we drove past each memorable landmark, while flashbacks of fond memories brought me back to happier days over the past decade. In my mind's eye, I watched a young Murray chase a bouncing, yellow tennis ball in my backyard or saw him take a belly-dive in the Slater Park pond when no one was looking to chase the resident swans or Canadian geese. These memories always put a smile on my face.

For 13 years, Murray, our "little boy," gave us comfort. He was always by our side. Now the time had come to put him down. On June 5, 2011, in the sparse examining room, we approached Murray, lying uncomfortably on top of a floor scale cushioned by an old blanket. He was panting with his eyes fixed straight ahead. I noticed the portal injected in his back leg, ready to accept the lethal dose. In a matter of seconds, as soon as I gave the doctor the OK, she would begin the medical procedure to put my pet out of his pain.

My wife, Patty, and her son, Ben, tearfully bent over, saying their good-byes, stroking Murray to make sure he knew he was not alone. Stroking his face, I whispered one last "good boy." With tears rolling down my cheeks, I knew it was time to end his suffering. Calling for the lethal pink drug led to a quick injection of that deadly substance. Within seconds, our chocolate labrador lay motionless on the blanket.

Murray's collar, plastic water bowl, worn black leash, chewy toys, and a few old photographs are the tangible items that remind us of his existence as a member of our family. Yet the memories are plentiful. While grieving his loss, those special times swiftly came back to me from over the years: his backseat rides in our car with his head hanging out the window, or saying the name "Sheba," our neighbor's female Yellow Labrador, which brought him to the window to look across the street at her house, and how he warmly accepted the adoption of a rescue dog, Abby, into our household. We adopted the younger chocolate labrador from the Paul J. Wildenhain Memorial Animal Shelter.

A pet's death, as my wife, Patty, and I recently experienced, has the same emotional impact as the loss of a parent, sibling, or even a close friend. However, we seemed to cope with this loss quickly, yet for many it often takes months or even years to heal. Some have even told me that they would never adopt or purchase another dog or cat because of the intense, emotional pain and trauma they experienced.

Murray was cremated, and his ashes have been placed in a wooden box, which sits on the fireplace mantle in our living room. Someday we plan to bury his ashes in his favorite stomping ground: our backyard. When this occurs, sitting outside on cool summer nights, Patty and I will surely remember our beloved chocolate lab, Murray.

Grieving Over Your Loss

My family and pet owners worldwide know it's painful to lose your pet, often considered to be one of the family. It even took a while for our grieving dog, Abby, to begin to normally eat her food. Sometimes she still walks the house wondering where her companion is, sniffing out areas that still have his scent.

Moira Anderson Allen, M. Ed., author of *Coping with Sorrow on the Loss of Your Pet*, states on her website that intense grief over the loss of your pet is both "normal and natural." While some people may not understand your strong emotional bond to your pet and pain after the pet dies, "all that matters is how you feel," Allen said.

According to Allen, grieving pet owners can also express their feelings and memories of their deceased pet in poems, stories, and letters to the pet. While feeling the loss, the person may feel guilt for not doing enough or denial of the death and anger at the veterinarian who failed to save the pet. Grieving can also cause depression.

Allen recommended, "Don't deny your pain and grief, and acknowledge your feelings." She recommended that a grieving pet owner work through feelings with family and friends, the veterinarian, or ask a local humane association to recommend a pet-loss counselor or support group. (For more information about pet loss, go to Allen's website, Pet Loss Support Page, at **www.pet-loss.net**).

As we grieve, life gets busy with the day-to-day activities of living, strangely healing our pain. Yet we will always remember Murray, the best dog and companion we have had in our more than five-plus decades of living.

10. RETIREMENT & LEISURE

ANTIQUING: A GREAT LEISURE ACTIVITY FOR BABY BOOMERS

Published June 29, 2012, in the *Pawtucket Times.*

When furnishing a home, some might be drawn to Scandinavian design at IKEA Stores. Personal taste and a love for traditional-design furniture might bring others to Ethan Allen. For those who like the more contemporary look, the Martha Stewart Furniture Collection may simply be their cup of tea.

However, for baby boomers Scott and Rae Davis, owners of Rhode Island's largest antique mall, antiques are the way to go when furnishing your home. For college students, young families, baby boomers, and even the retired, buying antiques can be a perfect solution to decorating your residence.

At 50, Scott Davis was an antique hobbyist for half his life before he opened up Rhode Island Antique Mall in Pawtucket. His love for antiques is apparent. When asked, he quickly said that "antiques make a house a home with their warmth, character, and charm." More important, the Pawtucket businessman said that antiques will hold their value or appreciate compared with new furnishings that begin losing value immediately upon purchase.

Antiquing can provide hours of entertainment, especially in winter and on rainy days. Antique-hunting can be a relaxing and enjoyable way to pass time without experiencing high-pressure salesmen or encountering large crowds while shopping at malls or large furniture stores, Davis said.

Today's furniture is not built to last a lifetime, Scott said. "Antiques were crafted to last generations, unlike today's foreign, imported products, carelessly made from particle board and drywall screws. "Antiques almost always become family heirlooms, he said. "New items rarely do," he observed.

"Antiques impart a pride of ownership that is rarely equaled by new items, especially those imported from Asia," Davis said.

Davis rattled off a long list of other reasons for people to consider antiquing as the way to go to when decorating a house. "Antiques teach us about history and preserve our heritage. They are also 'green' and help preserve our natural resources: the ultimate form of recycling," he said.

Antiques almost always cost far less than their new counterparts, Davis said. As an investment, antiques can even be considered assets by financial institutions and can become a significant part of one's wealth-building strategy.

The ABCs of Antiquing

According to Davis, finding the right antiques for your décor may well depend on where and how you shop. When visiting small, independent shops, you will usually get personalized service and advice yet sacrifice the variety and selection found in a larger establishment. Group shops or "antique malls" offer a greater selection with lower prices because dealers within the mall must compete with one another.

For those who go antiquing, the shopping experience is half the fun. Davis recommended that shoppers frequent shops that are enjoyable to be in (lighting, music, and air-conditioning). "Choose shops with a good reputation that have easy access, parking, and reliable hours. Small and out-of-the-way shops can be frustrating to find and disappointing once you get there," he said, adding that their hours and inventory can be inconsistent.

Why not map an antiquing route and spend the day shopping? Antique shops usually congregate near one another.

Davis cautioned antique shoppers to be wary of flea markets and auctions. Antiques found at these places often have hidden problems, and the sellers can be less than reputable, he warned. Avoid shops, especially those in "tourist traps" that sell reproductions because many times the "repros" are misrepresented as authentic or not clearly marked as reproductions.

Finding that Perfect Antique

Don't buy antiques from just anybody, warned Davis. Always seek advice from reputable dealers you can trust. Follow your gut and avoid advice from amateurs, he said.

When shopping, also buy things that you like. "Don't be swayed by others to purchase items you won't want to live with," Davis added. "Most important, buy the best you can afford. One exceptional piece will hold value better than 10 common pieces."

Davis said mixing and matching is the way to go when furnishing your home. "Don't be afraid to mix antique furnishings with new things. They'll work great together," he said, adding that new, upholstered furniture is brought to life when complemented with antique tables and cabinets.

He also recommended the Internet and books as keys to educate yourself about the world of antiques. "Today there are thousands of books and websites on every subject imaginable. Going on eBay can be a great way to learn about antiques and their values, but be careful when buying online." Davis noted: "Deals that seem to be too good to be true usually are."

Davis also warned shoppers to beware of reproductions, fakes, undisclosed repairs, and, "marriages" (mismatched parts). They are becoming increasingly common. "Avoid purchasing items like iron doorstops, mechanical banks, Asian artifacts, and other commonly reproduced items, unless you have a high level of knowledge in the field." Most of these on today's market are fakes, so buy them only from a dealer you can trust.

If You Love It, Haggle

If you like something you see, buy it while you can, Davis recommended. Haggle on price when appropriate. "Most dealers will accept offers of five percent to possibly 20 percent under their ticket price on higher-priced items, usually depending on what they paid for the piece," he said, or at least they will counteroffer. "Dealers want to sell yet replacing the sold items is becoming more difficult, so be reasonable."

Remember, good antiques sell very quickly and will likely not be there the next time you visit.

For more information, contact Scott Davis at RI Antiques Mall. Go to **www.riantiques-mall.com** or email **RIAntiquesMall@cox.net**.

CHILDHOOD PASSION FOR GARDENING BLOOMS IN RETIREMENT

Published June 21, 2013, in the Pawtucket Times

L ooking back more than 60 years ago, Michael Chute smiled when he remembered how a childhood hobby has firmly taken root in his retirement years. After 34 years, Michael and his wife, Angelina, closed their Pawtucket-based sign shop near McCoy Stadium in 2012. Now the retired couple makes use of their combined green thumbs, love, and knowledge of rose gardening, spreading the gospel of growing the perfect, healthy and attractive rose through their speaking engagements before garden clubs and in their writing in a blog, newsletters, and even a book.

Childhood passions can be reignited in later years, according to Michael. "When anyone is introduced to gardening or even sports or reading for pleasure, or art or writing at a very early age, it will stick with them for the rest of their lives." So true.

A Child's Chance Encounter

In the early 1950s, Michael's chance encounter with a "neighborhood dad" in his quiet Pinecrest neighborhood would ultimately lead to his lifelong hobby and passion for gardening. From this meeting, the 5-year-old child would take home a bit of knowledge about how to grow plants. Michael started his own small garden with a few leftover radish seeds given to him by the older man.

Michael said that tiny seedlings soon appeared from watering his seeds every day. "How else could those hard, little brown seeds turn into tiny green plants?" he wondered, believing that it must be the result of magic. His mother nodded when he told her this, agreeing with the child's assessment.

He began making daily trips to visit his "gardening mentor." Michael learned more about the basics of gardening, his new hobby. "I learned that tomatoes, corn, beans, squash, Ralph Kramden, Ike, and DeSotos were good; and that weeds, woodchucks, no rain, stray cats, slugs, grubs, and the Yankees were bad," he said.

The budding gardener ultimately learned to tell the difference between good bugs and bad ones. Even at his young age, Michael would realize that using horse manure, "gardener's gold," was one way to separate real gardeners from fakes. Lugging his bucketful of nature's fertilizer to his home, he dragged it right into the kitchen, saying, "Hey Ma, look what I've got." The "gardener's gold" went right out the back door, he said, because of his mother's stern command.

The radish seedlings were now six inches high in the backyard. He yanked one out, brushed off the dirt, and popped it into his mouth. Beginning to chew, the "incredibly sharp intensity of bitter flavor that only comes from very fresh radishes assaulted my tender tongue," he remembered. This resulted in his eyes watering and his ears ringing. He promptly spit out the radish.

Even with memories of eating the foul-tasting radish, the youngster continued to garden, learning the principles of germination. In time, he worked his own backyard garden. Over the years flowers, especially roses, have replaced the vegetable patch of his youth and middle years.

Michael would meet his wife, Angelina, a Newport native, at the library. She was a URI student who expressed little interest in gardening. The young couple, in their early 20s, married in 1971. One year later, they moved into their newly purchased ranch-style home in Riverside. The young man, remembering his childhood training, began to grow and harvest tomatoes, green peppers, eggplant, string beans, and even strawberries, plucked from his quarter-acre garden plot.

"I grew them; she cooked them," he said.

Michael's modest backyard garden steadily grew in size over 20 years with his renewed interest in gardening. Gradually his three rose bushes increased in number and would replace his tomato plants. Today the couple has grown hundreds of rose varieties in their backyard, even digging up their front yard six years ago and turning it into a trial area for gardening without pesticides, picking off pests by hand.

As to his philosophy of growing rose bushes in his home garden, "each rose bush gets two seasons to please me. If not, good-bye," he said, noting that he has only so many holes in the garden, and there is great competition for admission.

According to Michael, in the early 1990s, the URI Master Gardeners asked him to speak about roses at a meeting. Other speaking engagements followed for the couple. The flower-show bookings followed in the late 1990s, and the Chutes began traveling throughout New England and New York to spread the gospel about rose gardening. When Michael and his wife joined rose societies, they made new friends, yet also gained opportunities to share their growing knowledge about rose gardening with these individuals.

Nationally Recognized in the Rose Business

Today the Chutes are co-owners of RoseSolutions, a landscape-consulting company that offers educational programs, workshops, seminars, and consulting services o rose horticulture. They are both certified American Rose Society Consulting Rosarians and University of Rhode Island Master Gardeners. Michael is an accredited ARS horticultural rose judge. They served as guest editors of the American Rose Society 2008 Annual, wrote the chapter "Roses" in the University of Rhode Island Sustainable Gardening Manual, and are co-founders and past presidents of the Rhode Island Rose Society.

The Riverside couple maintain an active schedule of lectures and workshops through-out New England, including the Boston Flower & Garden Show, the Rhode Island Spring Flower & Garden Show, the Newport Flower Show, and the University of Rhode Island Symposium and Tower Hill Botanic Garden. They were recently featured on *Rose Chat Radio*, a nationally-broadcast Internet radio program.

Publishing the Definitive Book on Growing Roses

"From our many lectures on rose gardening, it became apparent to us from the same questions we got, that home gardeners wanted to grow roses, but did not know how," said Michael. "There was no definitive book specifically addressing rose gardening in New England," he added, noting that not even an easy-to-follow, well-written, hands-on guide to sustainable rose gardening (gardening without the use of pesticides) was on the market.

"There was a niche we needed to fill," Michael said.

Ultimately years of gardening experience would be detailed in a self-published book, *Roses for New England: A Guild to Sustainable Rose Gardening*. The idea of writing a book on rose gardening in New England initially came from people attending the Chutes' workshops, who requested their handouts. They recommended the handouts be compiled into a book.

It took the couple more than four years to write their first book, which was published by Forbes River Publishing in 2010. Four years earlier, they had vacationed in Sugar Loaf Mountain in Maine. During a blizzard that kept them away from the ski slopes, Michael and Angelina penned an outline of the book on a legal pad. Later, an Internet search would reveal that no book had been written about growing roses specifically in the New England region.

While the book probably could have been written in 15 months, the longer period of time it took to write gave "us an opportunity to see things we initially did not see," said Michael.

In the future, look for a sequel to their initial book, according to Michael. "We are on it now, the book," he added, noting that it will detail tips for easy-care rose gardening including lists of sustainable rose varieties, short bios of modern rose breeders of such roses, along with information on companion plants.

Do What You Love, But ...

Aging baby boomers, who are living and working longer, may find themselves in unfulfilling jobs. Michael warned those hoping to reignite a childhood hobby into a new, challenging career in their later years should proceed cautiously. "Do what you love, but be careful because hobbies do not always segue into businesses," he said.

For those learning the art of gardening, Michael recommended, "Don't make your first rose garden too big, even if you're going to plant lower-maintenance roses."

To purchase the 146-page book ($21.95 with free shipping), *Roses for New England: A Guild to Sustainable Rose Gardening*, go to **www.rosesolutions.net**. Visit the Chutes' blog at **www.therosejournal.wordpress.com**.

NO ROCKING CHAIRS FOR THESE COUNTRY FARMERS

Published May 11, 2012, in the Pawtucket Times

Some aging baby boomers can't wait to relax in their later years with visions of travel plans on the horizon or lists of hobbies and projects tucked away. Yet a growing number of seniors, like Ruth and George Handy, continue to work long after the traditional retirement age of 65 simply because they enjoy it.

Just 20 minutes from the City of Pawtucket, you will find a small, rural home situated on more than 100 acres of land. It is a "secret garden" of sorts that has widely become known as a gem of a place to purchase fine produce and beautiful, lush, unique plants. Just drive down a small country road off Mass. Route 118 in Attleboro, and you will find Ruth and George Handy hard at work in their greenhouses, pruning, primping, and selling thousands of flowering annuals, perennials, and tons of vegetables seven days a week from 8 a.m. to 7 p.m.

Mostly by word-of-mouth, customers make this yearly spring pilgrimage to Fine Farms, traveling from as far away as Vermont and Boston and then back home with their vehicles filled to the brim with colorful flowers and varieties you won't find in many big-box stores.

According to Ruth, her locally grown flowers and vegetables are fresher than those shipped to and sold by the growing number of supercenters, superstores, or mega-stores. "There really is a difference," she asserted. "We give daily, tender, loving care to our plants, and they usually tend to be healthier and even grow bigger."

Working Hard and Loving It

"Most people think that we go South for the frigid winters, but we are working hard for 10 months out of the year," said Ruth, a tanned, petite woman, who is wearing a pair of blue jeans, a sleeveless blue-cotton shirt and garden Crocs. Together Ruth and George, her husband of 43 years, are tilling 22 of their 120 acres by themselves. This acreage has been in Ruth's family since 1903, a legacy of which she is most proud.

"Retire? Never! We love what we do," said the 77-year-old farmer's wife. At 75, George begins his long workday at 4:30 a.m., usually finishing up and eating supper about 9:00 p.m. This is not a job for anyone to do, Ruth said.

According to Ruth, because of the economic downturn that caused the closing of many of their wholesale accounts, compounded with the spiraling price of fuel, the Attleboro couple shuttered two of their six greenhouses. However, "this year we still planted about 20,000 packs of flowers and vegetables and 1,500 hanging plants," said Ruth, who explained, "we start planting around January, and in March we begin to transplant the seedlings."

And that's not all. In between planting, harvesting, and then selling produce at The Corn Crib farm stand later in the summer, Ruth is a part-time instructor of water aerobics and chair exercises at the Attleboro YMCA. Ruth even penned *The Fine Farms Cookbook*, a compilation of 25 years of collected recipes. She is currently writing a novel with her cousin. George also is active and regularly works out in his home gym. Both are avid readers of mysteries and historic novels.

By mid-April, the four remaining greenhouses are filled with huge hanging baskets, including a variety of colorful plants from petunias, begonias, and impatiens to a variety of herbs. As Mother's Day approaches there still remains a large variety of flowers and baskets for the rest of the month. At the same time, George begins planting a couple of acres of corn to be harvested in July. When the greenhouses are depleted, usually in June, the couple shift their focus to their vegetable fields.

By mid-July, it is harvest time. Fresh vegetables are sold at The Corn Crib. The Handys offer many varieties of bicolored and white corn along with onions, potatoes, cucumbers, and tomatoes at this quaint farm stand, a mile down the road at the intersection of Tremont and Anawan Streets, off Route 118 in north Rehoboth.

Over the past 25 years, an avid gardener, Patty Zacks, has bought her flowers and vegetables from Fine Farms. Three generations of this Pawtucket resident's family have traveled into Massachusetts to visit the Handy's greenhouses. "This has been my spring ritual every year, first with my mom and now with my son. It is always a treat for the eyes to be one of the first customers in the greenhouses. The colors are breathtaking! In the summer I'll travel for their corn. There is nothing more enjoyable than vegetables freshly picked just hours before being cooked."

Take Time to Smell the Roses

Ruth explained that George has been farming the land for more than 60 years, since he was a teenager. Ultimately her husband bought The Corn Crib and the farm fields from her father, Hyman Fine, who continued to operate the flower business and greenhouses. In 1972, her father died suddenly at a school-committee meeting, and George became responsible for all aspects of the farm business.

"The first year was very difficult for us, but as each year passed, the farm became more profitable and better run," said Ruth. Even in their mid-70s, the Hardys continue to farm while the younger generations are going their own way. The couple have three children and six grandchildren, but no one is really interested in shouldering the long hours it takes to run the family farm.

While Ruth and George work hard in their later years, they believe in setting time aside to enjoy the simple pleasures of life.

"Slow down and enjoy nature that surrounds you," Ruth advised. As a child, she just could not wait to leave the farm to travel to the "big city." Yet now she appreciates the peaceful, rural life of the farm and "would not trade [her] lifestyle for anything else."

George urged aging baby boomers and seniors to look at their age as just a number. "Don't let [your age] limit you," he counseled, noting that he works as hard now in his senior years as he did in his 20s. "Work keeps me young," he added.

For more information about Fine Farms, call (508) 226-0616 or go to **f-i-s.com/finefarms/**. Or write 353 Smith Street, Attleboro, MA 02703. Or email **Finefarms@aol.com**.

REDISCOVERING PAWTUCKET'S RED POLLARD

Published June 22, 2012, in the Pawtucket Times

In 2003 a dramatic movie about a Depression-era racehorse and his oversized jockey became a top box-office film hit. This story of hope and perseverance was woven into a story about a down-and-out jockey, a heartbroken horse owner, a drifter horse trainer, and the eventual rise of a champion horse. It is no coincidence that near the former Narragansett Race Track in Pawtucket–now a Building 19 retail store–you will discover city streets named "War Admiral" and "Seabiscuit Place." Surprisingly many Pawtucket residents do not know that the real-life jockey whose story was told in this film lived out his middle years in their community. *Seabiscuit: An American Legend* was based loosely on the critically-acclaimed nonfiction book penned by Washington, D.C., writer Laura Hillenbrand in 2001, whose key figure resided in Pawtucket.

America's iconic jockey, John Pollard, whose moniker was "Red" Pollard, was known for his flaming red hair. He was taller, at 5'7", than most jockeys. Red and his wife, Agnes, called 249 Vine Street, located in Pawtucket's Darlington neighborhood, their home. Their two children, Norah and John, would grow up and receive their formal education in the city's schools. At the end of their lives, Red and Agnes would be buried a stone's throw from their modest Vine Street home in Notre Dame Cemetery on Daggett Avenue. Pollard died in 1981 and, two weeks later, Agnes would follow.

Pollard became a household name to tens of millions of aging baby boomers who either read Hillenbrand's book, ranked No.1 on *The New York Times* best-sellers list for a total of 42 weeks, or watched the 140-minute "Seabiscuit" film, which was nominated for an Academy Award.

According to Jockeys' Guild, Inc., the book-loving jockey, blind in his right eye, whose luck would lead to riding America's most beloved thoroughbred racehorse 30 times, accumulated 18 wins. Two films and a book would capture his great ride: winning $100,000 in 1940 at the Santa Anita Handicap. Over his 30-year career, fame and fortune would elude Pollard, who would suffer a lifetime of severe injuries from serious spills. He was hospitalized numerous times for a broken hip, ribs, an arm and a leg. One spill kept him bedridden for months before he could ride again.

For Pollard, "you just made your own luck and certain things that happen to you." Life to him was a crapshoot.

Coming to Pawtucket

The accident-prone Pollard was severely injured by the weight of a fallen horse in February 1938 at the San Carlos Handicap. Nine months later, back in the saddle, this unlucky jockey would shatter the bone in his leg during a workout from riding a runaway horse. This would ultimately keep him from riding in that legendary race between Seabiscuit and War Admiral. However, this severe leg injury would lead him to the love of his life, Agnes Conlon.

According to Norah Christianson, the jockey's daughter who now lives in Stratford, Connecticut, marriage would put Pawtucket on Pollard's radar screen. Recovering from the compound facture in his leg at Boston's Winthrop Hospital by reciting poetry, the jockey would capture the attention, fall in love and ultimately marry Agnes Conlon, his registered nurse, in 1936. The couple would have two children during their 40-year marriage.

Christianson, now 72, noted that it was easy for her mother to drive an hour from Pawtucket to visit her parents and 10 siblings, who lived in Brookline, Massachusetts.

Pawtucket was also an ideal place for Pollard to live because the city was centrally located to New England's racing circuit, added Christianson. Her father could easily get to the Narragansett Race Track and Lincoln Downs in Rhode Island, Suffolk Downs in Massachusetts, and Scarborough Downs Race Track in Maine. Moreover, in the winter season, he could easily travel to Florida and hit that state's racetrack circuit. Just five minutes from their home, Agnes took a job at Pawtucket's Memorial Hospital, working as a registered nurse in the emergency room.

Those riding injuries would keep Pollard from serving in the military during World War II, said Christianson, noting that her father worked as a foreman and would oversee the building of Liberty Ships at the Walsh-Kaiser shipyard in Providence. With the war's end, he continued to ride horses until the age of 46, when in 1955 he was just physically unable to do so. For a time, her father "worked at Narragansett mentoring young jockeys and then worked as a mail sorter at the track. After that, he worked as a valet for other jockeys until he finally retired for good. The track was always my dad's 'community' until it closed in 1978," Christianson said.

Sipping Whiskey, Reading Great Poetry

Pollard, whose education ended in fourth grade, had a love for poetry and the classics, recalled Christianson. Always on the move among racetracks, he could easily carry his favorite pocket volumes of Shakespeare, Ralph Waldo Emerson, Robert Service's *Songs of a Sourdough* and Edward Fitzgerald's *The Rubaiyat of Omar Khayyam*. Being a poetry lover, frequent stays at the hospital "allowed my father to read a lot and memorize," she noted.

She also remembered her father sipping a little bit of whiskey as he would recite poetry for the family after dinner. "We just absorbed the experience, not realizing we were learning."

Pollard traveled the racetrack circuit for months at a time, stated Christianson. When in town, her father would take her and her brother, John, to Pinault's Drug Store on Newport Avenue, enjoy a movie at the Darlton Theater, or visit Kip's Restaurant. "I remember Pinault's had a soda fountain that made the best homemade honeydew-melon ice cream." Many a day Pollard would stop at the Texaco gas station, located at Armistice Boulevard and York Avenue, to sit and talk for hours with his friends.

"Dad was a loner, a desperado, an extreme free spirit, a man obsessed with racing," recalled Christianson. Before he retired, Pollard's typical day started at 4:30 a.m. by heading to the track to exercise horses, later returning home with a few of his jockey friends in their work clothes, ready to eat a hearty breakfast cooked by Agnes and to "tell jokes and talk shop." His physically active and obsessive lifestyle in racing allowed him to enjoy "puttering around his basement workshop, mow the lawn, or even put up the storm windows," she said.

When Christianson was 17 years old, she had an inkling of her father's fame. Mr. Winters, her Tolman High math teacher, once asked her, "Is your father the jockey Red Pollard?" Looking back, she would realize that "her father did not make a fuss about his fame. He realized that when you stop being on the top, you are going to be forgotten, so winning that race was far more important than fame and recognition."

Being involved in local organized groups such as church, the Boy Scouts, and business clubs was alien to him, Christianson added. "As my brother once said to me when we were talking about our parents, "Ozzie and Harriet they were not.""

Protecting the Jockey Community
Yet Pawtucket's jockey was tapped to be on the first board of directors of the newly established national organization Jockeys' Guild in 1940, an enormously important guild for riders. This group was a nationwide organized union. Jockeys who were previously hurt had no financial recourse. Neither did the families of jockeys who were killed because they did not get any benefits before the Jockeys' Guild was created.

"In the early days, [the Nicholasville, Kentucky-based] guild was able to introduce safety measures such as better racing environments, monitor legislation concerning racing, and provide insurance for jockeys as well as decent wages. The great achievements of the Jockeys' Guild would be what you might call 'my father's community service'," added Christianson.

Red Pollard rode into American history, overcoming a physical disability of partial blindness, accepting intense physical pain caused by severe riding injuries that fractured his bones, while humbly accepting his role in racing history as the man who rode Seabiscuit.

TENNIS AND YOUR LATER YEARS

Published July 25, 2014, in the Pawtucket Times

Like bacon and eggs, AARP Rhode Island hopes to make tennis synonymous with AARP's "Life Reimagined" initiative. On Friday, July 11, Rhode Island's largest aging-advocacy group firmly tied its national initiative to the International Tennis Hall of Fame & Museum, seeing an immediate opportunity to be associated with one of the world's most high-profile tennis events, one that matched its age-50-plus membership demographic. The new relationship provided a unique opportunity for the Providence-based group to get the word out about its legislative advocacy and grass-roots community work.

This month, AARP Rhode Island unveiled its sponsorship with the Hall of Fame Tennis Championships, which drew 22,500 tennis fans from across the country to the International Tennis Hall of Fame & Museum in Newport, Rhode Island. A live telecast of the tennis matches and the tennis organization's Hall of Fame enshrinement ceremony, which honors the best of the tennis world, was beamed to millions around the tennis world on the Tennis Channel. AARP's sponsorship included center-court signage and 30-second spots on this channel.

"When we heard that tennis is promoted as 'the sport of a lifetime', we knew we were on the same wavelength," noted AARP State Director Kathleen Connell, who stressed "AARP is all about providing resources for a lifetime."

Anne Marie McLaughlin, director of marketing at the International Tennis Hall of Fame & Museum, agrees with Connell's keen assessment. "Tennis is very much in sync with AARP's "Life Reimagined" program. Perhaps people are seeking new ways to connect with friends once they've become empty nesters or a new hobby to keep them active and healthy. Tennis can provide so many benefits in these areas, and it's a great activity for people who are looking to reimagine and explore their life."

"We're proud to partner with AARP Rhode Island to showcase the game's many phys-ical, social, and mental benefits to their members," says McLaughlin, who agrees with Connell's take that tennis is a sport of a lifetime. "It can be played and enjoyed by a 5-year-old or a 95-year-old, and we are very excited to partner with AARP Rhode Island to engage and inspire their members," she says.

But Connell warns that "You cannot generalize about the athletic abilities of people over 50," noting that demanding sports such as marathons and distance swimming attract athletes in their 60s, 70s, 80s, and even older. "Tennis is a great sport for people over 50 because you can play at your own level with players of similar skill. To live longer and remain healthy we know that being and staying active is critical. AARP encourages people to find a sport or activity that can provide life-enhancing benefits, both physical and mental," added the Middletown resident.

Creating New Opportunities in Your Later Years

As a sport, tennis is a great fit for people looking to reimagine their life after 40. "Whether it's a job transition, career change, starting a dream business, adapting to being an empty nester, or making the switch to a retirement lifestyle, AARP 'Life Reimagined' provides online assessment tools, guidance, and resources to help people explore new opportunities, identify adaptable skills, and set new goals," Connell explained.

Connell says **www.Lifereimagined.org** is the go-to web address for feeling good about aging. "It's about you and what you want to accomplish," she says, noting that it helps put AARP's "Real Possibilities" into action.

According to Connell, AARP is no longer an organization for older people, but one for all people who want the best out of life, regardless of their age. Many AARP members are still working and do not plan to retire, others leave their jobs seeking new challenges or even establishing new businesses, she explains.

Over a year ago, AARP launched "Life Reimagined," a free program designed to help 76 million boomers easily navigate into new life experiences or reboot their professional lives into different directions. For the '60s generation, continuing to work a full-time job or even coasting into retirement is no longer an acceptable option. But AARP stressed that reinventing oneself is the way to go in your later stages of life.

The "Life Reimagined" website provides tools to help you make key decisions for your next direction and detailed resources to guide you through that journey, says Connell. "Whether your career has hit an unexpected bump in your 50s, or you are looking to start your own business or head down a new path into retirement, AARP can help," she said.

At the Hall of Fame Tennis Championships

AARP staff, and over 50 volunteers were on hand at the Hall of Fame Tennis Championships from Monday, July 7, through the tournament finals on Sunday, July 13. Being stationed at an AARP "Life Reimagined" booth, these individuals answered questions and distributed copies of *AARP Magazine* and other materials. On Friday, July 11, (AARP Day) Connell announced a new AARP membership benefit—a year-round discounted AARP member rate of $8 (instead of the standard $13 rate) for admission into the International Tennis Hall of Fame & Museum. The organization's museum is open daily and also offers special events including film, and music. Year-round tennis programming, including lessons and group play on the historic green courts are available, too.

Activities for AARP Day included a free 50+ tennis clinic led by legendary tennis coach and newly inducted Hall of Famer Nick Bollettieri, followed by a book signing and Q&A session (see Bollettieri in action on AARP Rhode Island's YouTube Channel, **www.youtube.com/aarpri**). That day, over 70 people attended an hour-long panel discussion in air-conditioned comfort of the Casino Theatre at the Hall of Fame about AARP's "Life Reimagined" initiative.

At the Friday panel, Connell noted that "It was a real treat for fans to get a chance to hear Hall of Famers Bollettieri, 82, (Class of 2014) and Owen Davidson, 71, (Class of 2010) talk about their careers. AARP volunteer Charles Dress, 76, of Warwick, also shared his thoughts about how tennis has played an important role in his later years, after retiring from a full-time career," said Connell. The panelists all agreed that tennis was "a natural outlet for the lifelong learners who want to work hard at improving their skills and staying mentally sharp."

Meanwhile, at Friday's tennis clinic, Bollettieri stressed to those attending, "age is only a number." Connell noted that this is in line with the messaging of AARP. "His enshrinement into the Hall of Fame is fitting not only because of his place as the coach of so many tennis champions, but also because he is a magnificent ambassador for the game. He inspires people with his energy and enthusiasm. We were thrilled that he made his way to our tent to join AARP," she says.

McLaughlin added that Bollettieri is "an amazing example of what 'Life Reimagined' can represent. At 82 years of age, Nick is still on court six days a week for 10 hours a day...and likely on the golf course the seventh day. He's living proof that it's possible and very positive for someone to stay physically active in older years. With this physical activity come great social and mental benefits as well."

Before the Hall of Fame Enshrinement Ceremony, Bollettieri gave this columnist a few pointers on living life in your later years. "Stay active and never, never, never use the word retire," he says, warning that once the word enters your vocabulary, you begin to decline.

Buying into AARP's "Life Reimagined" initiative, Bollettieri advises, "Don't retire, just change professions."

For more information about the International Tennis Hall of Fame & Museum go to **www.tennisfame.com/**.

AARP NO LONGER YOUR GRANDMOTHER'S MEMBERSHIP ORGANIZATION

Published March 15, 2013, in the Pawtucket Times

With the printing of a full-page, four-colored ad in the February 25, 2002, issue of *Newsweek* magazine, AARP, the nation's largest aging advocacy group, moved to reinvent its membership image by rolling out an ad campaign to lure the nation's aging baby boomers, those born between 1946 and 1964, into its rank and file. At that time the public viewed an AARP member as being in their 60s, gliding into the twilight of their retirement years. One simple ad consisting of a photograph of a shirtless, lean, aging baby boomer carrying his mud-caked mountain bike, worked effectively to change this misperception. AARP members were not moving into their twilight years, were still young, vibrant, and even active.

"Be Yourself," blared the ad's tagline, identifying the 50ish male with gray hair in the ad: "Peter Carlstrom, 51, cyclist, canoeist, an AARP Member."

In 2002 with the kickoff of this media campaign, the nation's largest aging group, which represented 35 million members that year, geared up efforts to recruit the nation's baby boomers into its membership ranks.

Baby boomers don't make compromises, according to AARP's membership recruitment ad more than a decade ago: "They make choices." Furthermore, the ad stated that AARP was there to help with fitness programs and provide information on making healthy choices in a myriad of ways, including eating right and staying fit.

"Real Possibilities" Ad Campaign Kicks Off

Today AARP continues to attack the misperception associated with its brand and with aging stereotypes by launching another national advertising campaign. According to the Washington, D.C.-based group, "Real Possibilities" aims to revitalize and reposition AARP as a membership organization that is relevant and can deliver messages of strength and empowerment. "Real Possibilities" will serve as the organization's new tagline and will be implemented into the existing AARP logo.

AARP's new public-relations campaign, created by GREY, seeks to show not only what the face of 50-plus looks like today, but more important, the new mindset of people entering or already in this life stage. It will run on television and digital media through October 2013.

AARP is putting one-third of its "Real Possibilities" media buy toward social and digital media, and the ads will appear on more lifestyle outlets as opposed to the news-focused outlets they've primarily appeared on in the past. Ads will drive consumers to a newly created landing page **www.aarp.org/possibilities**, where they will be able to access content that is most relevant to the 50-plus audience looking to achieve "real possibilities."

"People are looking for a trusted ally to help them turn their goals and dreams into real possibilities, and that's where AARP can help them and their families," said A. Barry Rand, CEO of AARP. "This is an opportunity to reintroduce AARP to the public and show the value that we provide to the 50-plus audience. We think this campaign effectively demonstrates how AARP is relevant to them."

AARP is shifting the focal point of the conversation from aging and advice to a deeper level of personal connection and empowerment. People age 50-plus don't want to be defined by age, and they don't want to live in fear that their possibilities become limited as they grow older.

"Possibilities are critical to this audience, and millions of people in their 40s, 50s, 60s and beyond are living in a new life stage: the age of possibility," said Emilio Pardo, executive vice president and chief brand officer of AARP. "We want to show how their life experiences have tremendous value and that possibilities should not be less, they should be ageless."

Reintroducing AARP to a Younger Crowd

While some may see AARP's new marketing effort as a way to expand its membership base to younger members, for AARP Rhode Island's John Martin, associate state director of communications, it is very practical to bring aging baby boomers in early.

"As AARP evolved it became evident that most things about 'retirement' require at-tention well before the day people retire," said Martin, citing his favorite example, retirement security.

"How can we help members plan for a secure retirement if we wait until retirement to reach out and offer resources and assistance? And then there is the more current question: If, say, at 52 you are working full time but feeling the weight of college tuition, rising taxes, and you've seen the equity in your home plummet, you should not wait until retirement age to make your voice heard on Medicare and Social Security. Most 50-year-old Americans now recognize they have a vital stake in the sustainability of these programs."

According to Martin, retiring in dignity also depends on one's health. "It's awfully hard to turn things around when you are 65, so AARP needs to connect with people earlier to provide health and fitness resources that might make life at 70 or 80 more enjoyable," he said.

"Another outcome of reaching those ages in better health is that people have created at least a better chance of saving on health care costs." He asked, "How can AARP promote the benefits of staying active and mobile if we have not been encouraging better diet, exercise, and preventative care as retirement approaches?"

Martin said people welcome such notions as "60 is the new 50." He points out that media images of the serene couple relaxing in easy chairs has been replaced by CNN stories about people skydiving to celebrate a 70th birthday or 80-year-old competitive swim champions. "We boomers live for the hope that we can reach retirement in better physical and mental shape than our parents. A generation ago, society was telling people to retire, collect Social Security and act their age, to accept the gold watch at 62 or 65 and ride off quietly into the sunset. No more," he said.

Great AARP websites

AARP is working hard to be the best resource, online, in-person and in communities to help aging baby boomers and those older to discover new possibilities, noted Martin. As part of the "Real Possibilities" initiative, AARP offers a way to reimagine your life (**www.lifereimagined.aarp.org**). This website offers someone over age 50 an opportunity to design his or her own reimagined life.

AARP also recently launched a dating service. And why not? asked Martin. "Happiness and romance is not reserved for those couples in the beer commercials. Think about online dating services of the past decade or two. Did many seem at all tailored to or comfortable for anyone over 50? The AARP brand and all that we stand for makes taking a chance a lot more comfortable."

With the graying of America, AARP has redefined its mission and repackaged itself twice in the past 13 years. The redirected membership organization, expanding its generational reach, strives to make a person's journey throughout their entire life span a little easier, a bit better and brighter.

Now isn't that worth the cost of an AARP membership? For more information about AARP membership and benefits, log on to **www.aarp.org/join** or call AARP Rhode Island at (401)248-2663 and request a membership application. AARP's website is in Spanish, too, at **www.aarp.org/espanol**.

11. SAGE ADVICE FOR GRANDCHILDREN

HERE'S MY ADVICE TO THE GRADUATING CLASS OF 2013

Published May 31, 2013, in the Pawtucket Times

L ast week, commencement speakers at colleges and universities around the country imparted their wisdom to tens of thousands of graduating college seniors. With the advent of social media and websites, millions more will receive advice from these commencement speeches given by well-known lawmakers, judges, television personalities, and CEOs, detailing simple tips and observations that, if taken, just might offer the young graduates a more rewarding personal and professional life.

Quotes in the Top 2013 Commencement Speeches

Often local newspapers report on commencement speeches delivered during each graduation season. According to Graduation Wisdom, a website that compiles the best commencement speeches and memorable quotes, some speeches are just better than others. Some of most memorable quotes taken from the top 2013 commencement speeches detailed on this website included:

John Green, educator and writer of adult fiction, who won the 2006 Printz Award for his first novel, *Looking for Alaska*, told Butler University's graduating class that "there are many more jobs out there than you have ever heard of. Your dream job might not yet exist. If you had told College Me that I would become a professional YouTuber, I would've been like, 'That is not a word, and it never should be.'

Eric Idle, British comedian and actor, who was a member of the British surreal-comedy group Monty Python, stated in his commencement speech at Whitman College: "Life has a very simple plot: First you're here, and then you're not."

Yes, more sage advice was given to graduating seniors this year by Dick Costolo, Twitter CEO, who stated in his commencement speech at the University of Michigan in Ann Arbor: "Believe that if you make courageous choices and bet on yourself and put yourself out there, that you will have an impact as a result of what you do. And you don't need to know now what that would be or how will it happen, because no one ever does."

Typical Advice in Commencement Speeches

If you look closely, you can find life lessons noted in commencement speeches given at colleges and universities over the years that just might lead to a happy and successful life, said Cristina Negrut, who penned "15 Rules for a Happy and Successful Life," which can be found on Graduation Wisdom's website.

Negrut noted that commencement speakers, usually at the top of their professional game, tell the graduating seniors a number of rules to prepare them for leaving the campus, assisting them to make their mark as adults. Specific advice includes: Don't worry, your life's passion will find you. Always trust yourself and learn to take bold action. Never let anyone define who you are. Chase your big dreams. Don't sit on the sideline; take the initiative and quickly get into the game. Be persistent, tenacious, and never give up. Don't fear failures in life, yet learn from them. Nobody is perfect, including you. Make use of your creativity and imagination. Remain in the present moment, not in the past or future. Don't play it safe; always take risks. Learn to embrace change. Work hard. Live selflessly and give back to others.

The Class of 2013 will begin their life journey with many challenges to face. Gas prices are now about $3.50 per gallon. Mortgage rates declined to the lowest level in decades, but many of the graduating seniors, burdened by huge student-loan debt, leave college without a job, an adequate credit rating, or a down payment to purchase a home.

Although the economy is slowly improving in the Ocean State, graduating seniors, like graduating classes before them, may be forced to relocate to other states to land their first professional jobs. The Ocean State continues to be one of the last states to see its economy revive.

My Tips for 2013 Graduates

At press time, I sit with a written commencement speech, yet with no invitation from a university or college to give it. If I were asked to speak before a graduating class, I would give tips on how to age gracefully throughout the accumulating years.

Aging can be viewed as a lifelong, unpredictable journey. Yet some people feverishly attempt not to embrace it, choosing instead to hold on to their gradually fading youth while fearing the onset of wrinkles, sagging stomachs, and even gray hair. As you move into your middle years and beyond, look at your life as a meaningful journey. Keep fo-cused on the present moment and don't be strapped to past experiences or future events.

When you confront life's health, financial, and professional challenges, keep a positive attitude rather than being overwhelmed by negativity. Each day you will make choices as to how you will tackle and react to your problems and life's difficulties. In every situation, you can see the proverbial glass as either being "half-full" or "half-empty." A positive attitude allows you to see a "half-full" glass, and this allows you to successfully age.

Savor Your Failures

As we grow older, sometimes we put too much energy into reflecting on our personal and professional defeats, focusing on the "bad hand" we were dealt in life. Each and every day, savor your victories. It is important for you to forgive yourself for your shortcomings and failures. Learning from your shortcomings will build a strong bridge to future success.

Also, forgive others who have hurt you personally and professionally. You cannot peacefully live or reconcile your life if you are still holding on to grudges, anger, and bitterness all tied to past relationships and negative employment experiences.

In your adult years, time flies rapidly by, as if in the blink of an eye. Amma, a Hindu spiritual teacher, teaches her followers to view life as a "cancelled check." Let go of those past regrets, forgive yourself for those mistakes, especially made in childhood and teenage years, and more important, those you made as you move into your middle or later years. Don't regret passing up personal or professional opportunities, for others will follow. Use your time on earth wisely; don't waste it carrying the burdens of past guilt or personal grudges.

As you grow older and accumulate more of life's experiences, share your story with others, especially those younger than you. You will have a huge reservoir of untapped wisdom gained through life's trials and tribulations. When taking on the role of parent or grandparent, continue to share your insights and lessons that you have learned throughout the cyclical ups and downs of your life. The generations following you will lose out if you choose to remain silent and keep your knowledge and history from them.

Stay Physically Healthy

Your health is the most important possession. Cherish it. URI Gerontologist Phil Clark once told me, "Use it or lose it. Stay as physically active as you can." Moreover, "If you rest, you rust," he said, noting that physical exercise elevates our mood and benefits our cardiovascular system.

The researcher on aging tells us that you "must also exercise your brain." Simply put, make time in your busy day to read newspapers, magazines, and books or play a challenging crossword puzzle, even chess.

Some graduating seniors will see their success tied to obtaining professional recognition, seeking to make far-reaching changes in their careers. Sometimes it is not the big things that you do that count, rather the simple, daily acts of loving kindness you give to all those around you.

Research also tells us that volunteer work can be a protective buffer from the curveballs that life may throw at us as we age.

Keep up and nurture your social contacts and personal connections with others. When you require help, don't be afraid to ask your family, friends or even professional colleagues for support and assistance. People will always move up the ladder of their careers, sometimes down, too. Take the opportunity to be there not only for people you know, but also strangers when they need a hand to jump-start their faltering careers.

Simplicity Is Key to a Good Life

Learn to slow down and enjoy the simple moments of your life. Nationally acclaimed author Connie Goldman stated that the simple act of watching a beautiful sunrise or sunset or even puttering around your garden can be as stimulating as a jam-packed calendar of activities.

There are no sure bets in one's life except death, taxes, and yes, growing older. So, Class of 2013, make the most of your life that is just beginning to unfold before you. Embrace and appreciate your later years and go for the gusto. Enjoy your new journey.

REGULAR FOLKS GIVE ADVICE TO GRADUATES

Published on May 23, 2014, in the Pawtucket Times

This month, commencement speakers at Rhode Island's colleges and universities will give the Class of 2014 their tips on how the graduates can successfully find their professional niche in a state with the distinction of having the worst employment rate in the nation and continues to be one of the last states to see an economic revival. Rhode Islanders are also known for their inferiority complex and general attitude about the quality of life in the state.

Robed graduating seniors will sit listening closely to commencement speeches given by very well-known lawmakers, judges, television personalities, and business CEOs, detailing their observations and advice, and how, if closely followed, just might give the graduates a more rewarding personal and professional life.

Typically a commencement speech (the length being about 10 minutes) is given by a notable, successful, stimulating figure well-known in the community, nationally or internationally. While some colleges and universities may enhance their prestige by bringing in high-profile speakers (University of Rhode Island, Rhode Island School of Design, Roger Williams University, and Providence College) sometimes at great cost; others like Brown University, unique among Ivy League institutions, features graduating seniors rather than outside dignitaries as their commencement speakers. This year, Rhode Island College undergraduate and graduate commencement speakers are Rhode Islanders.

So I say to presidents of colleges and universities, with your tight budgets you can save a little money by not bringing in highly-paid commencement speakers. As can be seen below, there are many potential commencement speakers in local communities throughout the state who fly below the radar screen and can give college graduates sound strategies for success gleaned from their life experiences. They give road maps on how one can live a more healthy, fulfilling life, mature in a way to realize their potential and age gracefully in a challenging and quickly-changing world.

Jesse Nemerofsky, 60, Providence, professional commercial photographer: "Always remember that everyone you meet in life can be a potential or future client. This being said, a positive introduction of yourself is a valuable way to be called to work together on projects, even to be hired for future jobs. George H. W. Bush, 41st President of the United States, has stated in interviews that when he meets someone he gets their business card and, at birthdays, Christmas time, or when the person is honored, he sends them a personal note. By taking time to acknowledge people over the lifetime of his career, the former president is highly respected by those he has encountered, even if his political position or business ventures were successful or not. Honesty and representing your capabilities are of course of the utmost importance, and small gestures like sending a personal note can ultimately have great impact, but excellence in your work should be your main goal."

Michael Cassidy, 66, Pawtucket, retired: "As you go into the 'real' world from the sheltered 'world of college' don't be too quick to judge the new people you meet in the workplace. People come in all types, sizes, shapes, temperaments, personalities, ages, and backgrounds; and they all have their own experiences from which you can learn. If you are smart enough to listen to what others have to offer, you can learn from them not only what to do, but what not to do. And most times learning what not to do is the most valuable lesson you can have."

Olon Reeder, 55, North Providence, Reeder Associates Public Relations: "Become adaptable to constant changes in your life. Today's global environment demands that you must become faster, better, and smarter and compete with yourself and everyone else to survive socially. You have to embrace nonstop learning, empower yourself with your own resources, have an independent attitude, and create value for who you really are and what you want to be to shape your quality of life for the future!"

Michelle Godin, 50, Vice President, New England Economic Development Services, Inc.: "Live each day of your life with integrity. Whether in your personal life or professional life, integrity will define you as a person. Never waiver. When your days on earth are ended, it is your integrity that others will remember. Those who live with integrity will be fondly remembered and missed, because with integrity comes many other admirable qualities such as compassion, empathy, tolerance, and understanding. Those lacking integrity will be discussed with disdain and quickly forgotten. Choose to become exemplary."

Paul Audette, 85, Pawtucket, semi-retired businessman: "The youth of today— from puberty to whatever age one reaches maturity—tend to see life as it pertains to them, yet each person is responsible for him or herself. While the youth may have the knowledge, they lack the life experience, which is the main factor in making good, sound judgments that ultimately affect [your] well-being as well as that of your loved ones. While experience cannot be taught, it cannot be overlooked as a major component in making sound decisions that affect your future. Experience comes from living—and life is a journey."

Joan Retsinas, 67, Providence, writer: "Savor, savor, savor. Savor the sunshine and the rain. Savor your friends, your family, your colleagues. Nurture the people close to you. Be a friend. Fall in love. If you fall out of love, fall in again. Read *Winnie the*

Pooh to a child. Eat ice cream. Ride a bike. Swim in the ocean. Laugh. As for fame, fortune, and success, don't fret. They don't really matter."

Rick Wahlberg, 61, senior project manager, Blue Cross & Blue Shield of Rhode Island: "Be useful, there is no feeling like making the world a better place. Be aware, strike a balance between career, family, friends, and community. Be grateful for what you have; don't be jealous of what you don't have, and share."

Wendy Jencks, 61, Cumberland, manager, Blackstone Valley Visitor Center: "There may be a time in young people's lives when they are nervous to take a risk; don't be afraid to take a chance. If an opportunity/life experience arises and you want it, take it even if it is unconventional. You may not get another opportunity again. Also, a person's first job is not the end all be all. Your dream job may actually be something you did not study. People confine themselves to their own walls."

Larry Sullivan, 49, Pawtucket, Director, Net Compliance Solution's Technical & Consulting services: "Recognize opportunity. If you can't identify opportunities, then they are very likely to sneak past you unnoticed. Most people's search criteria are so narrow in focus that it can essentially blind them to opportunities available right in front of their face. It's the old 'can't see the forest for the trees' scenario. Also, see yourself as a valuable asset. Your self-image will make a huge difference in the type of opportunities you attract to yourself. If you see yourself as a valuable asset, and you present yourself as such, others will see you that way as well."

Denise Panichas, 60, Woonsocket, executive director of The Samaritans of Rhode Island: "Respect cannot be given when asked for, it has to be earned. This is something you learn later in life. How do you earn respect from those around you? By being true to yourself–your values, beliefs, and most important to your commitments to family, friends, and the community."

Ken McGill, 51, Pawtucket, Registrar of Voters, City of Pawtucket: "Find time to give back to your community. In the years to come you will be looking for a good job, getting married, having children and getting on with life. Never forget those in need in your community. Mentoring children, giving time to a soup kitchen, volunteering to help civic groups in your city or town, or just helping a neighbor will give you more reward than any salary or position in the corporate world."

Gail Solomon, 59, Pawtucket, Gail Solomon, Inc., a graphic design company: "You're not the most unqualified or least knowledgeable person in the room. Everyone else thinks they are. And anyway it's much more elegant to ask questions than to behave like you know all the answers. Because nobody does. Ever."

Susan Sweet, 72, Rumford, former state administrator, nonprofit lobbyist and advocate; "In the short space that we are in the world, we must create meaning in our lives by contributing to the happiness and well-being of other people and other sentient beings. To do good and useful work, caring and acting for the betterment of others is the true goal of life."

Bob Billington, President of the Blackstone Valley Tourism Council who received his doctorate in education from Johnson & Wales University in 2005, says that "star power sells" when seeking out a commencement speaker: "We have regular people walking amongst us who do very extraordinary things every day but they may never get a chance to give a commencement speech at a college or university."

If so, I say that it's a shame.

SOME SIMPLE RESOLUTIONS CAN BETTER YOUR LIFE

Published on January 4, 2014, in the Pawtucket Times

E very year we see the Time Square ball swiftly drop as a million or so revelers loudly count down at the stroke of midnight. Also, we traditionally make New Year resolutions to perform acts of kindness and for self-improvement.

Making a resolution for positive change goes back for eons. According to Wikipedia, the act of making a resolution can be documented in Mesopotamia (the territory of modern-day Iraq). Babylonians made promises to their stone deities to start off a new year by returning borrowed goods and paying off debts.

The free Internet encyclopedia also notes that the Romans even carried out this tradition by making promises to Janus, the god of beginnings and transitions (for whom the month January is named). Knights during the Medieval era, from the 5th to 15th centuries, took a "peacock vow" after the Christmas season to re-affirm their commitment to knightly virtues of honor, courtesy, and love.

Wikipedia also reports that even "watch services" held late on New Year's Eve also provided an opportunity for Christian parishioners to review the past year and make confessions and prepare for the New Year by prayer. Judaism's High Holidays, from Rosh Hashanah ending with Yom Kipper, the Day of Atonement, gives worshipers an opportunity to reflect on their wrongdoings over the year to seek forgiveness and prepare for the upcoming year, adds the Internet website.

Memorable New Year Resolutions

Zoe Mintz, of the *International Business Times*, posted her thoughts about New Year resolutions, just hours before 2014, on the New York-based digital global publication's web. Like clockwork, many of the nation's newspapers and magazines printed articles detailing interesting, inspirational, and unusual resolutions from prominent people, from movies stars (they usually Tweet), artists, politicians, writers, and corporate leaders.

Mintz details some well-thought-out New Year resolutions from people whom you may well know.

"Let our New Year's resolution be this: We will be there for one another as fellow members of humanity, in the finest sense of the word."—Goran Persson, served as Prime Minister of Sweden from 1996 to 2006.

"New Year's resolution: To tolerate fools more gladly, provided this does not encourage them to take up more of my time."—James Agate, British diarist and critic.

"I made no resolutions for the new year. The habit of making plans, of criticizing, sanctioning and molding my life, is too much of a daily event for me."—Anaïs Nin, an author.

"One resolution I have made, and try always to keep, is this: to rise above the little things."—John Burroughs, an American naturalist and essayist important in the evolution of the U.S. conservation movement.

"I think in terms of the day's resolutions, not the years."—Henry Moore, an English sculptor and artist. He was best known for his semi-abstract monumental bronze sculptures, which are located around the world as public works of art.

"What the New Year brings to you will depend a great deal on what you bring to the New Year."—Vern McLellan, author of *Wise Words and Quotes*.

"Follow your passions, believe in karma, and you won't have to chase your dreams; they will come to you."—Randy Pausch, American professor of computer science and human-computer interaction and design at Carnegie Mellon University in Pittsburgh, Pennsylvania. He is author of *The Last Lecture*.

"Yesterday is gone. Tomorrow has not yet come. We have only today. Let us begin."—Mother Teresa, an Albanian-born, Indian Roman Catholic Religious Sister who founded the Missionaries of Charity which in 2012 consisted of over 4,500 in 133 countries.

"If you asked me for my New Year resolution, it would be to find out who I am."—Cyril Cusack, an Irish actor, who appeared in numerous films and television productions in a career lasting more than 70 years.

Everyday Resolutions

Resolutions may inspire or be a little bit ethereal, as detailed in the above listing compiled by Mintz. Simply put, our personal New Year resolutions help us cope with daily challenges to improve health, personal finances, and relationships, that is, to enhance our quality of life.

Many of your family and friends will be making their 2014 New Year resolutions to improve their health by eating healthy foods, losing weight, or ratcheting up their exercise regimen. Everyone knows someone who has made a resolution to either drink or smoke less, or not at all.

As the New Year approaches a person may say, "Life's too short," when they begin to craft their personal resolutions. Attitude adjustments may well occur, when the person resolves to see "a glass half-full rather than half-empty," making a commitment for the coming year to become a more positive person, one who looks forward to living life to the fullest. Some may explore ways to reduce the stress in their lives.

A 2014 New Year resolution for others may just be to dig themselves out of credit card debt (cut those cards in half), regularly put money away for retirement, invest in the stock market, or even to find a more satisfying job that pays better than their current one.

You might even see college students making their 2014 resolution to study harder to get that "A." Some baby boomers and seniors may even chose to make this year the time to enroll at a local college or university to get a bachelor's or graduate degree, or go to just learn new skills or sharpen up their existing skills.

For many, life may have become too routine and predictable, pushing them to schedule a trip to exotic places in the New Year. Some may choose to watch less television, committing to put their leisure time to a better use in 2014. One might resolve to becoming a volunteer at the local food kitchen, or helping the homeless, or even joining civic groups like the Pawtucket Rotary Club or Lions Club, or the Masons, to reach out to their community. Spending time helping those in need can also be a benefit for those volunteering—learning new skills, meeting new friends, advancing your career, or even improving mental and physical health.

New Year resolutions even help a person focus where their time, money, and energy are directed. Everyone knows someone who is resolving to spend quality time in 2014 with family members. Some may even make resolutions to get engaged or marry their long-time partner or to even begin a family.

With Christmas becoming so commercial, some may well make New Year resolutions that will push them away from materialistic pleasures, to exploring their spirituality.

Using Technology To Keep Resolutions

New technology can help keep us on track with keeping our 2014 New Year resolutions. With the growing popularity of cell phones (iPhone and Android) thousands of self-help apps are now becoming available on app stores for IOS and Android cell phones, reports business reporter Victor Luckerson in an article published on New Year's Day on **www.Time.com**.

Luckerson details apps that will keep you on track with keeping your 2014 New Year resolutions. Here is a small sampling:

For learning the basics of a foreign language to prepare for a vacation, Duolingo helps you to quickly learn the basics. Users can easily review lessons in vocabulary, pronunciation and basic grammar. Currently Duolingo offers lessons in English, Spanish, French, Portuguese, German, and Italian. Available for iPhone and Android.

MyQuitCoach was created to help you keep cigarettes at arm's length. The app uses data to help people curb their bad habit by allowing users to input how often they smoke and when they have their cravings. This information allows short and long-term goals to be set, enabling the smoker to reduce their daily cigarette use. Tying results to both Facebook and Twitter can increase support from social media friends. Available for iPhone.

For those who require motivation to go to their neighborhood gym, MapMyFitness is just the app for you. The app tracks 600 different fitness activities, from running, to ballroom dancing, to walking the dog. With this app you can even map out effective jogging routes. It even offers a social component that allows your friends to motivate you to exercise from within the app. Available for iPhone, Android, and BlackBerry.

For resolutions to tighten your belt to improve your personal finances, check out DailyCost. The app easily allows you to closely check ingoing and outgoing money in all your bank accounts. Moreover, you can easily log in all your daily expenses, too, categorizing them within seconds. Weekly and monthly spending charts allow you to closely review where you spend your money. Available for iPhone.

Finally here's an app to help you accomplish your resolution goals. Simply put, Lift helps you track how often you complete your tasks that you resolve to complete and rewards you with virtual check marks for achieving. Tasks can be drinking more water, praying, and other habits you want to change. App users who pursue the same goals can support each other via discussion groups. Available for iPhone and Android.

For this columnist, my 2014 New Year resolutions (like many) revolve around health, finances, and family. I resolve to become healthier by losing weight, eating healthier foods, and increasing my visits to the local YMCA; to get my financial house in order; and to spend more time with family and good friends. Maybe I might even write a book. As to my success, I will keep my fingers crossed.

THE LITTLE PLAID GUIDE
TO LIVING A BETTER LIFE

Published June 14, 2013, in the Pawtucket Times

I n two days, millions of Americans will celebrate Father's Day. As I penned this week's commentary thinking of the approaching holiday, I quickly began thinking of my Dad, who died of a heart attack more than nine years ago at the ripe old age of 89. While he had recently been ailing and was well along in years, it was quite a shock to receive the long-distance telephone call from my sister that he had died.

For many, Father's Day provides an opportunity to slow down and reflect on growing up with their father or stepfather, fondly recalling earlier times.

The Life and Times of Frank Weiss

There was one thing for sure that I know about my Dad: something I could literally take to the bank. Married for more than 62 years, he passionately adored his wife, Sally, whom he considered to be the most important person in his life. My twin brother, James, and two older sisters, Mickie and Nancy, and ultimately his five grandchildren and three great grandchildren would also be very important to him throughout his long life.

As a youngster, I remember Dad's work ethic, always working hard to support the family, often sitting at the wrought-iron-and-glass kitchen table late into the evening working on his weekly reports. Although he worked long hours, Dad always found time to go to a ball game or just spend time with his kids.

Dad was like the Energizer Rabbit: he kept working, working, and working. There was no retirement for this man who had worked for more than 33 years at Colbert Volks, a well-known women's clothing store in Dallas, Texas. Two years after his bypass surgery, my 70-year-old Dad wanted to chart a new career course, so he began a second job and worked at C'est Simone, a national manufacturer of women's apparel, until the mid-1980s. Amazingly, during his long career in women's retail, he could literally see a style or clothing trend long before it happened, always correctly predicting which new coat styles would sell in a particular season.

Looking Back Over the Years

I will always remember…

How we shot hoops in the backyard for ice cream. Dad always lost at the last moment. We always won and got that double-dipped chocolate ice cream as a prize.

At restaurants, I remember Dad drinking cup after cup of black coffee at Luby's Cafeteria, with the decaf coffee never quite being hot enough for his taste.

In his later years, Dad would often reach out to strangers in very simple ways. He always carried a roll of Susan B. Anthony dollars, giving out the coins to the lucky ones who crossed his path. "Don't spend them, they're lucky coins," he would say. Just before his funeral, we found his stash of coins. Everyone who attended the service received a "lucky coin."

He was a practical joker, yet at times a little too stubborn. As a very young child sitting at a street curb, he put his small leg in front of a truck, daring the vehicle to stop. This particular time the joke was on him. The truck moved; his leg didn't, and the bones in one leg were broken.

As a teenager, Dad would tip over outhouses throughout his neighborhood. He would assure me that nobody was in them. Always the practical joker, at his sister-in-law's house in Pikesville, Maryland, Dad walked over to her neighbor's house and, with a straight face, gave him advice on how to plant a tree. Heeding his authoritative advice, the neighbor kept digging the hole deeper, deeper, and deeper, until the ball of the tree was five feet from the top of the hole. Luckily a local landscaper would come by and inform the gullible neighbor that the hole was too deep.

Throughout his long life, Dad cared about people.

During his Army days, as an officer of the day, he ordered a cook to put cold cuts out for a group of soldiers who came by to eat after being out in the rain all day. The watery beef stew was not good enough for these guys, he would later tell me. While his superiors called him on the carpet for that act of kindness, he stood up to the military bureaucracy, demanding that they be accountable to their troops.

By tapping his business colleagues, Dad would successfully raise money for the AMC Cancer Society to help those battling this disease. Later he would be recognized by the organization for his fund-raising efforts. I often think perhaps that is where I get my skills in fund-raising.

Life's Little Lessons

I remember during the ups and downs in my brother's and sisters' personal and professional careers, Dad was always there giving practical advice, encouragement, and support, often through little gifts.

Last week, going through a cluttered desk drawer, I found a small book given to me by Dad almost 15 years ago. The inspirational book, *Life's Little Instruction Book*, penned by author H. J. Brown, Jr., from middle Tennessee, gave simple words of wisdom gleaned from his life experience as well as others.

This small tome caught the attention of my Dad along with the American public, becoming the first book ever to occupy the No. 1 spot on *The New York Times* best-seller list simultaneously in both paperback and hardcover formats. It logged more than two years on this prestigious daily newspaper's best-seller list, including more than a year at the No. 1 spot. The little plaid book was written as a going-away present for Brown's college-bound son, containing 511 simple suggestions, observations, and reminders on how to live a happy and rewarding life.

So as Father's Day approaches, memories of my Dad come to me again, giving me his sage advice on how to have a fulfilling personal and professional life. All I have to do is go through the pages of this long-lost book he gave me and read the following suggestions, observations, and reminders that he marked with a blue dot: the ones he liked the best.

Here Are some samples:

"When someone wants to hire you, even if it's a job you have little interest in, talk to them. Never close the door on an opportunity until you've had a chance to hear the offer in person."

"Never deprive someone of hope because it might be all they have."

"When starting out, don't worry about not having enough money. Limited funds are a blessing and not a curse. Nothing encourages creative thinking in quite the same way."

"Give yourself an hour to cool off before responding to someone who has provoked you. If it involves something really important, give yourself overnight."

"Don't waste time responding to your critics."

"Never give up on what you really want to do. The person with the big dreams is more powerful than one with all the facts."

"Give people a second chance but not a third."

"Read carefully anything that requires your signature. Remember the big print giveth, and the small print taketh away."

"Don't forget that a person's greatest emotional need is to feel appreciated."

"Don't burn bridges. You'll be surprised how many times you have to cross the same river."

"Judge your success by the degree that you are enjoying peace, health and love."

"Seek opportunity, not security. A boat in a harbor is safe, but in time its bottom will rot out."

"Just to see how it feels, for the next 24 hours refrain from criticizing anyone or anything."

"Don't be rushed into making an important decision. People will understand if you say, 'I'd like a little more time to think it over. Can I get back to you tomorrow?' "

"Send your loved one flowers. Think of a reason later."

"Be prepared. You never get a second chance to make a good first impression."

"Select a doctor your own age so you can grow old together."

"Get your priorities straight. No one ever said on his deathbed, 'Gee, if I'd only spent more time at the office.'"

"Don't flaunt your success but don't apologize for it either."

"Be bold and courageous. When you look back on your life, you'll regret the things you didn't do more than the ones you did."

Most important, "Never waste an opportunity to tell someone you love them."

Brown's book reminds us of the importance of taking simple actions that can lead to a more fulfilling life. It's a great gift for parents to give to their children.

To purchase *Life's Little Instruction Book*, go to **http://goo.gl/KshGhC..**

12. SPIRITUALITY & HELPING OTHERS

HINDU SPIRITUAL LEADER HEALS WITH HUGS

Published July 20, 2012, in the Pawtucket Times

Just shy of an hour's drive from Pawtucket, Rhode Island, thousands of spiritual seekers and devotees of Sri Mata Amritanandamayi, simply known to her followers as Amma (or "Mother" in Sanskrit), gathered at the huge conference and trade center at the Best Western Royal Plaza in Marlborough, Massachusetts, to sit before the Indian saint to experience her healing embrace and meditate.

Throughout the free public morning and evening programs held on July 14th, followed by a three-day retreat (which cost $360 for adults and included room and board; less for children), organizers estimated that there would be more than 10,000 hugs given to those attending this year's New England gathering for Amma's blessing. The New England program was the last stop on her North American tour, an annual tour since 1987.

Sitting Before Amma

Issac Amponsah, proprietor of Ama's Variety on Main Street, attends Roman Catholic services, meditates twice a day, and chants his Transcendental Meditation (TM) mantra along with following the teachings of Amma.

Last year Amponsah's car broke down on his way the to see Amma. Today he waits for hours in the 47,500-square-foot conference and trade center with his brother, Paul, to see Amma and receive her blessings. The Pawtucket businessman, casually dressed and wearing sandals, knelt before Amma, surrounded by swamis in orange robes, devotee-volunteers, and spiritual seekers, to receive her brief embrace, which lasted for less than a minute. Amma slowly rocked the Woodlawn resident as she chanted a mantra in his ear. When finished, he left carrying a spiritually-charged Hersey Kiss chocolate and a few flower petals from Amma.

More than 34 years ago, Amponsah said curiosity and a thirst for knowledge led him to Transcendental Meditation (TM), when he learned the art of meditation. In 1992, a fellow TM practitioner brought him to meet Amma in New York, where he got his first hug and listened to her Vedic philosophies. Over the years, he still travels to see her when she comes through New England.

"Knowledge, inspiration, and love are the things I take away from seeing Amma," stated Amponsah. He believes that she is a true expression of divine love, just like Jesus Christ.

"It was like soul connecting to soul," noted Amponsah, trying to explain his brief spiritual encounter with Amma. "She just radiates love."

Like Amponsah, other Rhode Island baby boomers came across the Massachusetts border to seek Amma's blessing, too.

For the past couple of years, Elizabeth Johanson, 50, a Pawtucket resident and a practicing Roman Catholic, has come for Amma's hugs and blessings. She considers this Hindu saint to be the incarnation of the divine mother in the Hindu tradition.

According to Johanson, "Amma's the real deal," who financially supports programs to promote nonviolence and social justice as well as feeding and housing the poor.

Johanson, wearing a white T-shirt sporting the word *love* and an Our Lady of Guadalupe medallion, strongly believes that her annual encounters with Amma and studying her teachings only strengthen Johanson's traditional beliefs in Roman Catholicism.

"I try to take Amma's love and unconditional compassion out into Pawtucket and Central Falls each day," noted the mental-health worker. "As I become more spiritually nourished, I am able to become more patient and tolerant in my everyday world," she said.

Fifty-seven-year-old Tommy Emmet, who grew up practicing the doctrine of the Church of England, is spiritually eclectic. Practicing Hinduism and Buddhism, the avid reader of tomes on the world's religions sees the thread of truth in all religious practices.

Wearing blue jeans and a colorful Hawaiian shirt, the aging baby boomer proudly wears an "Obama '08" button and sports a necklace showing his religious beliefs with dangling charms of images of Hindu deities, Native American symbols, and one of Amma.

In 2007 his wife, Karen Lee, owner of the Pawtucket-based Breathing Time Yoga Studio, introduced him to Amma. Emmet, an usher at National Amusement Theater at Providence Mall, has continued to come each year for Amma's healing hugs and blessings.

Emmet claims that sitting before this Hindu spiritual teacher enables him to more easily connect to his divine higher power and allows him to be more loving with himself and others. "Thinking about Amma just helps me get through the day," he said.

The Making of a Spiritual Teacher

Amma, who grew up in poverty, was born in 1953 in a remote coastal village in Kerala, South India. Her family's trade was fishing. As a young girl, she spent many hours in deep meditation on the seashore, where she began to compose devotional songs. Many of these compositions revealed depth and wisdom.

With an ailing mother, Amma left school to help with household tasks and take care of her seven siblings. As she went door to door gathering food scraps from neighbors for her family's cows, she saw intense poverty and suffering in her community. She brought people food and clothing from her own home, to the dismay of her family.

Amma began to spontaneously hug people to comfort them. People responded by calling her *Amma*. She had found her path of serving others.

Amma Recognized Around the Globe for Her Charity Work

In 1987, Amma toured the world, including the United States. With her home ashram in Kerala, South India, her ashrams, teaching her philosophy that all religions are one, are today scattered around the world. Her devotees say that Amma has never asked anyone to change religions, only that they go deeper into their own values and faith and live by those essential principles.

One of her initiatives, "Embracing the World Program" (ETW), funds humanitarian efforts throughout India. This program has provided more than $50 million in free medical care, built an 800-bed hospital, a medical school, and health clinics. Meanwhile it has provided more than 40,000 homes for the homeless throughout India and given financial aid to 100,000 people unable to care for themselves. ETW projects also fund vocational training and literacy training. The program also opens and operates orphanages, hospices, nursing homes, scholarship programs, and even plants trees.

Amma has received international praise. She has delivered addresses at the United Nations several times and has twice spoken at the Parliament of the World's Religions. She has also received the Gandhi-King Award for Non-Violence in Geneva and the James Park Morton Interfaith Award in New York. Two years ago, the Hindu spiritual leader was presented an honorary doctorate in humane letters at the University at Buffalo North Campus.

CHILDREN CAN BRING
MESSAGE OF LIFE AFTER DEATH

Published December 20, 2014, in the Pawtucket Times

The tragic, untimely death of a child will bring emotional pain and suffering to the parents. Yet amazingly through horrific experiences like this slowly comes a greater appreciation, understanding, and love of life.

Sixty-five-year-old Dave Kane and his wife, Joanne, know this so well. The fourth-largest nightclub fire in the nation's history, killing their son Nicky O'Neill, would propel the semi-retired radio talk-show host (he's on the air at WARL 1320 in Attleboro from 8 a.m. to 10 a.m. on Saturdays), comedian, performance artist, and author, with his wife on a journey of personal healing that would lead to their bringing comfort to others who grieve for lost loved ones.

Kane's 18-year-old son, Nicky O'Neill, was the youngest victim of the Station nightclub fire in which 100 people lost their lives over a decade ago. More than 230 people were injured. After this tragic event, Kane became a very visible proponent of fire safety and the enforcement of strict laws to ensure safety in public buildings. Three years later, he would publish his first book, *41 Signs of Hope*. In this book, Kane shares personal stories of synchronistic and, at times, seemingly spirit communication, around the number 41, which Kane and his family contend are contact from the spirit of his deceased young son Nicky.

The Number 41

Kane views the number 41 as an "incredible sign" from his deceased son that he still exists. Throughout the young man's life he always liked this number, he says, noting Nicky noticed that number everywhere, and he would let those around him know it.

"When he passed away Nicky was 18 years old and 23 days, that totals 41," notes Kane, a Johnston resident, who can reel off dozens of examples of the number 41 showing up around him. A videotape of Nicky as a baby discovered one year after his death shows him wearing a baseball uniform, and a baseball cap embroidered with the number 41.

At that time no one could figure out the significance. For more than a decade that followed Nicky's death, the number continued to appear. Although Kane and his family initially viewed the sightings as coincidences, they now see them as a sign of spirit contact. The book, *41 Signs of Hope*, followed by an hour-and-50-minute documentary released in 2005 (just called *41*), by Rhode Island filmmakers Christian de Rezendes and Christian O'Neill, is jam-packed with examples of the sightings of this number 41.

The First Contact

Detailed in Kane's book, *41 Signs of Hope,* shares how medium Cindy Gilman gave him a message from Nicky, who had died at the Station nightclub fire. A day before the deadly fire that occurred on February 20, 2003, Gilman smelled smoke as she walked through her office. The medium knew that a tragic event would happen close by and that she could not do anything to stop it.

The day after the tragic fire, while sitting in her kitchen drinking tea, a figure of a young man appeared to Gilman, with long blond hair, a glittery shirt, and a leather jacket, begging her to "call his father." Startled by this vision she did not know whom to call. A moment later the spirit reappeared showing her his charred body, then transformed back to his original form.

Gilman knew that the apparition wanted the East Greenwich medium to give his father a message, that Nicky had "crossed over and was not in pain." Picking up her personal phone book, she turned to "K" and immediately saw the name of a professional acquaintance, Dave Kane (the only name under that letter).

Kane recalls that she called his beeper. He returned her call and the medium offered to come on his radio show to identify the young spirit. The grieving father told her, "We had lost Nicky in a fire," with Gilman responding, "Oh, I should have said something." A very distraught Kane immediately hung up on her, thinking that he had a medium telling him she knew something that she really did not know.

Ultimately, he would call Gilman back, and she would describe the spirit to him. He confirmed to Gilman that this was his son.

Looking back, losing his son was the most horrible experience that Kane and his wife had experienced in their lives, he says. The morning after the deadly West Warwick fire, he stood in front of his bathroom mirror and cried, screaming, "Okay big shot, now what do you think?" Thirty years as a talk-show host gave him all the answers to any topic. But he had no answers to why his son died tragically and so young.

But the Number 41 would give Kane and his wife comfort that their son was reaching out, telling them that life does not end with death. Loved ones who have passed on never leave us, they are still with us, loving, supporting, guiding, and sending us signs each and every day, he says.

Rhode Island medium Gilman's confirmation of Nicky's definite proof of life after death was validated by a reading given to Kane and his wife by Robert Brown, an internationally acclaimed medium. The medium confirmed where Nicky had stood before he died, and that he helped a young woman during the fire, all confirmed months later.

Brown pointed at him at the end of the 45-minute reading and said, "Your son wants me to tell you one more thing, the show must go on." What Brown and nobody else knew was these words were spoken by Nicky to his father before he died at the Station nightclub, says Kane.

Just a couple of days before the tragic fire, Kane found out that his son was not getting paid much money to play in an opening act for the headlining band, Jack Russell's Great White. "You should not sell God's talent so short," said Kane jokingly. Nicky just hugged his father and kissed him, saying, "The show must go on."

Those last words, repeated by the British medium, confirmed the existence of spirit. Each and every day Kane and his family continue to receive signs from Nicky to continually validate this.

Spreading the Word

For more than 30 years Kane educated tens of thousands of Rhode Islanders on state and national topics on his radio show, "Kane and Company." Now he's traveling a new path in his later years, bringing the public awareness to more ethereal topics, like life after death.

With several of his own family members being cared for by Home and Hospice Care of Rhode Island, Kane wanted "to give back" and offered to share his *41 Signs of Hope* presentation to bereaved families, says Deanna Upchurch, grief counseling department manager at Home and Hospice Care of Rhode Island. After reviewing his "incredible" presentation, he was invited to share it to HHCRI's Loss of Parent, Loss of Spouse and Loss of Adult Child groups.

For more than one hour, Kane gives dozens of examples of how deceased loved ones can send you messages in many forms to validate their existence. Nicky shows up at Disneyland, at Chili's restaurant, even at a family Thanksgiving dinner, and when Kane was driving his car, reminding them he is still around as the number 41 pops up everywhere.

"It is up to us to acknowledge and know that they are here. We are so busy grieving and busy we just don't see our loved ones," he says.

Those attending HHCRI's grief counseling groups felt comfort in Kane's stories, notes Upchurch. "Grieving people often talk about ways they feel their loved ones are still connected with them after death," says Upchurch. "Whether it's a faint smell of a loved one's cigar or the sight of a cardinal, or butterfly, which they feel represents their loved one, people frequently share their experiences of sharing signs from their loved ones."

Upchurch says that Kane's presentation validates the experiences of the grieving. It helps them continue to feel connected to their loved ones and even keeps them open-minded for future signs from them.

After listening to Kane's passionate stories, it only reinforced my belief that "death is nothing at all," Kane's concluding words.

For more information about *41 Signs of Hope,* go to **www.davekane.net/41-the-book.html**. Or call (401) 965-0467.

CONQUERING CANCER THROUGH LIVING FEARLESSLY

Published November 9, 2012, in the Pawtucket Times

W e've heard it before: "Don't sweat the small stuff." "Do not fear death … only the unlived life." "Live life to the fullest." Anita Moorjani, 50, knows the truth behind these familiar sayings only too well because of a Near Death Experience (NDE) she had in 2006.

In Moorjani's book, *Dying to be Me: My Journey From Cancer To Near Death, To True Healing*, published in 2012 by Hay House, USA, the Hong Kong resident recounts stories of her childhood such as being raised Hindu while residing in a largely Chinese and British society in Hong Kong. Throughout her adult life, she faced challenges to find a profession and eventually found her one true love, husband Danny. She eventually fought devastating cancer, which resulted in her death, after which she ultimately came back to life and became healed, an outcome that today baffles the medical world.

The 191-page inspirational tome tells how Moorjani fought Stage IV lymphoma for almost four years, ultimately a terminal disease that spread from the base of her skull and traveled over her neck and down to her abdomen. Her body was riddled with malignant tumors, "some the size of lemons," she recalled.

As a result of her NDE and the publicity generated by her book, Moorjani speaks at conferences and events around the world to share her insights. She is also a frequent guest at the University of Hong Kong's department of behavioral sciences, speaking on topics such as dealing with terminal illness, facing death, and the psychology of spiritual beliefs.

Crossing Over

By the morning of February 2, 2006, Moorjani was wheelchair bound, on oxygen, and receiving full-time care at home. She was sliding in and out of consciousness while experiencing breathing difficulties due to fluid in her lungs. Her body was swollen with open skin lesions, and she was soon admitted to the local hospital in a coma. Her prognosis was grim, and the attending physician informed her husband that the doctor did not expect her to survive for 36 hours.

Placed in the Intensive Care Unit (ICU) and having been in a coma for nearly 20 hours, the forty-four-year-old woman's vital organs began to fail. In fact, she was ultimately pronounced dead. Moorjani recalled entering into an NDE and having a spiritual epiphany while on the other side of death's veil. She came to understand the ultimate cause of her devastating medical condition, which she reports as "being fearful of life." When she chose to return to her physical body, Moorjani knew she indeed had the power to heal her body of the spreading cancer and understood with certainty that this medical miracle would occur.

Over a six-month period after her NDE, Moorjani was given chemotherapy, even though every medical test revealed no trace of cancer. A lymph-node biopsy also revealed no cancer in any of her lymph nodes.

Like millions of others who have reported an NDE, Moorjani experienced many of its classic traits. She recalled having "an extreme sense of peace and well-being and an intense feeling of unconditional love," and she was reunited with deceased family members, friends, and spiritual guides.

Her book noted that even in a coma in this very deep NDE, she was acutely aware of her surroundings. She heard a physician tell her husband, who was outside her room in the corridor, that her organs were failing, and she would not last the night. In her NDE, she knew that her brother was on a plane coming to say good-bye.

On the other side, Moorjani recounts in this book how she received profound knowledge about her life, mission, and purpose of life with an understanding of the nature of the universe as well. When the terminally ill woman approached the boundary of no return, she remembers she had a decision to make: to stay and sever ties with her sickly body or return to heal and accomplish her life's mission. Choosing to voluntarily return to her disease-ridden body, upon regaining consciousness, she knew that her body would be quickly healed of cancerous tumors. She was released from the hospital within weeks, without a trace of cancer in her body.

With an increased belief in the God-force within, no longer would Moorjani fear death, and this experience fueled her desire to confront life fearlessly.

NDE: A Common Occurrence

Over the years, Jeffrey Long, M.D., a leading NDE researcher, has documented more than 3,000 NDEs, posted on the **www.nderf.org** website. The practicing radiation oncologist said that this database is by far the largest collection of NDEs, which is available in 22 languages and is publicly accessible. Readers from more than 100 countries access Dr. Long's website. More than 300,000 pages are read from this website every month.

Meanwhile Dr. Long's web site noted that although most people who come near death do not remember anything, about 18 percent later report that "something happened." That "something" is often an NDE, said Dr. Long. He noted a 1993 Gallup Poll that an estimated 12 million to 15 million Americans have personally experienced an NDE. As of 2001, almost 600 adults per day across the nation experience an NDE.

According to Dr. Long, who penned *The New York Times* best-seller, *Evidence of the Afterlife: The Science of Near-Death Experiences*, Moorjani's NDE is "one of the most profound NDEs ever reported. The insights she received during her NDE are profound, yet corroborated by the insights of many other NDErs."

Dr. Long noted, "I have carefully reviewed Anita Moorjani's incredible recovery and NDE. It is medically inexplicable. Doctors don't like to use the term 'miracle,' yet that is the best word to describe her experience."

While he did not review her original medical records, one physician did. In an email and a press release promoting a workshop to discuss Moorjani's rapid remission from an advanced stage of cancer, Dr. Peter Ko, an oncologist who reviewed her medical records, did not attribute her dramatic recovery to her chemotherapy. "Her recovery was remarkable. Based on what we have learned about cancer cell behaviors, I am unable to attribute her dramatic recovery to chemotherapy. I speculate that something nonphysical switched the mutated genes," said Dr. Ko, an oncologist of southern California.

Lessons Learned from Beyond the Veil

Moorjani believes her cancer manifested in her physical body due to the fear of being herself, displeasing others, not measuring up to their expectations, and fear of living life to the fullest. In fact, it was being "fearful of everything," said the internationally recognized writer, which blocked her greater essence from healing the physical body.

"Only when I realized my own magnificence, my own perfection, my own self-worth as a beautiful child of the universe, was I able to let go of fear and embrace life with all its uncertainties, ambiguities, joys, sorrows, and challenges. Seeing myself as perfection, as an exquisite manifestation of life led to my healing," she said.

A prevalent part of her NDE was the realization that we are all interconnected, and when she was not in her body, she was able to clearly see this.

Finally, "laughter and a good sense of humor can be your best medicine," she said. Moorjani recommends not taking your life too seriously. "Learn to lighten up and laugh. Don't be afraid of just being yourself."

For more details about Anita Moorjani's work, go to **www.anitamoorjani.com/**

BEFORE 'CROSSING OVER,' LEAVE A LEGACY OF LOVE

Published May 6, 2002, in the Pawtucket Times

D ead men (or women) tell no tales.

That's not true for millions of viewers who watch the syndicated hit series *Crossing Over* with John Edward. The 31-year-old internationally acclaimed medium has touched the hearts and souls of the American public as he uses his uncanny mediumistic ability to connect audiences with their loved ones who have "crossed over."

Believe him or not, this show is making waves throughout southern New England, according to Judy Shoemaker, director of promotions for ABC 6. The dead have something to say, and Edward is listening to what they say, she noted.

Attesting to the popularity of the show, 2,500 tickets costing $45 each were sold out in just one hour after being made available for yesterday's gathering at the Rhode Island Convention Center.

Edward was the sponsor of the Providence event. Before Sunday, tickets were sold on eBay, prices going for as high as $450 per ticket.

Edward's visit to the Renaissance City is the most anticipated promotional event that ABC 6 has sponsored in the past 30 years, noted Shoemaker. The Providence-based television station on Orms Street, which now airs Edward's one-hour show on weekdays at 4 p.m., received hundreds of letters, emails, and calls for the past several weeks from frantic fans wanting to attend the event.

"This show has moved and touched so many people, and it makes them feel good," Shoemaker said, explaining why the show sold out so quickly.

According to the Sci-Fi Channel, age-50-plus viewers watching *Crossing Over* represent 38 percent of the 503,000 viewers on late Monday through Thursday evenings, and 30 percent of the 553,000 viewers of the program in its late-Sunday-nighttime slot.

Rose O. Boucher, 84, a lifelong Pawtucket resident, regularly tunes into *Crossing Over* on the Sci-Fi Channel and on ABC 6. For her, Edward's show "is educational and relaxing to watch," she said. Boucher likes how it helps people who have worries and doubts. Responding to Edward's skeptics, she said, "There are a lot of things in the world that we don't know about."

According to Edward, at age 15 he tried to debunk a psychic who was doing readings at his grandmother's house. Going into his reading, he was skeptical, yet Edward came out impressed with the psychic's accuracy.

"The information that came through was factual and not generalities," Edward said, who noted that the psychic even predicted he would do the work if he chose to.

Even with 16 years of studying psychic development and metaphysics, Edward has never forgotten his Roman Catholic upbringing, and he believes that it has even enhanced his religious beliefs.

While he does not attend church regularly, he is constantly praying with his rosary and doing spiritual work. "Using your rosary and saying a repetition of prayers significantly helps raise your own vibration and frequency," he said.

"Everyone is psychic," Edward said. "Be open to learning about spiritual development. Go to a metaphysical bookstore, or the New Age section in a bookstore, and let the book pick you."

Edward looks at death this way: "Energy cannot be created or destroyed, yet it can change forms. I just look at death as a transition of the energy of the soul outside of the body." Over the years, Edward said he has found that his readings have solidified and strengthened the religious beliefs of many people.

Is there a heaven or hell? "No," said Edward. The other side is made up of different levels, and you gravitate to the level appropriate to your spiritual growth. "The higher, more-evolved levels might be deemed the heavenly levels, while the lower levels are for people who are not so (spiritually advanced)."

Edward urged people to take the opportunity to communicate and validate others in their lives before they "cross over," so that a medium is not required to do it for them.

Before you greet death, leave your legacy of love behind. That's what it is really all about, said the frequently humorous and down-to-earth medium.

Leaving your legacy of love behind is as simple as looking your loved one in the eyes and saying, "I love you."

THE WORLD ACCORDING TO A RHODE ISLAND MEDIUM

Published September 27, 2013, in the Pawtucket Times

C indy Gilman knew something was wrong but just could not put her finger on it. Three weeks before Tuesday, Sept. 11, 2001, when four coordinated terrorist attacks launched by al-Qaeda upon the Twin Towers in New York City and the Pentagon in the Washington, D.C. area, killing over 3,000 people, the well-known Rhode Island medium felt shaky and weak. The fifty-five-year-old medium had a metallic taste in her mouth, she even began to experience unidentifiable fear. Every time Gilman went into a meditative state to "spiritually lift herself up," her discomfort became even stronger. A series of blood tests just one week before the national tragedy, performed at her primary-care physician's office, found no medical irregularities.

When the huge passenger planes dove into their iconic targets, Gilman, like others across the country, learned about the Islamist terrorist attacks. Only then did she realize that her symptoms were what New York residents were now feeling, even down to the foul-tasting smoke and ash they breathed in from the falling, burnt debris.

One day before the mass shootings inside the Beltway, on Sept. 16, 2013, Gilman began to violently shake, even having an unidentifiable sense of fear, like she experienced 12 years earlier. The medium knew intuitively something was going to happen. The next day local radio, confirmed by CNN, validated her uneasiness that something was going to happen. It did. A lone gunman fatally shot 12 people and injured three others in Southeast Washington, D.C., at the headquarters of the Naval Sea Systems Command at the Washington Navy Yard.

Having the Gift

The petite, blond-haired medium, whose 37-year-old son, Danny, resides in the Boston area with his wife and one-year-old child, consciously began her spiritual journey in the early 1950s.

One of her first major spiritual experiences that she can recall, as a second-grader, the young student went up to her teacher and said, "I have to go home because my mother needs me; my grandfather just passed away." The teacher let the youngster walk home where her mother validated this death in fact did occur before her arrival.

At age 7, over 60 years ago, Gilman became aware of her spiritual gifts as she sang to a roomful of Holocaust survivors at a memorial service held in Boston. Standing on a milk crate to reach the microphone, the child singer brought tears to the eyes of many in the room, as she nervously sang lullaby songs they remembered being sung by their mothers while they were in captivity in German concentration camps. As the horrific, repressed memories came to the surface of the audience as she continued singing, a nervous Gilman remembered not seeing them as they were dressed that day but seeing them as emaciated, with shaved heads and wearing striped pajamas like they did in the camps. "I just closed my eyes and saw my maternal grandfather standing before me with my spiritual eye," said Gilman, seeing him as "young and healthy," not as a man whose body was once ravaged with cancer, who passed on months earlier. "My deceased grandfather nodded his head, and at that moment I knew that there was something more to life, more than just a person's physical body," added Gilman.

For a longtime the young child told nobody of this experience, but eventually brought it up with her paternal grandmother. "She started to cry and rubbed her hands on my face," she said, telling her that "God is with you." Later at a family gathering Gilman would walk up to an uncle and warn him of an impending heart attack. This happened. Her mother quickly told her not to say things like this. "I was told to sit on the couch and not put my intuitive foot in my mouth," she said. As to her spiritual verbal slips, Gilman now knows that "some things come through my higher intuitive self or through a spirit guide."

Looking back at her childhood, the seasoned medium thought "everyone had the abilities of being intuitive; it was a part of human nature," but life would teach her that this was not the case.

From Singer to Intuitive Pioneer

At age 17, Gilman would seek formal educational training to enhance her musical career by attending Emerson College where she once danced with Henry Winkler, "the Fonz," in a college production. "We remained in touch long after our college days," she says.

Ultimately, the college student transferred to the New England Conservatory of Music, where she graduated. Residing in New York City, the young college graduate honed her musical abilities by professionally performing in Miami, New York City, and the Catskill Mountains in Upstate New York and the Bahamas. At this time, before she became a professional medium, she would sometimes pick up things from the audience as she performed her repertoire of songs from the stage. In her late 20s she returned to Boston to begin to work as a professional intuitive spiritual medium.

"I really was a pioneer doing this type of work. People started calling asking me for readings," Gilman remembers. Both print and electronic media also began calling asking her for interviews on spiritual understanding.

For over 23 years, Gilman has brought comfort and insight to thousands of listeners as a radio talk-show host at WHDH–AM, Boston, (1972 to 1993), later moving to WHJJ-AM, Providence, (1984 to 1996). She used her intuitive and healing abilities, and her understanding of hypnosis and meditation skills, to assist in the healing process. She is a certified hypnosis counselor and meditation instructor. As an intuitive, her ESP expertise has been called upon to work with psychokinetic children in cooperation with Dr. J. B. Rhine (who coined the phrase "ESP") in the early 1970s and 1980s. Besides giving readings that bridge the physical world with spirit, Gilman has lectured at colleges on spiritual topics, also teaching psychic development classes and working with intuitively gifted children.

Gilman has even assisted police departments to solve crimes. In one instance, she traveled to Miami, Florida, to assist the chief of detectives in locating a murderer. Quickly looking at photographs of five suspects, Gilman intuitively described where the police could find the murderer, at a cottage she described in detail, including a printed sofa inside with three garbage cans in the back. The suspect was later captured at that location. However, she has retired her services working with law enforcement because "it is just too painful to do."

Successful Hits

While Gilman will tell you that no intuitive can be 100 percent accurate in their psychic predictions, she gives a few examples of intuitively zeroing in on major New England events. The medium gave a feature writer at the Boston Herald a prediction when he asked for one, that a big blizzard would happen in February 1978. "I clairvoyantly saw a newspaper headline that read, "This Is the Blizzard that Paralyzed Boston." Meanwhile, an image of Valentine cards on a shelf would date the event around February 14th, she noted.

Meanwhile, detailed in Dave Kane's book, 41 Signs of Hope, the former radio talk-show host, comedian, performance artist, and author, shares how Gilman gave him a message from Nicky, his son, who had died at the Station Nightclub fire. A day before the fourth-deadliest nightclub fire in United States history that occurred on February 20, 2003 killing 100 people and injuring 230 in West Warwick, Gilman smelled smoke as she walked through her office. The medium knew that a tragic event would happen close by and that she could not do anything to stop it.

The day after the tragic fire, a figure of a young man appeared to Gilman, with long blond hair, a glittery shirt, and a leather jacket. This spirit had just died at the Station Nightclub fire, begging her to "call his father." Startled she did not know whom to call. A moment later the spirit reappeared showing her his charred body, then transformed back to his original form.

The young man wanted her to tell his grieving father that he had "crossed over, was OK and not in pain," says Gilman. Picking up her personal phone book, she turned to "K" and immediately saw the name of a professional acquaintance, Dave Kane. She called his beeper. That evening Kane returned the call and the medium offered to help those who lost family members and friends in the fire. Kane told her "we had lost Nicky in a fire," Gilman remembered, "I knew it, I should have said something." Kane hung up but he ultimately called back the next morning, and she described the spirit to him. It was the spitting image of his son, he said. He confirmed to Gilman that this was his son, especially detailing how he had dressed the night he died.

A Few Thoughts and Observations

Gilman concludes my interview at the Kitchen Bar Restaurant on Hope Street, noting that there is definitely a spiritual, financial, and social shift happening across the world. Although horrific events, like earth changes, even terrorist attacks, like the recent shooting at the Washington Naval Yard, will still occur, she stresses that people will become more spiritually-inclined, too.

"Finding ways to become more grounded and focused will become more important," says Gilman, recommending meditation.

For more information or to book an appointment call Gilman at (401) 885-4115.

CHANGING THE WORLD
ONE PERSON AT A TIME

Published September 21, 2012, in the Pawtucket Times

You do not have to be in political office, a government official, own and operate a business, or run a nonprofit to make Rhode Island a better place to live and work. Individually we can work daily by performing good deeds to those who cross our paths that ultimately contribute to the greater good of our community.

Catherine Ryan Hyde's novel, *Pay It Forward*, published in 1999, was adapted into a Warner Brothers film (with the same title) one year later, bringing the *Pay It Forward* concept to millions of Americans. In the PG-rated film, young Trevor McKinney learns that positive community change can occur just by doing three good deeds. He sees the positive impact of *Pay it Forward* and learns that the practice of helping one another can "spread geometrically through society at a ratio of three to one, creating a social movement to making the world a better place."

We are drawn to the tormented 12-year-old Trevor McKinney, who is living with an alcoholic mother and conflicted by fears of his abusive, yet mostly absent father. The young boy takes on a school assignment given to his class by the new social-studies teacher, Mr. Simonet. The assignment is to "create something to change the world" and put it into action. For his project, Trevor embellishes on an idea in which, instead of repaying a favor or good deed back to someone, the recipient would *Pay It Forward* by doing good deeds to three new people. Ultimately McKinney sees the impact of this school assignment, like a rock skipping over a pond, making ever-widening ripples in the water.

This *Pay It Forward* concept is not a new one. According to Wikipedia, in a letter to Benjamin Webb dated April 15, 1784, Benjamin Franklin clearly penned his support of the concept in that correspondence.

The Founding Father wrote: "I do not pretend to give such a Sum; I only lend it to you. When you... meet with another honest Man in similar Distress, you must pay me by lending this Sum to him; enjoining him to discharge the Debt by a like operation, when he shall be able, and shall meet with another opportunity. I hope it may thus go thro' many hands, before it meets with a Knave that will stop its Progress. This is a trick of mine for doing a deal of good with a little money."

Like Franklin, university student Christopher Lo took this concept to heart. He was inspired by the unexpected return of a lost video camera, leading him to create the website **www.thekarmaseed.org** in 2010.The equipment was misplaced after he accidentally left it outside the university's library. Although it did not immediately turn up on the school's "lost and found" website, a stranger finally turned it in. Amazingly, that simple act of kindness of returning a lost video camera led to the creation of a website to track all the good deeds "passed forward" to illustrate the positive impact of the concept.

Lo created a "Karma Seed," a small, plastic card with a unique identification number, detailing the website location. If you perform a favor for someone, you just give them the plastic card and request that the person register the plastic card at the website. This person then "pays the good deed forward," requesting that the new recipient of kindness go online and register the card after they become the recipient of a good deed. Any recipient or giver of a Karma Seed card can go back to the website and see a detailed history of the good deeds that followed the original act of kindness.

Lo's Karma Seed organization contributes 50 percent of the profits to the Karma Seed Foundation to support social projects in communities surrounding Washington University in St. Louis.

One year later, a Louisiana affiliate of ABC News reported a story on the Newton Project, a 501(c)(3) outreach organization established to show that even with the world facing big problems, each person can make a unique, individual difference simply by taking the time to show love, appreciation, and kindness to those around them. Like Lo, the founder, Michael Phillips, based the mission of his organization on the classic *Pay It Forward* concept, yet demonstrates the impact of each act on the world by tracking each wristband with a unique identification number and quantifying the lives each has touched. The Newton Project's attempt to determine the benefits of a "Pay It Forward" system can be viewed by the general public at **https://goo.gl/nOUxyZ**.

Meanwhile the "Pay It Forward" movement got a jump-start with businessman Charley Johnson taking the helm of the Pay It Forward Foundation in 2012. He walked away from corporate America to change the world one person at a time. The former owner of a manufacturing company had an idea for encouraging kindness by creating a "Pay it Forward" bracelet that could be worn as a reminder of the importance of doing good deeds to strangers who cross your path. Today, more than 1.5 million "Pay it Forward" bracelets have been distributed in more than 112 countries, sparking some amazing acts of kindness. Few bracelets remain with their original recipients, however, because they circulate in the spirit of the reciprocal or generalized altruism.

Pay It Forward author Catherine Ryan Hyde, who also founded the Pay it Forward Foundation in 2000, sings his praises. "Charley says he's going to make this 'the biggest thing the world has ever seen.' If anybody else said that, I might not believe it. But nothing is out of the question when Charley goes after it."

Start today to make a difference in your neighborhood, office, and throughout your daily travels with a simple act of kindness to a stranger. Doing this and requesting that the beneficiary "Pay It Forward" may have major, positive implications for your neighborhood, city or town, the Ocean State and even the world. Amazing.

LOCAL FILMMAKER DOCUMENTS INNOVATIVE HUNGER PROJECT IN MAINE

Published on January 3, 2015, in the Pawtucket Times

L ast July, long-time Rhode Island resident John Martin, who filmed the 2013 web-based hunger documentary, *Hungry in the West End*, packed his bags and equipment to head off to rural Northern Maine. Martin, an award-winning AARP filmmaker and AARP's communications director, began filming a new short film to put a spotlight on the work of Dale Flewelling to feed Maine's hungry. The lifelong resident of Houlton in Aroostook County, who founded the Friends of Aroostook, a nonprofit agency, has worked for nearly seven years to provide fresh locally grown produce and emergency winter firewood to low-income families throughout Aroostook County.

Maine AARP's commissioned short film on Flewelling's efforts, titled *With Friends Like These: Dale Flewelling & Friends of Aroostook*, profiles the retired business-man's "passionate and charming crusade" to enlist friends, volunteers, leaders, and businesses to help seniors in Aroostook and Washington counties suffering daily from food insecurity.

After watching Martin's short film (just over 11 minutes), it gives a simple message. By bringing together the community and working together we can put nutritious, fresh food on the tables of the nation's needy. Creative ways of growing food, like at Aroostoock's farm, should be organized on farms throughout Rhode Island and the nation.

Yes, in hard times getting your hands dirty (by harvesting crops) rather than com-plaining may well be a simple solution to reducing hunger in America.

Stars Fall in Alignment

Looking back, Martin says, "Some things seem meant to be. There was a last-minute cancelation by a videographer who had been hired to shoot the film for our Maine state office. In a bind, they turned to me based on my, *Hungry in the West End*," he says.

Martin, a former *Providence Journal* reporter, says, "This was a dream assignment. The location was gorgeous. Overnight rain stopped right on cue. People were doing things more than talking about things, which is a lot better way of telling a story. I chose to follow Dale around during part of the day rather than sit him down for an interview. He is not big on sitting, and so that may have been the best decision I made. And at the end of the day he insisted on loading me up with green beans, Maine potatoes dug that very afternoon, tomatoes, and zucchini. How good is that?"

According to Martin, the first impression of the town of Houlton was that of a community hit hard by the nation's recent recession. "Last summer, no one was talking much about an economic recovery there," he remembers. After an overnight stay at a truckers' motel, Martin began his filming at Aroostook Farm at 5:30 a.m. "I was pretty shocked to see volunteers already at work picking string beans," he says.

Martin notes that Flewelling is as charming in real life as he comes across in the film, observing that his work has added tremendous meaning to his retirement.

"It only occurred to me recently that I thought I was making a hunger film, but as far as AARP is concerned, it also is a great example of "Life Reimagined" —AARP's resource for making life decisions, adapting to change, and developing next-chapter careers," says Martin, adding that Flewelling "personifies the benefits of identifying your "what next" opportunity and pursuing a dream."

"He is so connected to the earth and growing food. You have to give him credit for finding a great place to focus his energy in his life after running a business," states Martin.

"Also, for me the day at Aroostook revealed the great need the community faces," Martin added. "In contrast to the urban poverty that frames the issue in the West End of Providence, here you find people who lived well for generations in rural Maine, who are increasingly unable to meet their monthly expenses based on little or no personal savings and sometimes minimal Social Security benefits."

But either way, these seniors are worried about outliving their resources, he says.

We Can Be Part of the Solution

"My conclusion after spending six months reporting in the West End ('in Providence') was that government can do only so much; nonprofits are helping as best they can; but volunteers can make a huge difference. I hope that both *Hungry in the West End* and *With Friends Like These* spark recognition that when you volunteer to help feed struggling seniors, the feeling you get back is a tremendous reward. We all can be part of the solution. And younger people, especially, need to pay it forward because someday they may be the ones needing help," says Martin.

Dale Flewelling, executive director of the Friends of Aroostook, says "Generally speaking, a young organization such as Friends of Aroostook has to make a decision whether to utilize financial resources to build capacity or spend money on publicity and awareness. Like many, if not most, we choose to build capacity. To have John travel all the way from Rhode Island to Northern Maine and committing many hours and his talents to produce this film is almost overwhelming."

"Words can't describe the benefit this film brings to our programs. Friends of Aroostook and the hungry we serve owe a heartfelt thank you to John, AARP Maine State Director Lori Parham, and everyone at AARP who addresses the hunger needs within our less-fortunate population," adds Flewelling, noting that this problem "is not going away. But as you can see, people can make a big difference. So the film means a lot."

Getting People Involved

"One of the results of Dale's work at Aroostook Farm is that people see him in action out in the fields and better understand both the importance of the work and Dale's ability to get people involved," says Lori Parham, state director, AARP Maine.

Parham says actually seeing people work the farm land makes it far "less intimidating" for those who might be reluctant to seek out or ask for help. "As the film shows, the neediest seniors are actually helping others—they pick a bag for themselves and then pick a bag for someone else. We knew that capturing these images and sentiments in a short video would be a great way to illustrate Dale's efforts to relieve hunger in Maine," she says.

"John knows a lot about senior hunger, and he is a great visual storyteller. We hope that the film inspires people from across Maine and other parts of the country to join in similar movements to engage entire communities and create a shared resource that, quite literally, can grow from season to season," notes Parham.

To watch, *With Friends Like These*, go to **states.aarp.org/with-friends-like -these-picks-up-film-awards/**

RICHARD J. WALTON'S GREAT ADVENTURE IN LIFE AND DEATH

Published on January 4, 2013, in thePawtucket Times

Throughout his eighty-four years, Richard J. Walton served as a role model for generations of activists, watching out and protecting Rhode Island's voiceless citizens, showing all that positive societal changes could be made by making sound arguments. With his last breath, he even taught us how to face death. Walton, age 84, died on December 27 at Rhode Island Hospital. He had been treated for leukemia for about six months, says daughter, Cathy Walton Barnard, of Simsbury, Connecticut, who noted his last words, "I'm going on a great adventure."

Walton Touched Many Lives

Even with many in Walton's vast progressive and activist networks knowing about his illness, people were caught off guard by his sudden passing over a week ago, stated Rick Wahlberg, a computer consultant and a former president of Stone Soup Coffee House, who worked closely with Walton on the nonprofit's Board of Directors for over 20 years and developed close personal ties. "We considered him part of our family just like many others did," he said.

According to Wahlberg, a Cumberland resident, Walton was part of New York's intelligentsia scene (mingling with writers at the Lion's Head, a bar a few steps down from Christopher Street) in Greenwich Village, where he lived making a living as a writer.

Wahlberg viewed Walton as a "great example of morality, humanity, and a supporter of nonviolence," noting that his friend led an amazing life that helped shape his progressive point of view and that of his two daughters. When Wahlberg's oldest daughter, Corinne, heard of Walton's passing, she remarked, "He did more in one lifetime than most."

Over the years, Wahlberg, 59, and his wife, Barbara, attended Walton's birthday parties that would raise large sums of money for his favorite charities, attracting the state's powerful political and media elite right to his family compound, located at Pawtuxet Cove in Warwick. This legendary fund-raising event occurred from 1989 to 2011, bringing hundreds of people each year to celebrate his progressive causes. Due to his health in 2012, for the first time, Walton's birthday was held at the Roots Cultural Center in Providence.

Joyce Katzberg, 59, folksinger and a founding organizer of Stone Soup Coffee House, spent decades protesting with Walton at vigils, rallies, and picket lines. She remembers him as a kind, honest person. When necessary, he was not afraid of using the "F word," she quipped, noting that this word stood for "fascism." His social advocacy "has left many ripples and impacted many Rhode Island nonprofits," she adds.

"Richard called things for what they were, said things in ways that were hard to argue with because he had the facts, knew the background stories, and did his homework. He cared enough to tell the truth," said Katzberg, stressing how he excelled at moderating views between people with differing positions.

Bruce McCrae (aka Rudy Cheeks), a co-author of the "Phillip and Jorge" column in the weekly *Providence Phoenix*, who knew Walton for over 30 years as a social activist, educator, and a strong advocate for traditional American folk music, had his thoughts about his recent passing. "There is no doubt in my mind that Rhode Island would have been a much different and poorer place without his constant presence. He was a mentor to generations of students and social activists and one of the strongest voices for peace and equality that Rhode Island has ever known," he said.

McCrae, 62, says Walton's efforts for social change extended internationally to Africa where, in 1960, he worked on a number of documentaries on the emerging independence movements on that continent and to Latin America, where he started the Sister Cities Project between Providence and Niquinohomo, Nicaragua, helping to build a medical facility and school there.

One of the City of Pawtucket's most visible social advocates, Maggi Burns Rogers, remembers Walton as someone who worked hard to improve the world without forgetting how to enjoy it. "He loved to laugh, eat, drink, was an avid gardener, knew his music, read literature, and even traveled the world." (In between his social activism, teaching, and writing, during his long life Walton traveled to over 50 countries, making return trips to many of them.)

"Richard won't be remembered for just one thing because he brought his talent to so many different nonprofits," says Rogers, including Amos House, the George Wiley Center, Stone Soup Coffee House, Rhode Island Coalition for the Homeless, and the Pawtucket Arts Festival Executive Committee, to name just a few.

President Betsy Florin, of the Pawtucket-based George Wiley Center, viewed Walton with his long white beard as a Santa Claus-like figure. But unlike Santa, he gave every day of the year, all of his life, she said. "His real gift was not something tangible that could be wrapped in a pretty box and placed under a tree, it was, rather a gift of imagination combined with activism."

Walton "imagined a world of decency and fairness and then sought to make that happen," said Florin.

As to Walton's daughter, Barnard, 52, even in her earliest childhood memories she remembers her father as being an activist, who once marched with his young daughter at a gay pride parade. While not being an activist to "his degree" the preschool teacher is very politically active in her local community.

Today, Barnard is a diehard New York Mets fan. When Barnard and her brother visited their father in New York, he often took them to watch the team play at Shea Stadium. (As noted in an Op-Ed penned by Walton in 2000, throughout his life Walton's favorite baseball player and hero was Hank Greenberg, a Jewish baseball player who played in the major leagues in the 1930s and 1940s, primarily for the Detroit Tigers. He was considered to be one of the premier power hitters of his generation. Walton noted that Greenberg, who experienced anti-Semitism, would encourage another player subject to slurs from the sidelines. That was Jackie Robinson.)

Six Lifetimes Jammed into One

Walton's life is richly detailed in Wikipedia, a web-based free content encyclopedia.

Born in Saratoga Springs, New York, Walton grew up in South Providence in the 1930s, graduating from Classical High School in 1945. After taking a two year break from his studies at Brown University, serving as a journalist mate in the U.S. Navy, he returned to receive a bachelor's degree in 1951. He whet his appetite for music by working as disc jockey at Providence radio station WICE before enrolling in Columbia School of Journalism, where he later earned a master's degree in journalism in 1955.

Walton's training at Brown University and the School of Journalism at Columbia propelled him into a writing career. During his early years he worked as a reporter at the *Providence Journal*, and the *New York World Telegram* and *Sun*. At Voice of America in Washington, D.C., Walton would initially put in time reporting on African issues, ultimately being assigned to cover the United Nations.

The prolific writer would eventually publish 12 books, nine being written as critical assessments of U.S. foreign policy. In the late 1960s, as a freelance writer, he made his living by writing for *The Nation*, *The New York Times*, *The Washington Post*, *Chicago Tribune*, *Village Voice*, *Newsday*, *The [old] New Republic*, *Cosmopolitan*, even *Playboy*.

In 1981, after 26 years of living outside of Rhode Island, he would return, ultimately becoming one of the most recognizable social activists around, fighting against hunger, homelessness, and poverty. The journalist would run for political office and was active in the Citizens Party (the predecessor to the Green Party). He ran as the political group's vice presidential candidate in 1984 with the radical feminist Sonia Johnson. They did not win.

For over 25 years, Walton had taught writing to thousands of students at Rhode Island College (RIC).Walton fought to successfully establish a union at this university, hammering out a contract, ultimately serving as its first president until his death. With his death, RIC President Nancy Carriuolo called for lowering the flags on campus to half-staff in his memory.

Walton was married to Margaret Hilton and Mary Una Jones, both marriages ending in divorce. He is survived by his daughter Cathy Walton Barnard, son Richard Walton, and three grandchildren.

Big Shoes to Fill

Walton, with his long white hair and beard, wearing his trademark blue overalls, bandanna, and Stone Soup baseball cap, serves as a role model to the younger generations of social activists, those who will take up his worthy causes to fight for justice, end poverty, hunger, and homelessness. He taught us how to live life to the fullest, exploring the world while not forgetting to help those in need.

Walton's life turned out to be a grand adventure. But even with death approaching he taught us to take that leap of faith into the unknown, recognizing that death, too, can be an even grander adventure.

13. VETERANS

ATTACK STUNNED AREA VETS: PEARL HARBOR SURVIVORS RECALL HORROR OF DECEMBER 7, 1941

Published December 2006, in the Senior Digest

With the 65th anniversary of Pearl Harbor approaching, aging military veterans have planned a reunion, which may ultimately be the "last hurrah" to take place in Honolulu, Hawaii, in December. The reunion will commemorate Japan's December 7, 1941, surprise attack and the start of U.S. involvement in World War II.

According to the Pearl Harbor Survivors Project, in 1941 the youngest Pearl Harbor survivors were only in their teens and early 20s. Now their ages are approaching the early- to mid-80s, and frailties associated with advanced age may make this year's anniversary reunion and Survivors Summit the last official gathering.

On December 7, 1941, the surprise attack began at 7:55 a.m. For almost two hours, the Japanese aerial attack sunk or damaged 21 American ships of the U.S. Pacific Fleet. American aircraft losses totaled 188 destroyed and 159 damaged on that unforgettable day. A total of 2,403 military personnel lost their lives, including 68 civilians, with the number of wounded reaching 1,178. The Japanese would lose only 29 planes: less than 10 percent of their attacking force.

Dr. Gary Hylander, a professor at Stone Hill College, said, "With 30,000 World War II veterans dying each month, it's time to capture their stories." To commemorate and honor "The Day that Lives in Infamy," *Senior Digest* talked with three local veterans who shared their eyewitness accounts of the Japanese attack and reflected on Pearl Harbor, which happened 65 years ago this month.

At Schofield Barracks

At 84, Lincoln resident Leo Lebrun remembers Pearl Harbor as if it were yesterday afternoon. In 1941, unemployment would force this 19-year-old man to enlist at a U.S. Army recruiting office located at the main post office in the City of Woonsocket.

After basic training at Fort Slokum, the largest recruiting depot east of the Mississippi River during World War II, a five-day train trip would deliver Lebrun to San Francisco.

From there, the private would be stationed in Hawaii at Schofield Barracks, assigned to C Battery, part of the 8th Field Artillery Hawaiian Division. (Japanese planes would fly over Schofield Barracks on their way to bomb Wheeler Field and Pearl Harbor.)

Traveling 15 miles from the docks, Lebrun arrived at the Schofield Barracks complex, six months before the Pearl Harbor attack. "It was really a beautiful place, just like a college campus," remembered LeBrun.

On his way to Mass held in a theater at Schofield Barracks on December 7, 1941, Private Lebrun saw low-flying aircraft flying over the building. "We thought those planes were ours because it was not unusual to see planes flying overhead," he said. Strafing and dropping bombs forced the soldier to run for safety inside the theater. By seeing the "red zeroes" painted on the planes "we knew that they were Japanese," he said.

After the attack, Lebrun went outside to help the wounded and found his best friend, 19-year-old George Roberts of Los Angeles, had been killed by strafing. "We were shocked, scared and mad, but we were trained to handle it," he said. It took more than two weeks for the military to notify LeBrun's parents that he was not wounded in the attack.

According to Lebrun, the planes were flying so close to the buildings that some of his friends actually saw the faces of the pilots. If the Japanese planes came back in a second wave, he and the others who took shelter in the theater were ready. "We went to a supply room and grabbed .50-caliber machine guns. It was really difficult to hit or damage a plane with a .45-caliber pistol," he recalled.

After the sneak attack, Lebrun's artillery unit was assigned to defend the Punch Bowl, a site overlooking Pearl Harbor. In this position, large 155 mm howitzers would protect the island from invading troops. "The first night we shot at anything that moved. We killed a few mongooses." He noted that even a few days later his unit could still see heavy, black smoke and fire from the damaged ships in the harbor, which was almost two miles away.

Days after the attack soldiers from every outfit would travel to Akins Field and Heeler Field "to pick up plane pieces and clean up those areas," Lebrun added.

Lebrun would later participate in five major campaigns against the Japanese, earning five battle stars. Once discharged as a corporal in August 1945, he married Irene Froment from Woonsocket. The couple recently celebrated 61 years of marriage. The Pearl Harbor veteran would work as a meat cutter, and for the next 39 years made this work his career.

Serving on the USS *Bagley*

Carl Otto, 84, a former police officer who now lives at Attleboro-based Christopher Heights, an assisted-living facility, reflected on Pearl Harbor. From the stern of the USS *Bagley*, he remembered "seeing Japanese torpedo planes fire torpedoes at the ship and others at Pearl Harbor."

Fresh out of boot camp in Newport, Rhode Island, Seaman Second Class Otto chose to be assigned to the USS Bagley rather than being placed on a larger vessel such as an aircraft carrier or battleship. A five-day trip on a troop train would get the young sailor to the West Coast. Ultimately leaving Long Beach, California, the destroyer, manned by 150 sailors, set course for Pearl Harbor, the ship's home port.

The USS Bagley was moored at the Navy Yard in Pearl Harbor for repairs when the Japanese sneak attack began. That early morning, Otto, working as a mess cook, finished his duties and went to the rear of the ship to eat an egg sandwich and drink coffee, sitting on the gun mount by his friends. "At first we thought an approaching plane was Chinese. We just didn't recognize the Rising Sun emblem," he said.

"We actually saw the pilot waving to us, with his plane being only about 100 feet away from our ship," Otto noted, saying that "it shot a fish [torpedo] at us." A loud explosion a few minutes later confirmed to Otto that he indeed saw the torpedo that he believes hit the battleship the USS Tennessee.

General quarters called the sailors to their battle stations. Otto, serving as a powder man, quickly primed the five-inch .38-caliber gun with powder before the projectile was placed in it before firing. Otto recalled that more than 300 rounds of ammunition were fired from the ship's four gun batteries that morning.

"The battle went by so fast," remembered Otto, stressing that his gunnery training allowed him to go into "automatic mode" when preparing the powder charges at his gun battery. That day he clearly remembers looking toward Battleship Row and seeing heavy smoke, intense fire, and oil drenched water, with some spots on fire.

During the aerial battle, "we were credited with downing the first Japanese plane that day," Otto proudly recalled. Crew members armed with .50-caliber machine guns also were credited with destroying the second and third planes that approached the USS *Bagley*. Only four sailors were "nicked" by shrapnel, and the ship received no direct hits. (The ship would later be credited with downing five torpedo planes, one dive bomber, and a high-altitude bomber.)

According to Otto, the USS Bagley would leave the dock behind the USS Nevada. He watched that battleship run aground on the soft mud bottom of the harbor. If the battleship had sunk at the entrance of the harbor, "it would have made sitting targets of all the other ships (inside the harbor)," he said. Ultimately the USS Bagley would form a battle line with destroyers to stop any possible invasion.

Before being discharged from the Navy, Otto would participate in eight major battles in the South Pacific. Returning to North Attleboro, he would marry Pauline Dailey and, during their time together, Otto and his late wife would raise five children.

From the Rooftop of the Naval Hospital

Eugene Marchand, 87, credited appendicitis with keeping him off the USS Cassin, which was in dry dock at the Navy Yard on the day of Pearl Harbor. During the Japanese attack, bombs and fire caused the 1,500-ton destroyer to roll off the blocks and capsize against the destroyer USS Downes, which was alongside it, severely damaging both ships.

Recuperating from surgery, 21-year-old Marchand watched the attack from the third-floor rooftop of the Naval Hospital. At first the young sailor thought the flying aircraft were part of a "sham battle" between the U.S. Army and Navy. Ultimately seeing the "big red fireball" emblems on the low-flying planes and watching fire and smoke caused by dropped bombs and strafing brought home the point that the battle was not staged, but the real thing.

"The Japanese planes flew so close to us we could have hit the planes with rifle fire," Marchand claimed. Nurses and fellow patients urged him to return back inside by warning him to watch out for the deadly shrapnel. He noted that no bombs were dropped on the hospital.

While on the roof watching the battle, the First-Class Carpenter Marchand claims to have seen the first torpedo to hit Fort Island, a nearby amphibious base. After the attack, he was reassigned to the USS Whitney, a destroyer tender.

Being discharged from service after fighting in two South Pacific battles, Marchand would marry Elaine Degina from North Attleboro and raise six children. He was employed by local manufacturing companies, ultimately working for the city and retiring as a truck driver for the highway department.

THE GREATEST GENERATION'S LAST HURRAH

Published November 15, 2014, in the Pawtucket Times

The G.I. Generation, born between 1901 to 1924, (coined the "The Greatest Generation" by nationally acclaimed journalist Tom Brokaw), grew up in the Great Depression and went on to fight World War II, considered to be the largest and deadliest global military conflict in the world's history. The worldwide war directly involved more than 100 million people from over 30 countries.

With the enactment of a formal declaration of war in December 1941, the ranks of the United States military, by draft and voluntary enlistment, ultimately swelled to 16 million soldiers. Ultimately, those serving in World War II came from every state, ethnic group, and race, from poor and well-to-do families.

World War II veterans put their youth on hold to defend the country. Their ages ranged from 17 (with parental permission) to 37 years old. When discharged, a grateful country's G.I. Bill Education benefits would send them to college, propelling them into professional careers, giving them a good income to raise a family and to economically spur the economy.

Brokaw, a well-known American television journalist and author best known as the anchor and managing editor of "NBC Nightly News," who now serves as a special correspondent for NBC News and works on documentaries for other news outlets, claims that this was "the greatest generation any society has ever produced." He asserted that these men and women fought not for fame and recognition, but because it was just the "right thing to do."

The Last Man Standing

In their middle years, America's "Greatest Generation" would see the passing of the last Civil War veteran. On August 2, 1956, the 20th-century veterans would learn about the death of Albert Henry Woolson, 106, the last surviving member of the Grand Army of the Republic, who fought in the nation's bloody American Civil War. In 1864, Woolson had enlisted as a drummer boy in Company C 1st Minnesota Heavy Artillery Regiment.

Woolson is considered to be the last surviving Civil War veteran on either side whose status is undisputed. At least three men who died after him claimed to be Confederate veterans but their veteran status has been questioned.

According to the August 3, 1956 issue of the *St. Petersburg Times*, upon Woolson's death, President Dwight D. Eisenhower stated: "The American people have lost the last personal link with the Union Army. His passing brings sorrow to the hearts of all of us who cherished the memory of the brave men on both sides of the War Between the States."

In 2011, a World War I veteran was nationally recognized for being the last American doughboy. Frank Buckles, 101, had the distinction of being the last survivor of 4.73 million Americans who fought in the "War to End All Wars." The 16-year-old enlisted in the U.S. Army in 1917 and served with a detachment from Fort Riley, driving ambulances and motorcycles near the front lines in France. Buckles left military service with the rank of corporal.

In his final years, Buckles served as Honorary Chairman of the World War I Memorial Foundation. As chairman, he called for a World War I memorial similar to other war memorials inside the Washington, D.C. Beltway. He would campaign for the District of Columbia War Memorial to be renamed the National World War I Memorial.

Upon Buckles' passing, Veterans Affairs Secretary Eric K. Shinseki issued a release stating, "We have lost a living link to an important era in our nation's history," whose distant generation was the first to witness the awful toll of modern, mechanized warfare. "But we have also lost a man of quiet dignity who dedicated his final years to ensuring the sacrifices of his fellow doughboys are appropriately commemorated," adds Shinseki.

The Twilight Years of WWII Veterans

On November 11, there were fewer aging World War II veterans attending ceremonies held throughout the nation honoring them. With their median age pegged at 92 years, many of these individuals are quickly becoming frail, their numbers dwindling as the years go by.

Over the next two decades, America's World War II soldiers will be dying quickly. We will again see another generation of soldiers passing, like Woolson or Buckles.

At the end of World War II, there were 16 million who served our nation in that horrific war. Thirty years ago, when President Ronald Reagan traveled to the battle site of Pointe du Hoc, located at a 100-ft. cliff overlooking the English Channel on the coast of Normandy in northern France, there were only 10.7 million U.S. veterans left. The president came to celebrate the 40th anniversary of the Normandy invasion, recognizing the American Ranger team that took heavy casualties in capturing the German-occupied cliff.

According to the U.S. Veterans Administration, in 2014, our frail World War II veterans are dying at a quick rate of 555 a day. This means there are only 1.34million veterans remaining. By 2036, the National World War II Museum predicts there will be no living veterans of this global war that took place from 1939 to 1945 to recount their own personal battle experiences. When this happens, their stories, like Woolson and Buckles, will be told only in history books or by television documentaries or by historians and academics.

Last Tuesday, Veterans Day ceremonies and activities were held in 15 Rhode Island communities to honor those who served in the U.S. Armed Forces. Today, there are only 3,951 World War II veterans alive in the Ocean State. The elderly veterans' numbers dwindle at these celebrations and even at their reunions because of their frailty and health issues.

We are poised to see a generation of veterans vanish right before our eyes. I say, cherish them while you can. Urge those around you who fought in World War II to tell stories and oral histories for the sake of future generations. They have much to say; we have much to learn.

The National World War II Museum is in Louisiana. To learn more about the Greatest Generation and the global war they fought in, go to **www.nationalww2museum.org**.

My commentary is dedicated to Second Lieutenant Frank M. Weiss, my father, who died in 2003 at 89 years old.

SIPPING COGNAC SIGNALS AN END OF A GENERATION

Published on November 15, 2013 in Pawtucket Times

On November 11, fewer aging World War II veterans attended ceremonies held throughout the country honoring them. With their average age pegged at 92 years, many of these individuals known as the "Greatest Generation," are quickly becoming frail, their numbers dwindling as the years go by.

According to the United States Department of Veterans' Affairs, our elder World War II veterans are dying at a rate of just over 600 a day. This means there are approximately only 1.2 million veterans remaining out of the 16 million who served our nation in that war. By 2036, the National World War II Museum predicts there will be no living veterans of this global war which took place from 1939 to 1945 to recount their own personal experiences. When this happens their stories would only be told in some history books or by television documentaries.

The G.I. Generation, (coined the "The Greatest Generation" by nationally acclaimed journalist Tom Brokaw), grew up in the Great Depression and went on to fight World War II. Brokaw's 1998 best-seller, *The Greatest Generation*, put this generation, born between 1901 to 1924, firmly on the public's radar screen.

Brokaw, a well-known American television journalist and author best known as the anchor and managing editor of "NBC Nightly News," who now serves as a Special Correspondent for NBC News and works on documentaries for other news outlets, claims that this was "the greatest generation any society has ever produced." He asserted that these men and women fought not for fame and recognition, but because it was just the "right thing to do."

A Gathering To Remember

As with others of the G.I. Generation, old age and infirmity took its toll on the 80 members of the famed Doolittle Raiders. On November 9, three of the remaining survivors gathered once more on Veterans Day weekend to honor their 76 fallen comrades-in-arms and make a final toast to them. While not related by blood, these surviving members (plus one not attending) had history that bound them tightly together.

At this invitation-only ceremony at the National Museum of the U.S. Air Force at Wright-Patterson Air Force Base in Ohio, the surviving three members of the famed

Doolittle Raiders, Lt. Col. Richard Cole, 98, Lt. Col. Edward J. Saylor, 93, and Staff Sgt. David J. Thatcher, 92, coming from as far away as Texas, Montana, and Washington state, came to honor their 76 deceased bomber crew members.

Health issues would keep Lt. Col. Robert L. Hite, a native of Ohio, from attending the ceremony. Hite watched the ceremony with his family members from Nashville, Tenn. Wearing the traditional dress for reunions, a blue blazer and gray pants and a Raider tie, Hite gave his own personal salute to his fallen brothers with a silver goblet a few days earlier.

Thirty Seconds Over Tokyo

Over seventy-one-years ago, 16 U.S. Army Air Force B-25 Mitchell medium bombers, carrying 80 Army Air Force volunteers, took off from the aircraft carrier USS Hornet to bomb industrial and military sites in Tokyo and four major cities in Japan. This was America's first air raid on the Empire of Japan that took place 133 days after Pearl Harbor. The Doolittle Raiders bailed out or crash-landed their planes (that ran out of fuel) in China, and most were led to safety by Chinese villagers and soldiers. According to the Doolittle Raiders organization, over a quarter-million Chinese men, women, and children were killed by the Japanese for aiding the Raiders to escape.

Although the "psychological" air attack was in retaliation for the Japanese surprise attack on Pearl Harbor, this top-secret mission, led by Lt. Col. James Doolittle, had an added benefit of boosting the sagging morale of the American public.

Meanwhile, due to the surprise attack on the Japanese homeland, Admiral Isoroku Yamamoto, who planned the raid on Pearl Harbor, decided to save face by moving up his battle plans by eight months to attack Midway Island. American code breakers were able to give the date and location of this planned attack, allowing the U.S. Navy to move three carriers—USS Hornet, USS Enterprise, and the USS Yorktown —to ambush Yamamoto's naval force, ultimately sinking four Japanese carriers and destroying 350 airplanes.

Later on, the Tokyo raid was credited in turning the war around in the Pacific because of the devastating defeat of the Japanese at the Battle of Midway in June 1942. The Japanese military machine could neither replace those carriers nor could it replace the trained pilots and mechanics lost in the naval battle.

The Final Toast

According to Tom Casey, business manager for the Doolittle Raiders, on November 9, an estimated 10,000 spectators, many young children and aging veterans, lined the streets on the military base waving American flags, waiting to meet the three Lincoln sedans carrying the three Raiders who came to the National Museum of the U.S. Air Force near Dayton, Ohio.

After an afternoon memorial service with speeches and taps, a wreath was laid by the Doolittle Raider's monument outside the museum as five B-25 bombers flew low overhead in the famous missing-man formation as a tribute. The Raiders made their last toast that evening to comrades who died in the air attack or since their mission, says Casey.

The original plan for the last toast called for the last two Raiders standing to break open the bottle of cognac and toast each other and their departed members, stated Casey, who noted that this would signify the end of the Doolittle Raiders' mission.

However, Casey remembers two major changes were made last October at a meeting in Washington, D.C., by the four surviving Raiders. Their first decision was to schedule their last public reunion in April 2013 at Fort Walton Beach, Florida, the home of Eglin Air Force Base where the Raiders trained for their mission.

"They were also getting older, and travel was getting more difficult, so the second decision was made to not wait until there were only two standing members as initially planned," Casey recounts, stressing that it was important to bring together the five remaining Raiders while they were physically able to meet to officially close their mission. Unfortunately, Major Thomas C. Griffin passed away weeks later. With the urging of General Hudson, director of the National Museum of the United States Air Force in Dayton, Ohio, and with the agreement of the surviving members, the last toast would be scheduled for November 2013 on Veterans Day.

At the evening ceremony, before attending family members of their deceased crew members, Air Force leadership, and other invitees, a historian read the names of all 80 Doolittle Raiders, with the three surviving veterans calling out "here."

Among the many speakers, Chief of Staff of the Air Force Gen. Mark A. Welsh told over 600 attendees, "As far as I'm concerned, this is the greatest professional honor I've ever had to speak here with this crowd at this event."

Welsh admitted the first book he read as a youngster was *Thirty Seconds over Tokyo*. "It was given to me by my father, also a World War II vet, with the words that I should read it closely because this is what America is all about. I've never forgotten those words," he said.

"The Doolittle Raiders have been celebrated in books and in journals... in magazines... in various papers. They've had buildings named after them... had streets named after them. People play them in movies," Welsh added.

"They (the survivors) hate to hear this, but Jimmy Doolittle and his Raiders are truly lasting American heroes, but they are also Air Force heroes. They pioneered the concept of global strike ... the idea that no target on earth is safe from American air power," states Welsh.

Concluding the emotional ceremony, Cole, representing his fellow Doolittle Raider survivors, opened the 1896 Cognac (denoting Doolittle's birth year) and gave his final toast.

Casey notes that this bottle was presented to General Doolittle on his 60th birthday by a representative of the Hennessy Cognac Company. "That evening was the first time ever the bottle was taken out of its original box and shown to the public and displayed," he said.

"Gentlemen, I propose a toast," Cole told the remaining Doolittle Raiders. "To the gentlemen we lost on the mission and those who have passed away since. Thank you very much and may they rest in peace." Then he sipped the cognac from an engraved silver goblet.

The 80 silver goblets in the ceremony were presented to the Raiders in 1959 by the city of Tucson, Ariz. The Raiders' names were engraved twice, the second upside-down. During the ceremony, white-gloved cadets presented the personal goblets to the three survivors, while their long-time manager poured the 117-year-old cognac into the participants' goblets. Those of the deceased were turned upside-down.

The four remaining members of the Doolittle Raiders will continue to keep their heroic tales alive by personally sharing their experiences. When the last cup is turned upside down, it will be their oral histories, history books, or documentaries that will give us an impersonal small glimpse of what it took to answer the call to duty and to do that job well.

ABOUT THE AUTHOR

(Photo credit: Patty S. Zacks)

Herb Weiss has enjoyed a distinguished 36-year career in journalism, earning a national reputation as an expert on aging, health care, and medical issues. Over 600 articles that he has authored or co-authored have appeared in national, state, and local publications and newspapers. He is a 2012 graduate of the Theta II Class of Leadership Rhode Island.

Herb is a recipient of the 2003 AARP Rhode Island's Vision Award for his weekly commentary that appeared in the *Pawtucket Times*. He is a two time recipient (1994 and 1999) of the American College of Health Care Administrator's National Award for his coverage of long-term care issues. He was also awarded the Distinguished Alumni's Award by the

Center for Studies in Aging, North Texas State University, in 1997, for his career coverage of aging issues. In 1997, he was selected by the prestigious McKnight's LTC News to be one of its "100 Most Influential People" in Long-Term Care. In 2016, Governor Gina Raimondo appointed him to the Rhode Island Advisory Commission on Aging.

Today, Herb's weekly newspaper column appears in the *Pawtucket Times* and *Woonsocket Call,* two Northern Rhode Island daily newspapers.

Herb and his wife, Patty Zacks, reside in Pawtucket, Rhode Island.